THE TALL TALES OF DAVY CROCKETT

TENNESSEANA EDITIONS

THE TALL TALES OF DAVY CROCKETT

The Second Nashville Series of Crockett Almanacs

1839–1841

TENNESSEANA EDITIONS

An Enlarged Facsimile Edition, with an Introduction by Michael A. Lofaro

The University of Tennessee Press
KNOXVILLE

Publication of this book has been aided by a grant
from the Tennessee Historical Commission.

The paper in this book meets the minimum requirements of the American National Standard for Permanence of Paper for Printed Library Materials. ∞ The binding materials have been chosen for strength and durability.

Library of Congress Cataloging-in-Publication Data

The Tall tales of Davy Crockett.

(Tennesseana editions)
Bibliography: p.
Includes index.
1. Crockett, Davy, 1786–1836—Legends. 2. Crockett, Davy, 1786–1836—Humor. 3. Folklore—United States. 4. American wit and humor. I. Lofaro, Michael A., 1948–   . II. Series.
GR105.37.D3T35 1987   398.2′2′0973   86-30831
ISBN 0-87049-525-9 (alk. paper)
ISBN 0-87049-526-7 (pbk. : alk. paper)

For

Anthony L. Lofaro

Helen Wasson Lofaro

and

Ellen Margaret Lofaro

CONTENTS

PREFACE

Davy Crockett was a man in whom history and fiction met. He was both the civilized congressman from Tennessee who lost his life in the battle of the Alamo and the wild, untamed, comic spirit of the westering frontier of nineteenth-century America. The combination of these elements was noted even before his death when the author of a rather stodgy review of Crockett's autobiography commented upon the impropriety of a holder of public office making "himself a buffoon for the amusement of the public." The reviewer was favorably impressed with the autobiography, *A Narrative of the Life of David Crockett of the State of Tennessee* (1834), because it was intended as a corrective to the "odd sayings and whimsical doings of colonel Crockett. Many of these, of course, have been manufactured for him, and are extravagant caricatures of his real humor, and peculiarities of character."[1] Crockett himself noted in the preface to his *Narrative* that his book was meant to rectify the portrait painted of him in an earlier volume:

> I have met with hundreds, if not with thousands of people, who have formed their opinions of my appearance, habits, language, and everything else from that deceptive work.
>
> They have almost in every instance expressed the most profound astonishment at finding me in human shape, and with the *countenance, appearance,* and *common feelings* of a human being.[2]

The reviewer unwittingly went on to capture the beginning of the mythic process that eventually made Crockett the premier hero of the American frontier. He said that before the publication of the autobiography that Crockett, "by suffering such wretched caricatures to pass for likenesses, had tacitly assumed the character drawn for him by others."[3] Crockett and the reviewer had no idea of the immense power that his heroic death would soon invest in his image as a boasting, brawling

1. *The Western Monthly Magazine,* 2 (May 1834), 277. The reviewer was likely James Hall, the publisher of the magazine.

2. The best edition of Crockett's *Narrative* was edited by James A. Shackford and Stanley J. Folmsbee (1834; rpt. in an annotated facsimile edition, Knoxville: Univ. of Tennessee Press, 1973), pp. 4–5. Although Crockett pleaded ignorance as to the identity of the author of this book, it was surely he who provided the bulk of the biographical data to his friend Clarke (see Crockett, *Narrative,* p. 4, n. 3). The earlier volume that Crockett was reacting against was published under his name as *The Life and Adventures of Colonel David Crockett of West Tennessee* (Cincinnati: For the Proprietor, 1833).

3. *The Western Monthly Magazine,* 2 (May 1834), 277.

backwoodsman. The "wretched caricatures" soon became fantastic tall tales in the popular comic almanacs that bore Crockett's name. In these works Davy once again "assumed the character drawn for him by others"; it was, however, a character no longer bounded by the achievements of a mortal man, but only by the imagination.

The present edition places before the modern reader three of the early almanacs that are primary documents in the creation of Davy Crockett as America's first comic superman. The hope in reproducing these slim volumes in facsimile is to present them in the same format in which they first appeared to the eager readers who purchased them for their tall tales, fabulous woodcuts, and practical almanac information and, in so doing, to capture a true sense of their original appeal. The printed area of each of the pages is here enlarged twenty-seven percent to make the small typefaces more easily readable. The original dimensions vary, but are approximately 4 × 7 inches.

These three almanacs have never before been reproduced in facsimile, and two-thirds of their stories have never before been collected or reprinted in any readily accessible form. The accompanying essay examines the development of a tall tale Crockett in the almanacs in a wider cultural context. It investigates how this unique blending of history and fiction is both the result of the historical Crockett's participation in the evolution of his fictional counterpart and a further synthesis, one that combines tradition and innovation in regard to the making of almanacs in America and to the creation of Davy's adventures as parallels to Old World heroic narratives and to the escapades of the trickster-transformer characters of international folklore.

To facilitate access to the stories, two separate lists of the contents of the three almanacs are included in this edition. The first, "The Tall Tales of the Crockett Almanacs," records the stories in the order in which they appear. The second, "The Topics of the Tall Tales," groups the stories by topic for the convenience of the reader. Since several stories fall into two or sometimes three of the categories, the titles of those works are repeated under each appropriate heading. This second table, in conjunction with the index, should provide adequate access to the main characters and themes in the almanacs as well as to the titles of the stories and their illustrations. No tale-type and motif indices are included at this time; that work should necessarily be based on all thirty-one of the known Crockett almanacs.

ACKNOWLEDGMENTS

The three almanacs in this volume are reproduced from the originals in the collections of the University of Tennessee Library, Knoxville (1839), the Tennessee State Library, Nashville (1840), and the Barker Texas History Center at the University of Texas, Austin (1841). I thank each of these institutions for their kindness in granting permission to use their materials. I am very grateful to the Tennessee Historical Commission for the grant that provided the funds to photograph the almanacs and to the National Humanities Center, Research Triangle Park, North Carolina, for the fellowship under which a portion of the bibliographic research on the almanacs was conducted. Although it would be a lengthy task to acknowledge all those who have assisted and encouraged my research on the Crockett almanacs over the years, I would particularly like to thank the following individuals for their support: Keith Arbour; Charles F. Bryan, Jr.; Kathryn B. Croxton; Joe Cummings; the late Richard Beale Davis; John H. Dobson; Ralph Elder; Everett Emerson; David Harkness; Herbert L. Harper; Richard Boyd Hauck; John B. Hench; John N. Hoover; M. Thomas Inge; James C. Kelly; J. A. Leo Lemay; James B. Lloyd; Charles J. Maland; Marcus A. McCorison; Walter Pulliam; John Seelye; Fran Schell; and D. Strong Wyman. And, as always, my work was ultimately made possible through the help and insight of my wife, Nancy Durish Lofaro.

A CHRONOLOGY OF THE LIFE OF THE HISTORICAL DAVID CROCKETT

1786–1836

1786 On August 17, David is born to John and Rebecca Hawkins Crockett in Greene County, Tennessee.

1796 Tennessee joins the Union. The Crocketts open a tavern on the road from Knoxville to Abingdon, Virginia.

1798 John Crockett hires his son out to Jacob Siler to help drive a herd of cattle to Rockbridge County, Virginia. Siler tries to detain David by force after the contract is completed, but the boy escapes and eventually arrives home in late 1798 or early 1799.

1799 David starts school, prefers playing hookey, and runs away from home to escape his father's punishment. He works as a wagoner and a day laborer and at odd jobs for two and one-half years.

1802 David returns home and is welcomed by all his family.

1803 David willingly works and discharges his father's debts of seventy-six dollars.

1805 He takes out a license to marry Margaret Elder of Dandridge, Tennessee, on October 21, but she decides to marry another.

1806 Crockett courts and marries Mary (Polly) Finley on August 14 in Jefferson County, Tennessee.

1811 David, Polly, and their two sons, John Wesley and William, leave East Tennessee after September 11 and settle on the Mulberry fork of Elk River in Lincoln County, Tennessee.

1813 Crockett leaves Lincoln County to settle on the Rattlesnake Spring Branch of Bean's Creek in Franklin County, Tennessee, near the present Alabama border. He names his homestead "Kentuck." In September, Crockett enlists in the militia in Winchester, Tennessee, to avenge the Indian attack on Fort Mims, Alabama, and serves as a scout under Major Gibson. Under Andrew Jackson, he participates in the retributive massacre of the Indian town of Tallussahatchee on November 3. David's ninety-day enlistment expires on the day before Christmas, and he returns home.

1814 Jackson defeats the Creeks at the Battle of Horse-shoe Bend on March 28. Crockett reenlists on September 28 as 3rd sergeant in Captain John Cowan's company and serves until March 27, 1815. He arrives the day after Jackson's taking of Pensacola on November 7, 1814. Crockett attempts to ferret out the British-trained and -supplied Indians from the Florida swamps.

1815 Discharged as a 4th sergeant, Crockett returns home to find himself again a father. His wife, Polly, dies the summer after Margaret's birth, although David found her in good health on his return.

1816 Crockett is elected a lieutenant in the 32nd Militia Regiment of Franklin County on May 22 and marries Elizabeth Patton, a widow with two children (George and Margaret Ann), before summer's end. In the fall, he explores Alabama with an eye toward settlement, catches malaria, and nearly dies. He is reported dead and astonishes his family with his "resurrection."

1817 By about September, the Crocketts have settled in the territory soon to become Lawrence County, Tennessee, at the head of Shoal Creek. David becomes a justice of the peace on November 17.

1818 Crockett becomes town commissioner of Lawrenceburg before April 1. He is also elected colonel of the 57th Militia Regiment in the county.

1819 Crockett resigns his position as justice of the peace.

1821 On January 1, he resigns as commissioner, having decided to run for a seat in the state legislature as the representative of Lawrence and Hickman counties. After two months of campaigning, Crockett wins the August election. From the very first of his political career, he takes an active interest in public land policy regarding the West. The House adjourns on November 17, and David, his son John Wesley, and Abram Henry, explore the Obion River country.

1822 The Crocketts move west and settle near the Obion River after the second legislative session ends.

1823 Crockett defeats Dr. William E. Butler and is reelected to the state legislature.

1824 Crockett ends his state political career on October 22, when the House adjourns.

1825 In August, Crockett is defeated in his first bid for a seat in Congress.

1826 Nearly dying as his boats carrying barrel staves wreck in the Mississippi River, Crockett is brought to Memphis and is encouraged to run for Congress again by M. B. Winchester.

1827 Crockett defeats General William Arnold and Colonel Adam Alexander for a seat in the United States House of Representatives.

1828 Andrew Jackson is elected President.

1829 Crockett is reelected. He splits with Jackson and with the Tennessee delegation on several issues during this term in office.

1830 Crockett attacks the Indian removal bill.

1831 James Kirke Paulding's play, *The Lion of the West,* with James Hackett playing the Crockettesque lead, Nimrod Wildfire, opens in New York City at the Park Theater on April 25. In his campaign for a third congressional term, David speaks openly against Jackson's policies. He is defeated by William Fitzgerald in a close election.

1833 Mathew St. Clair Clarke's *The Life and Adventures of Colonel David Crockett of West Tennessee* is deposited for copyright on January 5. It is soon reprinted under the title *Sketches and Eccentricities of Col-*

onel David Crockett of West Tennessee. Crockett defeats the incumbent Fitzgerald and again wins a seat in Congress.

1834 Crockett publishes his autobiography, *A Narrative of the Life of David Crockett of the State of Tennessee,* written with the help of Thomas Chilton. On April 25, he begins his three-week tour through the eastern states in an anti-Jacksonian alliance with the Whigs.

1835 Two Whig books are published under Crockett's name: *Col. Crockett's Tour to the North and Down East* in late March and *Life of Martin Van Buren* less than three months later. The earliest known copy of "The Crockett Victory March" (*"Go Ahead" a march dedicated to Colonel Crockett*) and the first Crockett almanac are published. (The almanac was very likely published in 1834 for 1835.) Adam Huntsman defeats Crockett in the election for Congress, and Crockett, together with William Patton, Abner Burgin, and Lindsey K. Tinkle, sets out for Texas on November 1.

1836 In January, Crockett and Patton sign the oath of allegiance to the "Provisional Government of Texas or any future republican Government that may be hereafter declared. . . ." In early February, Crockett arrives in San Antonio De Bexar. On March 6, he is captured and executed after Santa Anna's army captures the Alamo. Early in the summer *Col. Crockett's Exploits and Adventures in Texas* is compiled and fabricated by Richard Penn Smith. That fall, Jackson's handpicked successor, Martin Van Buren, is elected President.

DAVY CROCKETT, TALL TALE HUMOR, AND THE SECOND NASHVILLE SERIES OF CROCKETT ALMANACS

"I'll have you understand that I'm a snorter by birth and eddycation, and if you don't go floating along, and leave me to finish my nap I'll give you a taste of my breed. I'll begin with the snapping turtle, and after I've chawed you up with that, I'll rub you down with the spice of the alligator. . . . I'll double you up like a spare shirt. My name is Crockett and I'll put my mark on your infarnal wolf-hide before you've gone the length of a panther's tail further."

These were the words that the legendary Davy Crockett used when he first met Ben Harding, his sea-going counterpart and faithful companion. In the tall tale world of ring-tailed roarers, such a rough and rowdy challenge to a fight was often the traditional greeting by which a backwoodsman took the measure of a new acquaintance. Ben gave back nearly as good a verbal barrage as he got, but when Davy identified himself, Ben "roared right out a laffing" and offered his hand in friendship. He said that he knew all about Davy and his wild adventures from the tales in the Crockett almanacs (1839, pp. 22–23).[1]

Published for the years 1835 through 1856, these works were the most influential source in the creation of a fictional Davy Crockett as our country's first comic superman. The first almanac, which bore the notation that it was printed in Nashville, began a series of seven such issues that possessed a certain uniformity of design and format not

1. References to the seven Nashville Crockett almanacs published for 1835 to 1841 will be included parenthetically in the text of the essay. The full titles of the first series of these almanacs are: *Davy Crockett's Almanack, of Wild Sports of the West, And Life in the Backwoods, 1835* (Nashville: Snag & Sawyer); *Davy Crockett's Almanack, of Wild Sports in the West, And Life in the Backwoods, 1836* (Nashville: Published for the Author); *Davy Crockett's Almanack, of Wild Sports in the West, Life in the Backwoods, & Sketches of Texas, 1837* (Nashville, Tennessee: Published by the heirs of Col. Crockett); and *Davy Crockett's Almanack, of Wild Sports in the West, Life in the Backwoods, Sketches of Texas, and Rows on the Mississippi, 1838* (Nashville: Published by the heirs of Col. Crockett). The most accessible source for these four almanacs is Franklin J. Meine, ed. *The Crockett Almanacks: Nashville Series, 1835–1838* (Chicago: Caxton Club, 1955). It is generally complete, but omits all almanac data, some non-Crockett narrative material, and is reset rather than printed in facsimile. See the facsimile title pages in this volume for the titles of the three Nashville almanacs in the second series.

present in any of the other almanacs.[2] This series was one of the most important forces in the development of the tall tale Crockett because it showcased him as the epitome of the boisterous backwoods hero and nurtured the growth of his legendary deeds in a medium that was arguably one of the most popular and widespread publishing enterprises of its day.

I

Previous almanacs exerted a powerful influence upon American culture of the seventeenth and eighteenth centuries.[3] As a source of information, the almanac was esteemed second only to the Bible, and, as the distance from civilization and printed materials increased, it became commonplace to observe that these two volumes formed the irreducible household library. Since almanac making was usually the most profitable venture that a printer could engage in, it was perhaps inevitable that the same commercial forces would inspire several of them to hit upon Crockett, one of the most popular figures of the Jacksonian era, as their subject and champion to meet the challenge presented by a triple threat to their prosperity—the increasing availability of newspapers, inexpensive watches, and advertising calendars.[4]

The content of the Davy Crockett almanacs was marked by both continuation and innovation in regard to the material included in their predecessors. As almanacs, the Crockett issues carried information on sunrise, sunset, the phases of the moon, and eclipses, together with astronomical calculations, weather predictions, and a family calendar. The tables of data indicated the intended range of the audience of the almanacs. The publishers' hopes of increasing sales by increasing the practical applicability of their volumes were noted in the first two Nashville almanacs in which the data was "Calculated for all the States in the Union" and the last two, which took in "The Canadas" as well. In general the calculations grew progressively more specific and expansive as the United States grew, so that by the last issue of 1856 the reader could survey data for the roughly rectangular area bounded by Massachusetts, Georgia, California, and Oregon. As if to demonstrate

2. For a discussion of the seven almanacs, see Michael A. Lofaro, "The Hidden 'Hero' of the Nashville Crockett Almanacs," in Michael A. Lofaro, ed., *Davy Crockett: The Man, The Legend, The Legacy (1786–1986)* (Knoxville: Univ. of Tennessee Press, 1985), pp. 46–79.

3. Marion B. Stowell, *Early American Almanacs: The Colonial Weekday Bible* (New York: Burt Franklin, 1977), pp. vii–xviii; Milton Drake, *Almanacs of the United States,* 2 vols. (New York: Scarecrow Press, 1962), I, v–xiv.

4. Drake, I, viii.

their traditional origins, these almanacs also intermittently included the droll anecdotes, homespun versification, and proverbial wisdom that had become a staple of the eighteenth-century almanac and almost inextricably intertwined in the mind of the modern reader with Benjamin Franklin's "Poor Richard" to the unfortunate neglect of the fine almanacs of the two Nathaniel Ames; Benjamin Banneker; William Bradford; Matthew Carey; John Dunlap; William Goddard; Jonas Green; Daniel, Titan, and Felix Leeds; Nathaniel Low; Isaiah Thomas; Peter Timothy; Robert Wells; and Benjamin West, to name but a few.

The Crockett almanacs were also clearly in the mainstream in the use of prefaces, receipts (recipes), and narratives. But sometimes the printer overdid. In the 1839 Nashville almanac, some of the data was squeezed out to provide more room for the stories. The error was remedied the next year.

The prefaces or introductions to all seven of the Nashville Crockett almanacs and to *Ben Hardin's Crockett Almanac. 1842* were delightfully overdone. Written in supposed backwoods dialect, they proved as entertaining as the stories they preceded.[5] These epistolary prefaces, in fact, carried on the tradition of the hoax and satire by variously claiming that Crockett had left enough manuscript material so that publishing of his work could continue after his death through at least 1843 (1837, p. 3; 1839, p. 2), that Crockett was still alive but a captive in a Mexican salt mine (1841, p. 2), and that Crockett was advising Ben Harding on making his almanacs through his letters from the mines (1841, p. 4).[6]

Continuity was also evident in the receipts that often parodied those of normal almanacs by giving ones with a particular frontier twist. Crockett's "A Receipt for the Cholera" told the reader to "Eat two cucumbers, dressed or raw, as you prefer; then take a quart of blackberries, four green corn, four raw potatoes mashed, a lobster or a crab, some ice water, and wash the whole down with a quart of buttermilk, and you will shortly have a touch of the real thing" (1836, p. 47). And who could argue with "Crockett's recipe for Cooking Bear-Steaks"? It

5. *Ben Hardin's Crockett Almanac. 1842* (New York, Philadelphia: Turner & Fisher; Baltimore: Turner). (Known variant imprints are given for the almanac entries and separated by a semicolon. The first imprint cited is that of the text used in this essay. The texts are usually identical, since some branch of the company of Turner & Fisher supplied the almanacs that were then issued by a local publisher. Most chose to make no alteration other than a change in imprint, although some would delete the woodcut on the rear cover to insert advertising.) Of the other Crockett almanacs only the *Crockett Awl-man-ax for 1839* (New York and Philadelphia: Turner & Fisher) and the *Crockett Almanac Improved 1842* (Boston: S. N. Dickinson) have prefaces, and these are not in dialect.

6. Another letter of advice from the mines was printed in *Ben Hardin's Crockett Almanac. 1842*, p. 4.

read: "Salt 'em in a hail storm, pepper 'em with buckshot, an' then broil 'em with a flash o' lightnin'!"[7]

It was perhaps in the use of narrative accounts that the Crockett almanacs most resembled their predecessors. Earlier almanacs had, on occasion, presented Indian captivity narratives and firsthand accounts of unusual people and events. Although both these groups of tales were usually included for moral instruction, the descriptions of providential deliverance from the savages were also a frame for graphic and detailed descriptions of torture that could turn the stomach of the supposedly squeamish, who, despite it all, probably refused to put the almanacs down. Likewise, the accounts of human deformities and the oddities of nature were precursors of the backwoods grotesques of the Crockett almanacs.[8] In addition to printing the story, Nathaniel Ames illustrated the cover of his Boston Almanac for 1772 with a woodcut of Emma Leach, a twenty-two inch dwarf who was so deformed that she was unable to walk; Benjamin West similarly featured Patagonian giants on his cover of *Bickerstaff's Boston Almanack* for 1768, and in 1772 gave the readers a full page illustration of "The Wonderful Man Fish" recently caught in England.[9]

Necessity was the mother of innovation in the almanac trade. By the third decade of the nineteenth century, it was apparent that one way in which to meet the competition due to the proliferation of general almanacs and the growth of the newspaper industry was to issue specialty almanacs such as those that bore Crockett's name. Robert B. Thomas' long-running *Farmer's Almanack,* first published in 1792 for 1793, was a harbinger of this trend at least in its title.[10] Although most almanacs

7. *Crockett Almanac. 1854* (Philadelphia, New York, Baltimore, Boston: Fisher & Brother; New York: Philip J. Cozans), p. [25]. Both are reprinted in Richard M. Dorson's *Davy Crockett: American Comic Legend* (New York: Spiral Press for Rockland Editions, 1939), pp. 152 and 100. Dorson's book is still the most extensive collection of the tall tales made to date.

8. Descriptions of ugliness were a staple of frontier humor and of the Crockett almanacs. For a prime example of the graphic quality of this humor, see Davy's adulation of Gum Swamps' own Jerusha Stubbs and note the grotesque symmetry of this ideal of backwoods beauty (1840, p. 21). For a wider view of the humor of ugliness, see Walter Blair and Hamlin Hill, *America's Humor: From Poor Richard to Doonesbury* (New York: Oxford Univ. Press, 1978), pp. 127–28, and Dorson's *Davy Crockett,* pp. xviii–xx.

9. Stowell, pp. 199–218. For additional background, see Catherine L. Albanese, "Davy Crockett and the Wild Man; or, The Metaphysics of the *Longue Durée,*" in Lofaro, *Davy Crockett,* pp. 80–101, and Barry Gaines and Michael A. Lofaro, "What Did Caliban Look Like?," *Mississippi Folklore Register,* 10 (Fall 1976), 175–86.

10. The same title, *The Farmer's Almanack,* was apparently used irregularly from 1713 through 1730 in Massachusetts by Nathaniel Whittemore. See Drake entry numbers 2952, 2956, 2957, 2958, 2974, 2992, 2998, 3006, 3011, 3016, 3023, and 3032. During these years Whittemore issued other almanacs as well. His last was published

at that time were issued with the farmer in mind due to the dominant agrarian nature of American society, changing demographics, particularly industrial development and the growth of cities, eventually transformed it into a true specialty almanac as well. By the 1840s, specialty subjects had gained a significant share of the almanac market and ranged over most current topics of the day. A brief sample of those works with the state and first year for which they were published included *The Physician's Almanac* (Mass., 1817), *The Health Almanac* (Mass., 1843), and, to promote the sale of Bristol's Sarasparilla as a literal cure-all, *The Free Almanac* (N.Y., 1843). Others were *The Christian Almanac* (Mass., 1821; N.Y., 1822), *The Whig Almanac* and *The Jackson Almanac* (both N.Y., 1835), *The Anti-Masonic Almanac* (N.Y., 1821), *The Temperance Almanac* (N.Y., 1831), and an anti-slavery publication, *The Liberty Almanac* (N.Y., 1844).[11]

As their titles clearly indicate, most of these almanacs were issued by or for special interest groups. Comic almanacs, which began in America with Charles Ellms's *The American Comic Almanac* in Boston for 1831, were intended for a far wider audience.[12] At first derived in the main from English comic almanacs, that in turn traced their lineage to jest and joke books, these works emphasized humor and hilarious illustrations over the propaganda and sales pitches of the other specialty issues while still seeking, quite naturally, to retain the utilitarian value of a traditional almanac.

Charles Ellms, a Boston illustrator and editor, also had a penchant for publishing sensational and nautical material. John Seelye's recent investigation of Ellms's *The People's Almanac* and works such as *The Pirates Own Book, The Tragedy of the Seas,* and *Robinson Crusoe's Own Book* revealed that Ellms was very likely the progenitor of the Nashville Crockett almanacs as well. The style of the woodcuts and the content and layout of his *The People's Almanac,* first issued for 1834, generally echoed that of the first series of Nashville Crockett almanacs for 1835 to 1838. Perhaps the strongest evidence, however, was the reuse of woodcuts from *The People's Almanac* and from *The Pirates Own Book* in the Nashville Crockett almanacs in identical or slightly

for 1741 (Drake 3064). Other uses of the word "Farmer's" in a title for or before 1793, the first date for which Robert B. Thomas' almanac was issued, include Drake entry numbers 470, 484, 501, and 6005.

11. For a larger sample of the specialty almanacs, see Drake, I, xii–xiii, and Robb Sagendorph, *America and her Almanacs: Wit, Wisdom & Weather, 1639–1970* (Boston: Little, Brown; and Dublin, New Hampshire: Yankee, 1970), pp. 236–58.

12. Drake, I, xiii. See also his entry number 3975.

modified form.[13] This argument would also explain why metaphors citing lobsters and crabs appeared as common in these Crockett almanacs as those that cited animals more likely encountered on the Tennessee frontier and why it was entirely appropriate to have Ben Harding, the sailor, assume the editorship of the second series of Nashville almanacs.

Ben had appeared only once before he supposedly met Davy in the tale that began this essay. Three years earlier in the 1836 Nashville almanac, he was featured in a story entitled "The Early Days, Love and Courtship of Ben Harding, Member of Congress from Kentucky, as related to Col. Crockett by himself" (1836, pp. 14–19). It took no great leap to connect this Ben Harding with the actual colorful congressman from Bardstown, Kentucky, named Ben Hardin.[14] In all the other stories, however, Ben was cast as a swaggering sailor who edited and published Crockett almanacs. The second series of Nashville Crockett almanacs, reproduced in facsimile in this volume, marked, therefore, a significant break with the original depiction of Ben Harding and the beginning of a new group of outlandish tales intimately connected with and second only to those of Crockett himself.

Although the Crockett almanacs originally incorporated some of the same types of materials found in Ellms's publications and in other early comic almanacs, as a specialty almanac they were still most definitely a group apart. Their initial focus upon a current American hero, their descriptions of wild beasts, and their rough and tumble tales of hunting, adventure, and hairbreadth escapes in the backwoods, expanded quickly into the realm of the humorous tall tale. These characteristics, when combined with the longevity of a twenty-two-year run of thirty-one different issues, made the Crockett almanacs unique and influential.

Their success was also due to a coincidental master stroke of timing. The first issue came out for 1835, the same year that A. B. Longstreet's sketches were collected into book form and published as *Georgia Scenes*. Both marked the official beginning of what was termed the "Humor of the Old Southwest" that was the dominant force in tickling America's funnybone for the next quarter century. For many it also marked the beginning of a truly American humor, one based on indig-

13. John Seelye, "A Well-Wrought Crockett: Or, How the Fakelorists Passed Through the Credibility Gap and Discovered Kentucky," in Lofaro, *Davy Crockett*, pp. 34–43. See also Drake entry number 4061.

14. See Lucius P. Little's *Ben Hardin: His Times and Contemporaries, With Selections from his Speeches* (Louisville: Courier-Journal Job Printing Co., 1887) and John Seelye's "A Well-Wrought Crockett," in Lofaro, *Davy Crockett*, pp. 26–28.

enous characters, scenes, and language. Parts of the broad comic farces, outrageous character sketches, and outlandish exaggerations were even to live on well after that period because of the formative influence that this type of humor exerted upon Mark Twain who was born that very same year.

A final reason for success was that in 1835 the fame of the historical Crockett had reached its zenith. The newspapers were alive with his presence, and two books about his life and adventures published in 1833 and 1834 had sold so well that new editions of the *Sketches and Eccentricities of Col. David Crockett, of West Tennessee* and of his *A Narrative of the Life of David Crockett of the State of Tennessee* (the only one that he wrote) were printed.[15] Crockett felt confident enough about his political fortunes to test the waters for a presidential bid on a tour through the Northeast, a journey that was recorded in *An Account of Colonel Crockett's Tour to the North and Down East*.[16] Defeated, however, in his congressional campaign, Crockett rode off to Texas to underwrite the popularity of the almanacs at a heavy price. His death at the Alamo assured him a preeminent place in both American history and myth and increased the sales of all works bearing his name.

II

The fictional *Davy* Crockett was a radical but still somewhat recognizable version of the historical *David* Crockett. Born on August 17, 1786, in Greene County in East Tennessee, David was a first rate but relatively obscure backwoods hunter and Indian fighter who had progressively moved across the entire state in search of a better life for himself and his family. Having fought in the Creek Indian War and held several local political posts, Crockett turned his knack for storytelling and politics to his advantage. He parlayed his reputation into a state and then national political career and became the representative symbol of the frontier hero in Jacksonian America. Sensing the power of this image,

15. *Sketches and Eccentricities* (New York: J.&J. Harper, 1833) is the best known title of the work first published as [Mathew St. Clair Clarke], *The Life and Adventures of Colonel David Crockett of West Tennessee* (Cincinnati: For the Proprietor, 1833). The best edition of Crockett's 1834 *Narrative* was edited by James A. Shackford and Stanley J. Folmsbee (rpt. in an annotated facsimile edition, Knoxville: Univ. of Tennessee Press, 1973). See also the preface of this volume, note 2.

16. (Philadelphia: Carey & Hart, 1835). The other of "Crockett's" Whig books is not included in this list because it consists mainly of artless invective rather than tales. See [Augustin Smith Clayton], *The Life of Martin Van Buren, Heir-Apparent to the "Government," and appointed Successor of General Andrew Jackson* (Philadelphia: R. Wright [Carey & Hart], 1835).

Crockett often encouraged the growth of his legend by promoting himself as a simple down-home country boy whose superb marksmanship was an extension of his character. He was a straight shooter.

How well he manipulated his image quickly became apparent in his early campaigns. In his run against Dr. William E. Butler in the state elections of 1823, for example, Crockett played up his backwoods roots and labeled Butler as an aristocrat luxuriating in the decadent life associated with cities and civilization. When visiting his opponent's house and noting the expensive furnishings, Crockett refused to walk upon a particularly handsome rug and subsequently incorporated a telling comparison as a high point in his speeches: "Fellow citizens, my aristocratic competitor has a fine carpet, and every day he *walks* on truck finer than any gowns your wife or your daughters, in all their lives, ever *wore*!" He once even memorized Butler's standard campaign speech and delivered it word for word just before it was Butler's turn to speak.[17]

Elected to represent his district in Congress in 1827, 1829, and 1833, Crockett eventually broke with President Jackson, whom he sarcastically called "the 'Government,'" and with the Tennessee delegation on several important issues. He fought unsuccessfully for a land bill that would guarantee squatters' rights in West Tennessee and opposed Jackson on the "spoils system" of political patronage, on the power wielded by Jackson's "kitchen cabinet," on the removal of federal deposits to undermine the Bank of the United States, and on the Indian removal bill that led to the infamous "Trail of Tears."[18] Nowhere was the vehemence of Crockett's opposition to Jackson more evident than in the conclusion to his autobiography. After gloating a bit in regard to his reelection in 1833 over Jackson's candidate, William Fitzgerald, who had unseated him in 1831, Crockett said that what was even "more agreeable to my feelings as a freeman" was that

> I am at liberty to vote as my conscience and judgment dictates to be right, without the yoke of any party on me, or the driver at my heels, with his whip in hand, commanding me to ge-wo-haw, just at his pleasure. Look at my arms, you will find no party hand-cuff on them! Look at my neck, you will not find there any collar, with the engraving

17. James A. Shackford, *David Crockett: The Man and the Legend,* ed. by John B. Shackford (1956; rpt. Chapel Hill: Univ. of North Carolina Press, 1986), p. 64.

18. Crockett, *Narrative,* pp. 29, 93–95, 112, 124, 131, and 133; Shackford, pp. 116–18.

MY DOG.

ANDREW JACKSON.

But you will find me standing up to my rack, as the people's faithful representative, and the public's most obedient, very humble servant,

DAVID CROCKETT.[19]

Even in defeat his "go ahead" spirit of independent action and sense of humor never completely deserted him. When he lost his bid for reelection to the House of Representatives in 1835 by 252 votes to Adam Huntsman, a peg-legged lawyer supported by Jackson and Governor Carroll of Tennessee, he might have become despondent or bitter. Instead, he decided to explore Texas and to move his family there if the prospects were pleasing. On November 1, 1835, Crockett, together with William Patton, Abner Burgin, and Lindsey K. Tinkle, set out to the west. He did so because, as he wrote on the eve of his departure, "I want to explore the Texes [*sic*] well before I return."[20] At this point he had no intention of joining the fight for Texas independence.

The foursome reached Memphis the first evening, and, in company with some friends in the bar of the Union Hotel for a farewell drinking party, Crockett offered his now famous remark: "Since you have chosen to elect a man with a timber toe to succeed me, you may all go to hell and I will go to Texas."[21] They set off the next day. Their route was down the Mississippi River to the Arkansas and then up that river to Little Rock, overland to Fulton, Arkansas, and up the Red River along the northern boundary of Texas; they then crossed the river, entered Clarksville in North Texas, and proceeded south to Nacogdoches and San Augustine; and finally went on to San Antonio and then the Alamo.[22]

At San Augustine the party evidently divided. Burgin and Tinkle went home; Crockett and Patton signed the oath of allegiance, but only after David insisted upon the insertion of the word "republican" in the document. They thus swore their allegiance to the "Provisional Government of Texas or any future *republican* Government that may be

19. Crockett, *Narrative*, pp. 210–11.
20. Shackford, pp. 210–11.
21. [Richard Penn Smith], *Col. Crockett's Exploits and Adventures in Texas . . . Written by Himself* (Philadelphia: T.K. & P.G. Collins [Carey & Hart], 1836), p. 31; Shackford, p. 212.
22. Shackford, pp. 212–13.

hereafter declared. . . ."[23] Crockett had balked at the possibility that he would be obliged to support some future government that might prove despotic.

That Texas had changed his plans was indisputable. His last surviving letter written on January 9, 1836, was quite clear:

> I must say as to what I have seen of Texas it is the garden spot of the world. The best land and the best prospects for health I ever saw, and I do believe it is a fortune to any man to come here. There is a world of country here to settle. . . . I have taken the oath of government and have enrolled my name as a volunteer and will set out for the Rio Grand [*sic*] in a few days with the volunteers from the United States. But all volunteers is entitled to vote for a member of the convention or to be voted for, and I have but little doubt of being elected a member to form a constitution for this province. I am rejoiced at my fate. I had rather be in my present situation than to be elected to a seat in Congress for life. I am in hopes of making a fortune yet for myself and family, bad as my prospect has been.[24]

Texas would allow him to rejuvenate his political career and, as he clarified elsewhere, would serve as well as his future home and the means of acquiring the affluence he had unsuccessfully sought all his life. He intended to become land agent for the new territory.[25]

In early February, Crockett arrived at San Antonio De Bexar; Santa Anna arrived on February 20. On the one hand, Crockett was still fighting Jackson. The Americans in Texas were split into two political factions that divided roughly into those supporting a conservative Whig philosophy and those supporting the administration. He chose to join Colonel William B. Travis, who had deliberately disregarded Sam Houston's orders to withdraw from the Alamo rather than support Houston, a Jacksonian sympathizer. And, on the other hand, he saw the future of an independent Texas as his future, and he loved a good fight.[26]

The details of the famous battle of the Alamo are so often recounted that they need no reiteration here. Crockett's part in the battle and particularly the circumstances of his death on March 6, 1836, however, continued in uncertainty until the publication in 1975 of the translation

23. Ibid., pp. 213, 216–18.
24. Ibid., p. 216.
25. Ibid., pp. 214–15.
26. Ibid., pp. 220–28; Richard Boyd Hauck, *Crockett: A Bibliography* (Westport, Conn.: Greenwood Press, 1982), reissued in paperback as *Davy Crockett: A Handbook* (Lincoln: Univ. of Nebraska Press, 1986), pp. 49–50. It will be cited as *Crockett* in these notes.

of the diary of Lieutenant José Enrique de la Peña.[27] When this eyewitness account was placed together with other corroborating documents, Crockett's central role in the defense became clear. Travis had previously written that during the first bombardment Crockett was everywhere in the Alamo "animating the men to do their duty." Other reports told of the deadly fire of his rifle that killed five Mexican gunners in succession, as they each attempted to fire a cannon bearing on the fort, and that he may have just missed Santa Anna, who thought himself out of range of all of the defenders' rifles. Crockett and five or six others were captured when the Mexican troops took the Alamo at about six o'clock that fateful morning. Santa Anna had ordered that no prisoners be taken and was so infuriated when some of his officers brought the Americans before him to try to intercede for their lives that he ordered them executed immediately. The prisoners were bayoneted and then shot. The whole episode likely took no more than a few minutes.[28] Crockett's reputation and that of the other survivors was not, as some have suggested, sullied by their capture. It required more military ability to survive the siege than to be killed in it. Their dignity and bravery was, in fact, further underscored when de la Peña recounted that "these unfortunates died without complaining and without humiliating themselves before their torturers."[29]

Ironically, a work mostly of fiction masquerading as fact had put the truth of Crockett's death before the American public in the summer of 1836. Despite its many falsifications and plagiarisms, [Richard Penn Smith's] *Col. Crockett's Exploits and Adventures in Texas . . . Written by Himself* had a reasonably accurate account of David's capture and execution. Many thought the legendary Davy deserved better and provided it, from thrilling pictures and tales of him clubbing Mexicans with his empty rifle and holding his section of the wall of the Alamo until cut down by bullets and bayonets—the Fess Parker-John Wayne image so dear to most Americans—to his previously mentioned survival as a slave in a Mexican salt mine in the Crockett almanacs.[30]

27. José Enrique de la Peña, *With Santa Anna in Texas: A Personal Narrative of the Revolution,* trans. and ed. Carmen Perry (College Station: Texas A&M Univ. Press, 1975). The original Spanish edition was published in 1955.

28. Dan Kilgore, *How Did Davy Die?* (College Station: Texas A&M Univ. Press, 1978), pp. 12, 15–21, 47; Hauck, *Crockett,* pp. 52–54; see also Paul Andrew Hutton, "Davy Crockett, Still King of the Wild Frontier," *Texas Monthly* (Nov. 1986), 122–30, 244–[48].

29. De la Peña, p. 53.

30. *Col. Crockett's Exploits and Adventures in Texas,* pp. 203–205; Richard Boyd Hauck, "The Man in the Buckskin Hunting Shirt," in Lofaro, *Davy Crockett,* pp. 11–13; Shackford, pp. 228–36; "Battle of San Antonio de Bexar, Heroism and Death of

III

The first two Nashville Crockett almanacs and a competing issue published in New York were already in the hands of the public when the historical Crockett died at the battle of the Alamo in 1836.[31] His heroic death, the crucial element in the elevation and recreation of any man into a national myth, loosed the floodgates for the unrestrained expansion of Crockett's legend in the popular media of his day and ours.

David had, in fact, already become Davy to a certain extent. "His" major books—the *Sketches and Eccentricities, A Narrative,* the *Tour,* and the posthumously published *Col. Crockett's Exploits and Adventures in Texas*—contained a number of tales that had taken root in fertile soil. A number of these stories were reprinted in the early Nashville almanacs and, within a few years, flowered into tales with Davy as a full-blown ring-tailed roarer.

This Crockett of the Nashville almanacs was no relation to the Walt Disney-Fess Parker version of the frontiersman. He was a screamer who could "run faster,—jump higher,—squat lower,—dive deeper,—stay under longer,—and come out drier, than any man in the whole country." Although he came out wet in another adventure, he did manage to kill a twelve-foot long "monstratious great Cat-Fish" in an underwater battle of epic proportions. He also saved the United States from destruction by wringing the tail off Halley's Comet and flinging it back into space (1835, p. 2; 1836, pp. 6–7; 1837, p. 2).

In later non-Nashville almanacs the stories sometimes grew taller yet, as Davy saved the solar system by unfreezing the "airth" and sun that had "friz fast" to their axes with hot bear "ile." He then reenacted the role of Prometheus as he "walked home, introducin' the people to fresh daylight with a piece of sunrise in my pocket. . . ." Davy even wrapped his giant alligator's tail around his body and rode his pet up the face of Niagara Falls, and, in other episodes, he treed a ghost and drank up the Gulf of Mexico.[32]

Col. Crockett" (1837, pp. 44–46, 48); "Introduction—by Ben Harding" (1841, p. [2]). "Colonel Crockett's Trip to Texas and Fight with the Mexicans," *Davy Crockett's Almanac, 1845* (Boston: James Fisher; Philadelphia and New York: Turner & Fisher; New Orleans: Magee, Kneass & Co.), p. [29]; "Death of Crockett," *Crockett Almanac. 1848* (Boston, James Fisher; Philadelphia: Philip Borbeck; New Orleans: Magee and Kneass [a significant textual variant with much advertising inserted and with a rearrangement of the stories]), pp. [33, 35].

31. The competitor was *Crockett's Yaller Flower Almanac, for '36* (New York: Elton).

32. *Crockett Almanac, 1854,* p. [25]; *Crockett's Almanac, 1846* (Boston: James Fisher; Philadelphia and New York: Turner & Fisher; Richmond: Drinker & Morris), pp. [32–33]; *Davy Crockett's Almanac, 1844* (Boston: James Fisher; Philadelphia and

"Crockett's Wonderful Escape, by Driving his Pet Alligator Up Niagara Falls," from *Crockett's Almanac. 1846. Scenes in River Life, Feats on the Lakes, Manners in the Back Woods, Adventures in Texas, &c. &c.* (Boston: James Fisher), p. [32]. American Antiquarian Society.

While the language of Crockett's boasts and the setting and events of his battles and epic exploits had a decidedly American twist in these tales, the form of his heroism harkened back to Old World myth, saga, and romance. Davy's life, as described in the almanacs, contained the

New York: Turner & Fisher; Philadelphia: Turner & Fisher; New York: Turner & Fisher), p. [33]; *Crockett's Almanac, 1846,* p. [33]. An earlier reference to the parallel between Crockett and Prometheus in the almanacs occurs in *Ben Hardin's Crockett Almanac. 1842,* p. [9]. All but the story from the 1842 almanac are more readily available in Dorson's *Davy Crockett,* pp. 16–17, 10–12, 159–60, 157–58.

key features of heroic narrative and shared common ground with the likes of Cu Chulainn, Prince Marko, Siegfried, Beowulf, Roland, El Cid, and especially Antar. Crockett's remarkable birth, his incredible boyhood deeds, his extraordinary abilities in individual combat with man and beast, his travels, his pride in his women, his weapons, and his animals, his mighty oaths and boasts, and, most importantly, his tragic and noble death in a battle against overwhelming odds, all conformed to typical heroic pattern.[33]

Davy "war the biggest infant that ever was, and a little the smartest that ever will be"; he was weaned on whiskey mixed with rattlesnakes' eggs and had a twelve-foot long cradle that was made out of the shell of a snapping turtle, "kivered with wild cat-skins," and had an alligator-hide pillow stuffed with Indian scalps.[34] He killed three wolves when he was six years old and said that when he was eight, he "weighed about two hundred pounds an fourteen ounces, with my shoes off, an my feet clean, an stomach empty."[35] Davy's mature deeds were the focal point of most of the almanacs and are amply represented in this volume in the topical sections entitled "Davy Challenging Man," "Davy Challenging Beast," and "Davy and the Indians." His adventures took him throughout the United States, to the Carribean, South America, Europe, the islands of the Pacific, and to the Far East. Throughout it all, his pride in himself and in those who constituted his nuclear family was unflinching. His wife, Sally Ann Thunder Ann Whirlwind Crockett, was a patriotic treasure of a screamer, who celebrated the annexation of Texas with a drink of "Eagle egg nog" and his youngest daughter could fricassee a bear by grinning a "double streak o' blue lightnin into his mouth" at the age of six.[36] As a traditional warrior, however, Davy's most constant companions in his adventures were his prized weapons and animals: his rifle, Killdevil; his knife, Big Butcher; his pet bear, Death-Hug; and his dogs, Tiger, Grizzle, Rough, and others.

33. Richard M. Dorson, "Davy Crockett and the Heroic Age," *Southern Folklore Quarterly,* 6 (June 1942), 95–102; see also J. DeLancey Ferguson, "The Roots of American Humor," *American Scholar,* 4 (Winter 1934–35), 41–49, and Constance Rourke's reply, "Examining the Roots of American Humor," *American Scholar,* 4 (Spring 1935), 249–53. Both are conveniently reprinted in William B. Clark and W. Craig Turner, eds., *Critical Essays on American Humor* (Boston: G.K. Hall & Co., 1984), pp. 51–58, 58–62.

34. *Crockett Almanac, 1851* (Philadelphia, New York, and Boston: Fisher & Brother), p. [14]; *Crockett's Almanac. 1848,* pp. [8, 9]; *Davy Crockett's Almanac, 1845,* p. [5]. See Dorson's *Davy Crockett,* pp. 3–8, for a more readily available version of these texts.

35. *Crockett's Almanac. 1848,* p. [13]; *Crockett Almanac, 1851,* p. [14]. Davy's horse helped by killing the fourth wolf.

36. *Crockett Almanac, 1854,* p. [7]; *Davy Crockett's Almanac, 1845,* p. [33].

Two of the most interesting facets of Crockett's participation in Old World heroic narrative were the mighty boasts that often complemented his mature deeds and the extraordinary nature of his death at the Alamo. Taking a cue from the introductory "'Go Ahead' Reader" section of the first Nashville almanac quoted above in which Crockett could "run faster,—jump higher . . . than any man in the whole country," the 1837 Nashville almanac made apparent how quickly such boasts could expand to epic proportions in the "Speech of Colonel Crockett in Congress" and how, at the same time, they could reveal much about the beliefs of the writers of the tales in regard to frontier humor, cultural stereotypes, and prejudices.

Mr. Speaker.

Who–Who–Whoop–Bow–Wow–Wow–Yough. I say, Mr. Speaker; I've had a speech in soak this six months, and it has swelled me like a drowned horse; if I don't deliver it I shall burst and smash the windows. The gentleman from Massachusetts (Mr. Everett) talks of summing up the merits of the question, but I'll sum up my own. In one word I'm a screamer, and have got the roughest racking horse, the prettiest sister, the surest rifle and the ugliest dog in the district. I'm a leetle the savagest crittur you ever *did see*. My father can whip any man in Kentucky, and I can lick my father. I can outspeak any man on this floor, and give him two hours start. I can run faster, dive deeper, stay longer under, and come out drier, than any *chap* this side the big *Swamp*. I can outlook a panther and outstare a flash of lightning: tote a steamboat on my back and play at rough and tumble with a lion, and an occasional kick from a *Zebra*. To sum up all in one word *I'm a horse*. Goliah was a pretty hard colt but I could choke him.—I can take the rag off—frighten the old folks—astonish the natives—and beat the Dutch all to smash—make nothing of sleeping under a blanket of snow—and don't mind being frozen more than a rotten apple. Congress allows *lemonade* to the members and has it charged under the head of *stationary*—I move also that *Whiskey* be allowed under the item of *fuel*. For *bitters* I can suck away at a noggin of aquafortis, sweetened with brimstone, stirred with a lightning rod, and skimmed with a hurricane. I've soaked my head and shoulders in Salt River, so much that I'm always corned. I can walk like an ox; run like a fox, swim like an eel, yell like an Indian, fight like a devil, and spout like an earthquake, make love like a mad bull, and swallow a nigger whole without choking if you butter his head and pin his ears back.

(1837, p. 40)[37]

While the backwoods boast was a mainstay of the Crockett almanacs and of much of the "Humor of the Old Southwest," this hallmark of the American frontier had at least three primary antecedents. Davy's savagery in the often ritualistic combat that followed the boasting linked

37. The tale is reprinted in Dorson, *Davy Crockett,* pp. 29–30.

The savage Crockett as depicted in "Crockett's Fight with the Indian Chief, 'Wild Cat,'" from *Davy Crockett's Almanac. 1845* (Boston: James Fisher), p. [9]. American Antiquarian Society.

Crockett's "Fight with a Puke [a Missourian]," from *Crockett's Almanac, 1850* (New York, Philadelphia, and Boston: Fisher and Brothers), p. [23]. St. Louis Mercantile Library Association.

him to the ancient tradition of the wild man as posited by civilized society, the New World American as popularly conceived of by the European. Additionally, his boasts drew upon both the heroic nature of the flyting of the Old World epic as one of its ancestors and upon the Aristotelian character type of the *alazon* for the comic spirit invested in Crockett as a swaggering, blustering, and sometimes cowardly braggart.[38] In this instance, the Crockett of the almanacs was again a syn-

38. Albanese, "Davy Crockett and the Wild Man," in Lofaro, *Davy Crockett,* pp. 80–101; Dorothy Dondore, "Big Talk! The Flyting, the Gabe, and the Frontier Boast," *American Speech,* 6 (October 1930), 45–55; William F. Thompson, "Frontier Tall Talk," *American Speech,* 9 (October 1934), 187–99; Dorson, "Davy Crockett and the Heroic Age," 97–101; and Walter Blair, "Americanized Comic Braggarts," *Critical Inquiry,* 4 (Winter 1977), 331–43. A slightly different version of Blair's article appears in Blair and Hill, *America's Humor,* pp. 122–42. For traces of the wild man in the life of the historical Crockett, see Catherine L. Albanese, "Citizen Crockett: Myth, History, and Nature Religion," *Soundings,* 61 (Spring 1978), 95–97.

thesis, the end product of a historical process transformed to suit the tastes of nineteenth-century American readers.

Perhaps the best example that combined the ritual aspects of the boast and the no-holds-barred backwoods brawl occurred when Davy described his "Fight with a Puke [a Missourian]":

> One day as I war settin' in the door of my cabin, and sharpening out my thum nale, I felt wolfish about the head and shoulders, when I seed a Puke and a Wolverine goin' by. The Puke cocked his eye, and looked sassy. I looked at him and snorted like a wild hoss. Sez he—"I guess you feel wholesome this mornin'." Sez I—"I feel as if I could double up any Puke that ever walked between here and a generation of vipers." That made him feel ugly, and he moved his ears like a Jackass, and sez; "stranger, I think I shall go home with one of your eyes in my pocket." I stood up and spit in his face. He pulled up his breeches, and crowed three times. I felt my flesh crawl over, and my toe-nails moved out of place. I moved my elbow in scientific order, and got ready to take a twist in his hair. When he seed that, he squealed and ran around me three times. I jumped up, and planted my heels in his bowels. That made him feel dissatisfied with me, and he caught me 'round the thigh and war goin' to throw me down: but I stooped over and cotched him by the seat of his trowsers and held him up in the air, when he squirmed like an eel, and tried to shoot me with his pistol. I twisted him over, and took his knee-pan in my mouth and bit clear through to the bone. He squawked and begged for mercy, and then I let him down, and give him a kick that sent him half a rod, and he run like a deer.[39]

In not killing his less skilled opponent, the tall tale Crockett revealed something of the nobility in the "noble savage" aspect of his character that in turn reflected the heroism of the historical Crockett in his stand at the Alamo.

Without question, the actual Crockett's death was the single most important event in establishing his fame and served as well as the cornerstone and primary source of the myths that developed about him. As with the Old World heroes, Davy's death fittingly crowned his career rather than simply ending it. The almanacs caught the tone perfectly. They showed him dying in combat and provided a fitting mythic eulogy:

> Down fell the Kurnill like a lion struck by thunder and lightning. He never, never spoke again. It war a great loss to the country and the world, and to ole Kaintuck in particklar. Thar war never known such a member of Congress as Crockett, and never will be agin. The painters and bears will miss him, for he never missed them.
>
> He died like a member o' Congress ought to die. While he war about to do

39. *Crockett's Almanac, 1850* (New York, Philadelphia, and Boston: Fisher & Brothers), p. [23]. Another example of ritualistic boast and battle is found in Davy's

"Death of Crockett," *Crockett's Almanac. 1848* (Philadelphia: Philip Borbeck), p. [33]. St. Louis Mercantile Library Association.

his country sum sarvice, and raise her name high as her mountains, he war cut down in the prime o' life, and at a time when he war most wanted. His screams and yells are heard no more, and the whole country are clouded with a darkness for the gallant Kurnill. He war an ornament to the forest, and never war known to refuse his whiskey to a stranger. When he war alive, it war most beautiful to hear his screams comin through the forest; it would turn and twist itself into some o' the most splendifferous knots, and then untie itself and keep on till it got clar into no war. But he are a dead man now, and if you want to see old Kaintuck's tears, go thar, and speak o' her gallant Kurnill, and thars

---

"A Love Adventure and uproarious fight with a Stage Driver" (1836, pp. 43–44). See also Lofaro, "The Hidden 'Hero,'" in Lofaro, *Davy Crockett,* pp. 54–55.

not a human but what will turn away and go behind some tree and dry up thar tears. He are dead now, and may he rest forever and a day arter.[40]

One almanac account stated the "facts": "Thus perished Crockett, in a noble cause. Fear was a word he knew not the definition of. It was calculated that during the siege he killed no less than 85 men, and wounded 120 besides . . ." (1837, p. 46). And another that had Davy defeat Santa Anna and survive the battle of the Alamo brought Crockett back for a rematch with his nemesis in the Mexican War. Riding his pet bear, Davy singlehandedly routed the entire army: "for I out with my bone scythe, an if I didn't make Mexican heads fly about as thick as horse chestnuts in a hurrycane, then melt me into iron for steambilers. I fed five hundred flocks o' wolves on their meat, made a thousand quail traps o' their bones, wiped the sweat off with uncle Sam's striped handkerchief, and come home to Kentuck as fresh as old Niagara."[41]

IV

The three almanacs of the second Nashville series reprinted here have relatively little of the jingoistic and expansionistic rhetoric of the Turner & Fisher almanacs. Instead, they capture the mythical Davy in a state of transition. They contain none of the "autobiographical" stories that echo those that appeared in "Crockett's" major books nor any of the descriptions of wildlife or of other unusual or interesting occurrences in the backwoods that so distinguished the first series. And neither do they yet depict him as fully evolved into the nearly invulnerable comic superman who ranged over the whole world doing impossible deeds. What these three Nashville almanacs do establish, however, through the plots, language, and humor of their tales, is a pattern of oppositions that would define Davy as one of the legendary trickster characters of folklore and as a cultural mirror of his times.

As one reads these stories, Davy's affinities with other trickster-transformers of various folk traditions becomes clear. Like Coyote, the best known of the tricksters in North American Indian lore and like the less familiar Hare, Spider, Raven, and Turtle of that same tradition, he is creator and destroyer, giver and taker, benefactor and buffoon, one who is cunning and then is a dupe, and one who is all-powerful one moment and cowardly the next. In this dualism, Davy is in good measure a lineal descendant of the trickster as divine culture hero, an inte-

40. *Crockett's Almanac. 1848*, p. [35].
41. *Davy Crockett's Almanac, 1845*, p. [29].

gral part of the origin myths of many primitive societies.[42] Crockett also participates in this mythology by exemplifying the comic and picaresque traits of the trickster. He combines the nineteenth-century American version of the medieval jester with that of the wandering hero. In one tale, Crockett even becomes something of a transformer in order to escape from a "passel of Injuns." While not a literal shape-shifter, a god-like being truly without a fixed form, Davy certainly demonstrates his malleability in this instance:

> I cut dirt around amongst sum bushes, and then I seed that one eend of a log was open, and the open eend war hid in the bushes. But I found that the hole war very small. So I stuck my finger down my throte and threw up all the vittles that war in my bowels. But I war not small enuff yet, and I tride to think of the meanest thing I ever did, so as I might feel small. By them means I got in a proper fix for squeezing in, but arter all it war like spiking a cannon. (1840, p. 29)

Further parallels to the trickster tradition abound in the Crockett almanacs. Like the European character of Reynard the Fox and the Afro-American characters of Anansi the Spider and the famous Brer Rabbit, Davy leapfrogs from one adventure to the next for the sheer thrill that each conquest or defeat provides. He is impulsive, often at the mercy of his passions, and generally exhibits unconscious or preconscious behavior, all classic traits of the trickster.[43] At times, he seems the embodiment of the motto of the historical Crockett gone wild. "Be always sure you're right, then go ahead" effectively becomes "Go ahead whether you're right or not" in the almanacs. And like all these tricksters, Davy shows no real concern for material advancement or wealth, no desire to rise in society like many of the heroic protagonists in the tales of the Brothers Grimm or of Jack, in the Jack Tale cycle of the Southern Appalachians, who is the American counterpart to Jack in English tales such as "Jack and the Beanstalk." Just as in the wonderful tale of his unexpected ride on the horns of an elk, Davy moves through his world either free of all restraint or simply out of control, all the while reveling in the problems that he more often than not creates (1841, pp. 21–22).

42. Paul Radin, *The Trickster: A Study in American Indian Mythology* (London: Routledge and Kegan Paul, 1956); Roger L. Welsch, *Omaha Tribal Myths and Trickster Tales* (Chicago: Sage/Swallow Press, 1981).

43. Davy's behavior, however, does not completely prove a true fit to the classic unconscious or preconscious mold of the trickster. He has a code of moral and social values and a clear sense of the difference between good and evil not present in the classic trickster myths. On the other hand, his code and concepts of good and evil are at considerable variance with the civilized cultural norms of his day. He is again best seen as a composite creation.

The pattern of oppositions in the three almanacs is seen most easily when examining Davy at his best and at his worst. While there are none of the extraordinary, outrageous tales that would fall into the category aptly termed "The Legend Full-Blown"[44] in this transition period, there are several tales which show Davy off to advantage, not the least of which is his famous shooting match with Mike Fink. Davy's sharp-shooting has given him the edge in a fabulous contest until Mike shoots half the comb out of his wife's hair and dares Davy to duplicate the feat. But Davy can't. "'No, no, Mike,' sez I, 'Davy Crockett's hand would be sure to shake, if his [shootin] iron war pointed within a hundred mile of a shemale, and I give up beat, Mike . . . '" (1840, p. 11).

When the possibility of harming the fair sex was not an issue, however, Davy excelled. His true grit was apparent particularly in his hand-to-hand combat with bears. In one fierce tussle, Crockett was surprised and captured "by a great bear that war hugging me like a brother, and sticking as close to me as a turcle to his shell." Happy at first to have his dinner so close at hand, Davy declared that his confidence shrank when the bear increased his hold and "drew his tongue across my throat to mark out the place where he should put in his teeth." Nonetheless, with the distraction provided by his dog, Rough, he was able to throw the bear and kill it with his knife (1841, pp. 9–10). In another episode, Davy fell into a tall hollow honey tree and onto a hibernating bear. He escaped by sinking his teeth into the bear's tail and encouraging it out of the tree with "an awful fundamental poke" in the rump with his butcher knife. Davy let his transportation live, "for it would be onmanly to be onthankful for the sarvis he done me," especially since chewing two inches of the bear's tail cured his toothache (1840, pp. 25, 28).

At his best, Davy was also helpful and compassionate. She-screamer Grace Peabody was so grateful that he saved her from a pack of wolves that she sent him a fine new pair of stockings that she knit out of wolf sinews (1840, p. 20). This Crockett even saved the lives of Indians on occasion (1839, p. 10) and in "Indian Notions" went so far as to describe a brave and his small daughter as more than "varmints": "They lookt more like human creturs with human feelings, than any of the breed that I ever noed before." And after hearing the brave relate the sentimental tale of his great love for his deceased wife, the Colonel could only say: "Davy Krockitt is none of your whimperers, but if I

44. Dorson created the category; see his *Davy Crockett*, p. v.

didn't drop tears as big as a bullet, I hope I may be shot" (1840, pp. 12–13).

As a trickster, Davy's character moves quickly from one extreme to another. The heroic, noble hunter of the almanacs is also a coward and a fool, as well as a savage and a bigot. In these three issues, Crockett is shamed by an elk, scared by an owl, saved by his wife, and duped by a pedlar (1839, pp. 25–26; 1840, pp. 2, 8–10, 29). He is also cast as the country bumpkin in the traditional tale of the fool who continues to spit on an expensive carpet rather than soil a decorated spittoon and gets so mad at the servant who keeps moving the spittoon into his line of fire that he yells, "'if you put that ere box in my way agin I'll spit in it'" (1839, p. 12).

Perhaps most offensive to modern sensibilities are those tales that showcase vulgar and savage behavior or center upon prejudice. It would be hard not to shudder when Davy forces a squatter to eat "every atom" of a freshly fallen cow pie because he asked Crockett to support his false land claim, or not to express some shock when Davy kills an Indian because the brave taunted the whites by exposing his "posterum" and asking them to kiss it (1839, pp. 11–12; 1841, pp. 4, 6). Like most tricksters, his responses are seldom in proportion to the offense.[45] This excess is also visible in an early version of the savage nationalism that the Turner & Fisher almanacs would perfect. After Davy survives the fierce combat in "Tussle with a Bear" alluded to earlier, he says that "When I cum to strip, arter the affair war over, the marks of the bear's claws war up and down on my hide to such a rate that I might have been hung out for an American flag. The stripes showed most beautiful" (1841, p. 10) The disregard that he displays for his own well-being and that of others is also typical behavior for a trickster.

The darkest side of Davy's character lies in the attitude that the writers of the tales invest in him to make his extreme deeds seem logical. He kills or abuses "red niggers" with impunity because Indians, like blacks, are regarded as subhuman "ignorant wretches" (1841, p. 6; 1839, p. 18). He also insults and mistreats "Yankees," "Paddies" [Irishmen], preachers, and anyone with an education (1840, pp. 29, 33; 1841, p. 22; 1839, pp. 34–35; 1841, pp. 23–24). Indeed, anyone that differs from the ideal citizen of the backwoods is sure to receive cruel treatment.

45. Perhaps the epitome of extreme behavior occurs when Davy kills and boils an Indian to make a tonic to help cure his pet bear's stomach disorder. The tale is in *Davy Crockett's Almanac, 1847* (Boston: James Fisher; New York and Philadelphia: Turner & Fisher), p. [25].

A face to face confrontation with the brutality, racism, chauvinistic humor, and comic stereotypes that many nineteenth-century Americans regarded as funny is a disturbing experience. But rather than ignoring history, the reader should view the best and the worst elements of the stories together as a cultural whole. Then compare the extreme violence of some of the tales and the audacity of the woodcuts that illustrate them to that of the Saturday morning cartoons on television and the superheroes in present-day comic books before rendering a final judgment and realize that these fictions and fantasies are in many ways the direct descendants of the Crockett almanacs. Remember that the "Nashville" Crockett almanacs were written and published in Boston and that the mythic West and legendary tall tales of Davy Crockett are creations filtered through eastern perceptions and prejudices. And recall how the Davy of the almanacs is both an American and a composite creation. He is startlingly new and familiar at the same time, a firm link between the present of the nineteenth century and the history and the traditions of almanac making, Old World heroic narrative, and the international folklore of the trickster. Combine all these elements and then gaze into the almanacs as a fun house mirror of America's cultural past. They offer an image that is part truth, part distortion, and always interesting.

While not forgetting the problems raised by the stories, remember too that the almanacs were designed as entertainment and meant to appeal to a broad audience for the widest possible commercial success. They reflected the attitudes of their day but were not produced with malicious intent. In the final analysis perhaps Ben Harding the sailor best explains the purpose of the stories when he sums up his editorial method: "I meen to crack on all I no, under a full press of canvass, till I giv the bografy of every wild cretur in these landings, and make the whole *world laugh and dance for joy.*" And the Nashville Crockett almanacs succeed so well along these lines that in many instances the reader might wish to take the precautions that Ben urges before examining these "terrificashus" yarns: "You had best to hoop your ribs before you reed em or you will shake your bowels out a laffing" (1841, p. 2; 1839, p. 2).

Michael A. Lofaro
University of Tennessee
October 21, 1986

BIBLIOGRAPHIC NOTES ON THE TEXTS

The rarity and fragility of the Crockett almanacs, in combination with their desirability to private collectors of almanacs, Americana, and items dealing with Davy Crockett, create difficulties both in attempting to locate existing copies and in formulating a complete bibliographic description of the existing texts of the second series of Nashville almanacs.

In research conducted from January 1981 to September 1986, it became apparent that changes had occurred that significantly altered the list of libraries that hold these three almanacs as noted in Milton Drake's standard bibliography of *Almanacs of the United States* (New York: Scarecrow Press, 1962). For the separate entries for the 1839, 1840, and 1841 Nashville almanacs, Drake cited 40 locations (15, 16, and 9 respectively). Of these, 9 (2, 4, and 3) no longer hold or never held the almanacs. However, 20 new locations (8, 10, and 2) have been unearthed to yield a present total of 51 locations (21, 22, and 8) of 53 almanacs (2 archives have duplicates, one of an 1839 and one of an 1840 issue). Since several libraries hold almanacs for two or three of the years and each year is listed individually in Drake's bibliography, there are only 33 different archives that collectively hold all these items. An updating of Drake's entries that incorporates all new information is found in this book in the section entitled "A Checklist of the Locations of the Second Nashville Series of Crockett Almanacs."

The almanacs are also quite popular with individual collectors and occasionally are offered at auction or for sale by booksellers. For example, nine Crockett almanacs, including a copy of the 1839 and of the 1840 Nashville imprints, appeared as item 35 of Sotheby's May 23, 1984 auction (sale #5187). The estimated sale price for the lot was $7,500 to $10,000. The total number of verified Nashville almanacs of the second series would likely thus increase to at least 55. The actual number of extant almanacs would be significantly higher due to those held in private hands.

This preliminary survey does not represent a complete canvassing of all libraries in this and in other countries and does not attempt to locate those almanacs held in private collections. It does include a survey of all the repositories listed in Drake's bibliography as holding any of the thirty-one different issues of the Crockett almanacs for 1835 to 1856 and their variant imprints (based on the supposition that these institutions might wish to strengthen their holdings in this area). It also includes a personal survey of over ninety libraries (with some overlap with those surveyed by mail) located mainly east of the Appalachians and of a few other major research facilities such as the Huntington Library in San Marino, California, and the Newberry Library in Chicago.

The ideal situation of gathering all of the originals together for examination (or photocopies or microfilms of those items whose condition would permit duplication) was simply not possible in this case. Because the bibliographic analysis had to proceed in a piecemeal fashion without the opportunity for rigorous comparative study, the following observations must be regarded as tentative. Based on a personal examination of 24 copies of the almanacs (10 [plus 1 variant at the same location], 10, and 3) at 23 locations and a survey by mail of the remaining 29 copies at 28 locations,[1] it appears likely that the versions of the second series of Nashville almanacs reprinted in facsimile in this volume are the primary texts. There are no variants in the publishers' imprints for these almanacs and none for the corresponding first series of Nashville issues of 1835 to 1838 as well. Such is not the case for the majority of the other almanacs, particularly those issued in the 1840s by the firm of Turner & Fisher.

The only variants for the second series of Nashville almanacs appear in the first number and are minor. In the 1839 edition, the primary text (version A) has "A Pretty Predicament" as the title for the tale on page 14 and the reference at the bottom of the illustration for the same story on page 16 tells the reader to "See Account of the Predicament, at Page 14." The St. Louis Mercantile Library Association has a second copy of the almanac (version B; their call number AA/C8/2) that changes the title on page 14 to "A Bundling Match" and similarly changes the caption at the bottom of the woodcut on page 16 to "See Account of Bundling Match, Page 14." Versions A and B bear the same title of "A Pretty Predicament" for the otherwise identical illustration on page 16. The only other variant thus far uncovered is the misprinting of page 8 on the verso of page 5 in the copy of the John Hay Library of Brown University. No variants for the 1840 and 1841 almanacs have yet been found.

1. As previously noted, the term "location" reflects the structure of Drake's bibliography. The 53 almanacs are held by 33 libraries.

A CHECKLIST OF THE LOCATIONS OF THE SECOND NASHVILLE SERIES OF CROCKETT ALMANACS

The following list updates Drake's entries for the 1839, 1840, and 1841 Nashville Crockett almanacs, his numbers 13414, 13416, and 13420 respectively, by repeating his original entries and adding all new locations and information uncovered through September 1986 in brackets. Needless to say, the list is still a preliminary one. It alphabetizes the symbols for the convenience of the reader. It also continues Drake's use of the National Union Catalog's standard symbols for libraries (an explanatory list of the symbols follows the entries) and the use of the abbreviation "frag." for fragment, "impf." for imperfect, and "ll." for leaves. Each of these three almanacs was issued with 18 ll. (36 pages). Please consult the facsimile title pages for full title and imprint data.

1839

The CROCKETT Almanac for 1839. Nashville: Ben Harding. 18 ll. [CSmH]; CtY; DLC; [GEU]; InU [actually InU-Li (17 ll.)]; MB [impf.]; MBAt; MH [actually MH-H]; MWA; MoSM (two varieties); [see the last paragraph of "Bibliographic Notes on the Texts" for an explanation of the MoSM varieties. Version A is complete; version B has 17 ll.—pages 35 and 36 are missing]; N; NHi; [NcWsW]; [NjP]; RJa [no copy located]; [RPB (misprints page 8 on the version of page 5)]; T; [TKL (McClung Collection)]; TN [no copy located]; [TU]; [TxU (Barker Texas History Center)]; TxWB; WHi.

1840

The CROCKETT Almanac for 1840. Nashville: Ben Harding. 18 ll. [CSmH]; CtY; DLC; [GEU]; [ICU (two copies)]; ICHi; InU (impf.) [actually InU-Li (17 ll.)]; MB [15 ll.—missing pages 31 through 36]; [MBNEH]; MDedHi [no copy located]; [MH-H]; MWA; MoSM; N; NB (10 ll.) [no copy located]; NHi; [NcU]; NjP; RJa [no copy located]; [RPB (15 ll.—missing pages 31 through 36)]; T; [TKL (McClung Collection)]; TMC (17 ll.) [now TM, but no copy located]; [TU]; [TxU (Barker Texas History Center)]; WHi.

1841

The CROCKETT Almanac for 1841. Nashville: Ben Harding. 18 ll. CtY; InU (frag.) [actually InU-Li (14 ll.)]; MB; MBAt [no copy located]; [MH-H]; MWA; MiD-B; Ms-Ar [no copy located]; PHi; T [no copy located]; [TxU (Barker Texas History Center)].

LIBRARY SYMBOLS

CSmH / Henry E. Huntington Library, San Marino, Calif.
CtY / Yale University, New Haven, Conn.
DLC / Library of Congress, Washington, D.C.
GEU / Emory University, Atlanta, Ga.
ICHi / Chicago Historical Society, Chicago, Ill.
ICU / University of Chicago, Chicago, Ill.
InU-Li / Lilly Library, Indiana University, Bloomington, Ind.
MB / Boston Public Library, Boston, Mass.
MBAt / Boston Athenaeum, Boston, Mass.
MBNEH / New England Historic Genealogical Society, Boston, Mass.
MDedHi / Dedham Historical Society, Dedham, Mass.
MH-H / Houghton Library, Harvard University, Cambridge, Mass.
MWA / American Antiquarian Society, Worcester, Mass.
MiD-B / Burton Historical Collection, Detroit Public Library, Detroit, Mich.
MoSM / St. Louis Mercantile Library Association, St. Louis, Mo.
Ms-Ar / State Department of Archives and History, Jackson, Miss.
N / New York State Library, Albany, N.Y.
NB / Brooklyn Public Library, New York City, N.Y.
NHi / New York Historical Society, New York City, N.Y.
NcU / University of North Carolina, Chapel Hill, N.C.
NcWsW / Wake Forest University, Winston-Salem, N.C.
NjP / Princeton University, Princeton, N.J.
PHi / Historical Society of Pennsylvania, Philadelphia, Pa.
RJa / Jamestown Philomenian Library, Jamestown, R.I.
RPB / Brown University, Providence, R.I.
T / Tennessee State Library, Nashville, Tenn.
TKL / Knoxville-Knox County Public Library, Knoxville, Tenn.
TMC [TM] / Memphis-Shelby County Public Library, Memphis, Tenn.
TN / Nashville-Davidson County Public Library, Nashville, Tenn.
TU / University of Tennessee, Knoxville, Tenn.
TxU / University of Texas, Austin, Tex.
TxWB / Baylor University, Waco, Tex.
WHi / State Historical Society of Wisconsin, Madison, Wisc.

THE TALL TALES
OF THE CROCKETT ALMANACS

1839

1840

1841

THE TOPICS
OF THE TALL TALES

Davy Challenging Man

Davy Challenging Beast

Davy in Lighter Moments

Davy and the Indians

Ben Harding

Riproarious She-Males

Other Ring-tailed Roarers

Yankees, Pedlars, Preachers, and Eddycated Fools

THE TALL TALES OF DAVY CROCKETT

The Second Nashville Series

Vol. 2.] "GO AHEAD!!" [No. 1.

THE CROCKETT ALMANAC 1839.

An Unexpected Ride on the Horns of an Elk. See Page 25.

Containing Adventures, Exploits, Sprees & Scrapes in the West, & Life and Manners in the Backwoods.

Nashville, Tennessee. Published by Ben Harding. See Page. 2

INTRODUCTION——-by Ben Harding.

Once when I was cruising doun the Massippy on a raft, I fell in with a roaring feller in them parts, and arterwards I found out he was Kurnel Krockett; a glorious prize he was and had more whiskey in his barrel than some craft has when they are going on a India viage. So I kepp my land tacks aboard till I had sounded the old feller pretty well, and found him a wise one—you know it takes a long head to make a Allmyneck. Well I seed very little of the Kurnel arterward till I started on my last viage. When we was out to see on my last viage, I fell from aloft and broke both legs, and put my hip out of place. I thort this misfortin was a sign that somethin bad was goin to happin, and true enuff, when I got home I heered how my old friend the Kurnel had run agin a snag, as he used to call it, and had lost the number of his mess amongst the Texicans. It made me feel pleggy bad, and I went rite off and got drunk in honor of the Kurnell's disease. So I went on a cruize doun into Kentuck, and there I cum across the Kurnel's papers, so as I was knocked up with one game leg and a short hip, and as the doctor pronounced me unseaworthy, I thort I would keep up the Allmynick out of respect to the old Kurnel. I shall cruize about among the gravers and printers in person, and shall see every thing done ship-shape and Bristol fashion. I have got the papers into rail fust rate hands, and as I shall always keep an eye out to windward, I think they will do about what's right. I've got good paper, good gravers, and all that; besides there is a rigular built feller that lives in New York who is a dabster at Matthewmattocks and sifering, and next year he is to make the calkulations for four pints of the compass, so that enny body can find the way out of the woods in the darkest night by jist looking at his Allmynack. I showed a leg all I knew to get 'em rigged out that way for this year in time for the printers; but was obleeged to give up the ship for this time. If the Allmynacks stood in the store all the time, the kalkulations for one place wood do very well; but somehow they wont stick to the bookseller's shelves no time at all, and they goes into all parts like a Jim Crow that is travelling all over the Union. We left out the kalkulations for the moon this year, for the eclipse will happen out of sight and nobody wont see it no how you can fix it; and because it would only be of any use in one part of Amerrykay. The kalkulations for the sun are ship shape. You cant say of them that black is the white of their eye; and next year and ever after till next day arter etarnity the kalkulations for the sun and moon shall be fust chop and shall show up them two glims all the way from Maine to New Orleans. If there is any mistake in the sigh-for-inn for 1840, you may set Ben Harding down for one of Joe Bowers's men with a cod's head on his shoulders. I shall keep all your low slang out of the book, and make it read as slick as a greasy bed-blanket, and as strait as a frozen nigger. All the stories will be as beautiful as a red eel or a painted monkey, so that I think I have hit the mark and shall give my readers **Satisfaction.**

Among the papers yet to print are the drollest yarns about wild scrapes, terrible fights with the wild varmints of the west, both two legged and four legged, and some with no legs at all, that ever was heerd tell of. They are raal terrificashus. So much so that you must reed em through a pare of spektakles or they will make your eyes ake. It like to have broke the press down to print them, they are sich hard karakters. A little dog that swollered one of the leaves of the proof sheet was taken with the kollery morbuss, and his tung hung out haff a yard till he died in the cutest aggunny. You had best to hoop your ribs before you reed em or you will shake your bowels out a laffing. But I'll not be polavering enny more about em here, but just let em speak for themselves in the All-mynack, as it comes out. And now, deer readers, I hope you will be satisfied with matters and things, and if you are not you may just top your boom, and make **A General clear out.**

1839. JANUARY, FIRST MONTH. 3

Days mo.	Days of the week.	Sun rises,	Sun sets.	Days increase.	Sun slow.	☉ declin South.	Length of Days.
1	Tuesday.	7 30	4 38	0 5	3 43	23° 3'	8 58
2	Wednesday.	7 30	4 39	0 6	4 11	22 58	8 58
3	Thursday.	7 30	4 40	0 7	4 39	22 53	9 0
4	Friday.	7 30	4 40	0 8	5 7	22 47	9 0
5	Saturday.	7 30	4 41	0 9	5 34	22 40	9 2
6	**Sunday.**	7 30	4 42	0 10	6 1	22 33	9 2
7	Monday.	7 30	4 43	0 11	6 27	22 26	9 4
8	Tuesday.	7 30	4 44	0 12	6 53	22 18	9 4
9	Wednesday.	7 30	4 45	0 13	7 18	22 10	9 6
10	Thursday.	7 30	4 46	0 14	7 43	22 2	9 8
11	Friday.	7 29	4 47	0 16	8 7	21 53	9 8
12	Saturday.	7 29	4 48	0 17	8 31	21 43	9 10
13	**Sunday.**	7 29	4 49	0 19	8 57	21 33	9 12
14	Monday.	7 28	4 50	0 20	9 16	21 23	9 12
15	Tuesday.	7 28	4 51	0 22	9 37	21 12	9 14
16	Wednesday.	7 27	4 53	0 24	9 58	21 1	9 16
17	Thursday.	7 26	4 54	0 26	10 19	20 50	9 18
18	Friday.	7 26	4 55	0 28	10 38	20 38	9 20
19	Saturday.	7 25	4 57	0 30	10 54	20 25	9 22
20	**Sunday.**	7 24	4 58	0 32	11 15	20 13	9 24
21	Monday.	7 23	4 59	0 34	11 33	20 0	9 26
22	Tuesday.	7 23	5 0	0 36	11 49	19 46	9 28
23	Wednesday.	7 22	5 2	0 38	12 5	19 33	9 30
24	Thursday.	7 21	5 3	0 40	12 20	19 18	9 32
25	Friday.	7 20	5 4	0 42	12 35	19 4	9 34
26	Saturday.	7 20	5 5	0 44	12 48	18 49	9 36
27	**Sunday.**	7 19	5 6	0 46	13 1	18 34	9 38
28	Monday.	7 18	5 8	0 48	13 13	18 18	9 40
29	Tuesday.	7 17	5 9	0 51	13 24	18 2	9 42
30	Wednesday.	7 16	5 10	0 53	13 35	17 46	9 44
31	Thursday.	7 15	5 12	0 55	13 44	17 30	9 46

Col. Crockett's Adventure with a Grizzly Bear.

RELATED IN A MENAGERIE.

You may say what you please and be d—d, Mr. Stranger, about your hannycondy, the great terrificacious sarpint of Seelon in South Ameriky, and your rale Bengal tiger from Afriky. Both on 'em heated to a white heat and welded into one would be no part of a priming to a grizzly bear of the Rocky mountains. He'd chaw up your roonosseros and your lion and your tiger as small as cut tobacco, for breakfast and pick his teeth with the bones. The cretur's rale grit and don't mind fire no more than sugar plums, and none of your wild beastesses can say that for themselves. I've killed one or two on 'em myself, which ar not a thing many pukes or suckers can bost on, tho they are pretty good at scalping injuns. I was delightfully skeered by the fust I ever saw—no, that ar a d—d lie, tho I say it myself.—Davy Crockett was never skeered by anything but a female woman, but it ar a fact that I war tetotaciously consarned for my life.

You see it war when I war young I went to massacree the buffaloes on the head of Little Great Small Deep Shallow Big Muddy River, with my nigger b'y Doughboy, what I give three hundred dollars for. I'd been all day till now, vagabondizing about the prairie without seeing an atom of a buffalo, when I seed one grazing in the rushes on the edge of a pond, and a crusty old batchelder he was. He war a thousand year old at least, for his hide war all kivered with skars, and he had as much beard as would do all the dandies I've seen in Broadway for whiskers and mustashes a hull

[Continued on page 6.

Col. Crockett's Adventure with a Grizzly Bear. See Page 3.

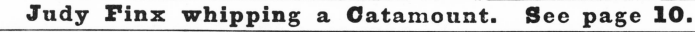

Judy Finx whipping a Catamount. See page 10.

FEBRUARY, SECOND MONTH. 1839.

Days mo.	Days of the week.	Sun rises,	Sun sets.	Days increase	Sun slow.	☉ declin. South.	Length of Days.
1	Friday.	7 14	5 14	0 57	13 53	17° 13′	9 48
2	Saturday.	7 13	5 15	1 0	14 1	16 56	9 52
3	**Sunday.**	7 11	5 16	1 2	14 8	16 38	9 54
4	Monday.	7 10	5 18	1 4	14 14	16 21	9 56
5	Tuesday.	7 9	5 19	1 7	14 19	16 3	9 58
6	Wednesday.	7 8	5 20	1 9	14 24	15 44	10 2
7	Thursday.	7 7	5 22	1 12	14 27	15 26	10 4
8	Friday.	7 6	5 23	1 14	14 30	15 7	10 6
9	Saturday.	7 5	5 25	1 17	14 32	14 48	10 8
10	**Sunday.**	7 4	5 26	1 19	14 33	14 29	10 12
11	Monday.	7 2	5 27	1 22	14 34	14 9	10 14
12	Tuesday.	7 1	5 28	1 24	14 33	13 49	10 16
13	Wednesday.	7 0	5 30	1 27	14 32	13 29	10 20
14	Thursday.	6 58	5 31	1 30	14 30	13 9	10 22
15	Friday.	6 57	5 32	1 32	14 28	12 49	10 24
16	Saturday.	6 55	5 33	1 35	14 25	12 28	10 28
17	**Sunday.**	6 54	5 34	1 38	14 21	12 7	10 30
18	Monday.	6 52	5 35	1 40	14 16	11 46	10 32
19	Tuesday.	6 51	5 37	1 43	14 10	11 25	10 36
20	Wednesday.	6 50	5 38	1 46	14 4	11 4	10 38
21	Thursday.	6 48	5 40	1 48	13 58	10 42	10 40
22	Friday.	6 47	5 41	1 51	13 50	10 20	10 44
23	Saturday.	6 45	5 42	1 54	13 42	9 59	10 46
24	**Sunday.**	6 44	5 44	1 57	13 34	9 37	10 50
25	Monday.	6 42	5 45	2 0	13 25	9 14	10 52
26	Tuesday.	6 41	5 46	2 3	13 15	8 52	10 54
27	Wednesday.	6 39	5 47	2 6	13 4	8 30	10 58
28	Thursday.	6 37	5 48	2 9	12 54	8 7	11 0

year. His eyes looked like two holes burnt in a blanket, or two bullets fired into a stump, and I see he was a cross cantankerous feller, what coodent have no cumfort of his life bekays he war too quarrelsome. If theres ennything Davy Crockett's remarkable for its for his tender feelings, speshally toward dum creturs, and I thort it would be a marcy to take away his life, seeing it war onny a torment to him and he hadent no right to live, no how. So I creeps toward him like a garter snake through the grass, tralein killdevil arter me. I war a going to tickle him a little about the short ribs jest to make him feel amiable, when out jumps a great bear, as big as Kongress Hall out of the rushes and lights upon the old Jew like a grey winged plover. He only hit him one blow, but that war a side winder. I wish I may be kicked to death by grasshoppers if he didn't tare out five of his ribs and laid his heart and liver all bare. I kinder sorter pitted the old feller when I see him brought to such an untimely eend, and I didn't somehow think the bear done the thing that war right, for I always does my own skalping and no thanks to interlopers. So sez I, 'I'm a civil man, Mr. Bear, saving your presence, and I wont come for to go to give you no insolatious language; but I'll thank you when we meet agin, not to disremember the old saying, but let every man skin his own skunks,' and with that I insinnivated a ball slap through his hart. By the ghost of the great mammoth of Big Bone Licks, your'd have thort, by the way he nashed his teeth, I'd a spoken sumthing onpleasant to him. His grinders made a noise jest as if all the devils in hell war sharpening cross-cut saws by steam-power, and he war down upon me like the whole Missouri on a sand bar. There's no more back out in Davy Crockett than thar ar go-ahead with the Bunker Hill Monument, and so I give him a sogdologer over his coco nut

Days mo.	Days of the week.	Sun rises,	Sun sets.	Days increase.	Sun slow.	☉ decl'n South.	Length of Days.
1	Friday.	6 35	5 50	2 12	12 42	7° 44′	11 4
2	Saturday.	6 34	5 51	2 15	12 30	7 21	11 6
3	**Sunday.**	6 32	5 52	2 18	12 18	6 59	11 10
4	Monday.	6 31	5 54	2 20	12 5	6 36	11 12
5	Tuesday.	6 29	5 55	2 23	11 51	6 12	11 14
6	Wednesday.	6 28	5 56	2 26	11 38	5 49	11 18
7	Thursday.	6 26	5 57	2 29	11 23	5 26	11 20
8	Friday.	6 25	5 59	2 31	11 8	5 3	11 24
9	Saturday.	6 23	6 0	2 34	10 53	4 39	11 26
10	**Sunday.**	6 21	6 1	2 37	10 38	4 16	11 30
11	Monday.	6 17	6 2	2 40	10 22	3 52	11 32
12	Tuesday.	6 17	6 3	2 43	10 6	3 29	11 36
13	Wednesday.	6 15	6 4	2 46	9 49	3 5	11 38
14	Thursday.	6 14	6 6	2 49	9 32	2 42	11 40
15	Friday.	6 12	6 7	2 51	9 15	2 18	11 44
16	Saturday.	6 10	6 8	2 54	8 58	1 54	11 46
17	**Sunday.**	6 9	6 9	2 57	8 41	1 31	11 50
18	Monday.	6 7	6 10	3 0	8 23	1 7	11 52
19	Tuesday.	6 5	6 11	3 3	8 5	0 43	11 56
20	Wednesday.	6 3	6 12	3 6	7 47	S. 20	11 58
21	Thursday.	6 2	6 14	3 9	7 29	N. 4	12 0
22	Friday.	6 0	6 15	3 12	7 11	0 28	12 4
23	Saturday.	5 59	6 17	3 15	6 52	0 51	12 6
24	**Sunday.**	5 57	6 18	3 18	6 34	1 15	12 10
25	Monday.	5 55	6 19	3 21	6 15	1 39	12 12
26	Tuesday.	5 53	6 20	3 23	5 57	2 2	12 16
27	Wednesday.	5 52	6 21	3 26	5 38	2 26	12 18
28	Thursday.	5 50	6 22	3 29	5 20	2 49	12 22
29	Friday.	5 49	6 23	3 32	5 1	3 13	12 24
30	Saturday.	5 47	6 24	3 35	4 43	3 36	12 26
31	**Sunday.**	5 45	6 25	3 37	4 25	3 59	12 30

with the barrel of old killdevil that sot him a konsidering, and he thort better on it and sot off after Doughboy as if the devil had kicked him on eend. It's true Doughboy slipped a ball inter his ampersand jest as I struck him; but that war not what turned him, I grinned him out a countenance, so he thort it war safer to make his breakfast on Doughboy than me, which war a thing oncreditable to his taste, seeing I war a white man and he only a nigger. Well, I hadn't time to load my iron before he gathered upon Doughboy like a Virginny blood mear, and the nigger give himself up for a gone sucker, and fainted away. The bear got up to him jest as I war putting down my ball, and I expected to see him swaller the b'y without greasing; but he no sooner smelt of him than he turned up his nose in disgust, as Isaac Hill did when Mr. Upham hosswipt him, and run away howling as if his delicacy was hugaceously shocked. By this time I felt most inticingly wolfy and savagerous, and I jest giv him a hint that no man could neglect that it war best to turn in his tracks, and I waited for him jest on the edge of Little Great Small Deep Shallow Big Muddy. He pitched inter me like the piston of a steam injun, and we both rolled into the drink together. Onluckily for him I didn't lose holt of killdevil, and when he raised his head and tried to get over his astonishment, I clapt the barrel right across his neck to shove his visnomy under water. I'll be shot with a packsaddle without benefit of clargy if the ridiculous fool didn't help me himself; for he clapped both hands on the eends of the barrel and pulled away as if it war a pleasure to him. I had nuthing to do but hold on to the stock and float alongside of him till he war drowned. Dont you come for to say that I'm teliing the least of a lie, for every fool knows a grizzly bear will live an hour with a ball through his heart, if so be he's onny mad enuff.

Adventure.---Ride on the Back of a Buffalo. See Page 10.

Desperate Fight with two Catamounts. See page 10.

Whipping a Catamount.

There war a gal named Judy Finx, that lived down to Mud creek. Every body has hearn on her, and every body has seen her, too, except them what her brother carries their eyes in his pocket. It's concluded that she takes the rag off quite, all along up and down the creek and something of a piece beyond. Judy went out one arternoon to a tea squall. As it war at a near neighbor's who lived only about five miles off, she did not take her rifle with her; she only put her butcher knife in her bosom; but she wore that as much for ornament as anything else. On the way home it war quite dark, and her neighbor where she had been let Judy have a tame bear to see her home, as there war no other beau present. They were going through a piece of woods together, when they heard a squalling like a woman's voice, and Judy knew it was a catamount right off. So she jumped on the bear's back, being intarmined that the varmint should have a chase before he got her. The bear knew what she wanted, and he set out at full speed. They had not gone fur before a great snake seized the bear by the hind leg and stopped his progress. The bear turned around and caught the snake by the neck with his teeth, and held on upon it. The snake thrashed about, and jest as the catamount came up, Judy caught the cretur by his long tail, and begun to chastise the catamount with it as if it had been a cowskin. The catamount squalled and grinned and snapped at the snake's tail whenever it came down upon his head and shoulders, and at last he caught it in his teeth. The bear then let go of the sarpent and he wheeled upon the catamount. The way them two made the leaves fly war a caution, and Judy did not stop to see which would gain the victory. She drove forward the bear and soon got home, safe and sound.

Ride on the Back of a Buffalo.

About ten years ago I fell in with a camp of Konzas, a good piece off the north fork of the Canadian. The injuns a kyind a sorter give me a sorter tanyard grin, and the old chief specially puckered up his pictur like a green persimmon, but there were three raal roarers from Salt River with me, so I didn't care a picayoon if it cum to skulpin. Besides I was tetotaciously tired, and I slepp so sound that I wish my rifle may hang fire forever, if I dont think it would have took the second blast of the last trump to wake me. So I lay till after daylite, and then one of me comrades shook me, to tell me the Injun boys had found a huraah's neest. I took up old killdevil, and out I went, and about a hundred yards from the camp there war an old buffalo bull with a hundred little screeching imps about him, with their bows and arrows. They'd stuck so many arrows in him that he looked as thorny as a honey locus or a porky-pine; but they hadnt got deep enough to touch the rite spot. First the old turk would go arter one full chizzle; but then another would stick an arro into his posterity, saving your presence, and round he would turn and arter the little torment like an ate horse baggage waggin. I railly pitied the old cretur, and sez I, it are railly a shame to let this uncircumsised Fillistin defy the army of Israel in this ridiculous way. I'll let him know there's a warrant out arter him, and I wur gwine to blaze away; but an old injun kort me elbow, and axed me if it were the way in Kentuck to hinder the children from having a little dust of diversion that did no harm to no one. Truth are the truth, sez I, if an injun do speak it, and my sarvis to you for the complement. After a wile the old devil's baby of a bull laid down, for he'd lost a purty smart chance of blood, and what doz one of the bys do, but gits astraddle on his back. The way he riz up warnt slow, and off he sot as if the prairie were afire behind him. I've a notion the b'y never rode so sharp a rail before as that bull's hump. The old injun the b'y belonged to wur as white as a lump of chalk for fear his b'y would be killed, and he bangs away at the bull and hits him in the belly, for he wur afraid of breaking the by's leg if he squinted at the heart. That maid the cretur as ugly as a copperhead in July, and he takes arter the old hero like a whole team of thunderbolts. 'Run! run, father,' screeches the young varmint to the old one, 'or I'll be down on ye like a falling star, and I begun to see the old one was in danger pretty considerably much. So I sung out to the b'y to raze his leg, cause it kivered the critter's heart, and I wish I may be shot if he didn't do it as cool as if I held the breech of the rifle at him and not the muzzle, but that's the nature of an injun. Bang goes old killdevil and down comes old bull-beef; but the b'y couldn't walk for a week, and he kyind of thort he'd never ride bairbacked on a buffalo agin, without he seed some special casion.

Fight with two Catamounts.

A Hunter of old Kaintuck set out one morning to go down by Swamp creek with his dog arter some wild fowl. He come to a place where he knew there was most always a smart chance of catamounts, but he didn't care to look for any of them, as they aint good eating for enny body that dont like them. Howsomever his dog seemed to be of a different notion, for he went barking up a tree, and the hunter was forced to look arter him. As soon as he cum to the spot he seed two catamounts on one branch. They looked down at the hunter and his dog and seemed to be quite rageoriferous. So the hunter raised his rifle and took aim at one of 'em. He hit the varmint on the leg, and he set up a squall, and made a dive rite at the face and eyes of old Kaintuck. The dog seized him by the tail, and he whirled around and tore the dog most ridiculous; but the hunter levelled a blow at the varment with the breech of his rifle, and telled him jest to hold still a minnit and he would settle his coffee for him without a fish skin. But the catamount turned agin toward the man, and then his feller citizen dropped doun from the limb, and both came at the hunter at onct. He howsomever gave the fust one a rap on the head and knocked quite a conflaggeration out of his eyes, and he winked like it felt very uncommon. But the dog was wide awake, and ketched the reserve by the hind leg, and he begun to tune up like there was a disturbance begun. But the dog held on, and finally both of the varmints turned upon the dog. Then the hunter ketched hold of the fust catamount's tail and took a turn with it around a young sapling and tied a knot that held him fast a while. He had to be pesky quick in doing this, for the cretur wouldn't hold still a minnit. Then the hunter went to help his dog, who had got the other varmint by the lip, and held on upon it as if it had ben an apron full of Jackson currency. The hunter loaded his rifle, and put it agin the varmint's backside and fired. It was sich a fire and brimstone glister as put him out of pain in a wonderful quick time—though he kicked and squirmed most beautiful at fust. By this time the other catamount had jerked out his tail, and the dog was just giving up the ghost, and the hunter thought it was quite unsartin what would happen. So he made a blow at the cretur with the breech of his rifle, and the varmint caught it in his teeth; the hunter let him get it away, as he knew the cretur wouldn't know how to use it arter he got it. He left his rifle with the catamount, and put down his legs one arter the other, for home, as fast as if a Yankee pedlar was drinking up his whiskey and chewing the barrell.

Col. Crockett and the Squatter.

Once upon a time Kongress made a law to give away part of the public lands in old Kentuck—that is, if a feller could prove that he'd made an improvement and growd corn on it, he war to have the first rite to buy. They called this the rite of pre-emption, which war no rite at all in some cases; as I shall exemplify to you presently.

One day in 1829 Jim Hickory came into my clearing, the same Jim they called the Riproarer of Salt River, and axed me if I knowed the Piankashaw Bottom on Bears Grass, and the places adjacent. 'Do you think Davy Crockett's a fool?' sez I. 'No,' sez he, 'I wouldn't be so imperlite as to say that, and it would be a d—d lie if I did; but the fact ar, I'm going to buy the bottom of the land agent, and I want your testification that I had an improvement thar.' 'When war that, Jim,' sez I, 'for I never heerd tell of it before.' 'It war between 1825 and 1826,' sez Jim. 'Now, Jim, I wont be such a blackguard as to tell you you lie,' sez I, 'or anything of that ar sort; but it ar a fact, you don't speak the truth, or anything within a thousand mile of it. You know you war gone to Santa Fee that ar year.' 'Kurnul,' sez he, 'that's a small bit of a mistake.' 'Do you mean to tell me I lie?' sez I; 'because if you do there will be trouble between us in less time than hell would scorch a feather!' Lord forgive me for swearing—it ar a thing I'm not used to; but it made my bristles stand rite up to think Jim wanted me to swear to a no-such-a-thing. 'Kurnel,' sez Jim, for he see that my temper war in a state of pretty considerable mollification; 'I don't want to entice you to do anything agin your conscience. Just go with me to the ground, and if I don't satisfy you I had corn growing thar between twenty-five and six, I'll give you my skin to make razor strops of, that's all.'

Well, thought I, it will do no harm to go with him, any how he can fix it, and as it war a magnificent day, I shouldered old killdevil and went along with him. When we got to the spot, he had built up a shanty there, and had a cow, and showed me three stalks of corn growing between two pepperage trees. 'Thar,' sez he, 'Kurnel; did you ever see finer corn in your life?' 'The corn ar well enuff,' sez I; 'but it war not growing here three or four year ago, for sartin.' With that the infarnal varmint showed me whar he had cut 1825 and 1826 in great figures on the trees with his knife, and the corn war growing between them, sure enuff, and then I begun to feel awful conscientious.

'Look you, Jim Hickory,' sez I; 'you've barked up the wrong tree this time. Do you know what youv'e done, you cussed, illiterate, unscrupulocious offscowring of creation and crooked barrel of a shot gun? You've axed Davy Crockett to swear to a lie. Don't come for to go to be wolfy or cantankerous at what I say; for there can't be no scalping between us. I stand on the caracter of a gentleman and the univarsal dignity of human natur, and I can't condescend to chaw you up, for you're no gentleman, and what's more, no man—not the least indefinite article of a man. You're a fool, and can't dance, and your daddy's got no peach orchard, and I think it ar my duty to bring you to justice. Do you see what that cow has just let drop? It ar not honey

Raising Corn between two years.

or apple sarse, ar it? Now if you don't sit down and eat every atom of it, I'll make daylite shine through you quicker than it would take lightning to run round a potato patch.' And so I cocked my rifle and drew a lead on the white of his eye. Jim didn't much like to do it, but he see my back was up, and he knew there was no mistake about Davy Crockett. He tried hard to beg off, but that was neither here nor there, and so, as there was no help for it, rather than have his soul-case bored through with my screw auger, he sot down to his confectionary, and I didn't spare him a spoonful of it, though he did make awful ugly faces. He was so ashamed of the whole affair that he axed my pardon for what he'd done, and I never had a better friend arterwards. I kinder think he'll never forget the taste of parjury as long as he lives.

Col. Crockett in the Parlor.

When I first went to take a squint at Kurnel Korpussle I some expected to see a grand place, something like our court house, but that wasn't the smallest part of a circumstance to it. My eyes, if there wan't a looking glass in it Jemmy Tweed might a seen himself in from the buck tail in his hat to his shoe sole, and he's the tallest man in all Kentuck; but I can whip him though. It was all sot in solid goold. The Kurnel was as perlight as all out doors, and ses he, 'How do you kyind a sorter found yourself, Crockett?' 'A kyind a sorter middling,' ses I, 'I giv you kyind thanks. How is it with yourself?' Then he axed me to smoke a segar, and I thanked him I would, but it was warm enuff to roast injuns and I'd take a flem-cutter first. Then we sot down to smoak and talk over the affairs of the nation.

I was hugeously ashamed to spit on that splendiferous carpit, but there was no help for it, tho' he didn't kyind of seem to like it, nor the sarvunt nither. Howzever, the nigger cum in with a beautiful tin box with a leetle hole in the top of it, and sot it down rite where I'd been spitting. It are a fact it wur painted all over with flowers so scientifically I thought there war something to eat in it, so I turned round and spit on the other side of my cheer. When the nigger saw that he cum and put the box where I'd spit, and I had to turn round agin. And what do you think he done? Why, he put the box afore me once more, a purpose to set my bristles up. 'I'll tell you what, Mr. Nigger,' ses I, 'it's well known I'm a peaseable man and I know better what belongs to good manners than to scalp you rite afore your master, but if you put that ere box in my way agin I'll spit in it.'

Colonel Crockett in the Parlor. See Page 12.

1839

A Pretty Predicament.

When I was a big boy that had jist begun to go a galling, I got astray in the woods one arternoon; and being wandering about a good deel and got pretty considerable soaked by a grist of rain, I sot down on to a stump and begun to wring out my leggins, and shake the drops off of my raccoon cap. Whilst I was on the stump I got kind of sleepy, and so laid my head back in the crotch of a young tree that growed behind me, and shot up my eyes. I had laid out of doors for many a night before with a sky blanket over me—so I got to sleep pretty soon and fell to snoring most beautiful. So somehow or somehow else I did not wake till near sundown, and I don't know when I should have waked had it not been for somebody tugging at my hair. As soon as I felt this, though I wan't more than half awake, I begun to feel to see if my thum nail was on, as that was all the ammunition I had about me. I lay still to see what the feller would be at. The first idee I had was that a cussed Ingun was fixing to take off my scalp, so I thought I'd wait till I begun to feel the pint of his knife scraping against the skin, and then I should have full proof agin him, and could jerk out his copper-colored liver with the law all on my side. At last I felt such a hard twitch that I roared right out, but when I found my head was squeezed so tight in the crotch that I could not get it out, I felt like a gone sucker. I felt raal ridiculous, I can assure you; so I begun to talk to the varmint and telled him to help me get my head out, like a man, and I would give him five dollars before I killed him. At last my hair begun to come out by the roots, and then I was mad to be took advantage of in that way. I swore at the varmint till the tree shed all its leaves and the sky turned yaller. So in a few minutes I heerd a voice, and then a gall cum running up and axed what was the matter. She soon saw what was to pay, and telled me that the eagles were tearing out my hair to build nests with. I telled her I had endured more than a dead possum could stand already, and that if she would drive off the eagles I would make her a present of an iron comb. That I will, says she, for I am a she steamboat and have doubled up a crocodile in my day. So she pulled up a small sapling by the roots, and went to work as if she hadn't another minnit to live. She knocked down two of the varmints, and screamed the rest out of sight. Then I telled her the predicament I was in, and she said she would loosen the hold that the crotch had on my head. So she took and reached out her arm into a rattlesnake's hole, and pulled out three or four of them. She tied 'em awl together and made a strong rope out of 'em. She tied one eend of the snakes to the top of one branch and pulled as if she was trying to haul the multiplication table apart. The tightness about my head begun to be different altogether, and I hauled out my cocoanut, though I left a piece of one of my ears behind.

As soon as I was clear, I could not tell which way to look for the sun, and I was afeared I should fall into the sky, for I did not know which way was up, and which way was down. Then I looked at the gal that had got me loose. She was a strapper. She was as tall as a sapling, and had an arm like a keel boat's tiller. So I looked at her like all wrath, and as she cum down from the tree, I says to her, 'I wish I may be utterly onswoggled if I don't know how to hate an ingun or love a gal as well as any he this side of roaring river. I fell in love with three gals at once at a log rolling, and as for tea squalls my heart never shut pan for a minnit at a time; so if you will bundle with me to-night, I will forgive the tree and the eagles for your sake.' Then she turned as white as an egg-shell, and I seed that her heart was busting, and I run up to her, like a squirrel to his hole, and gave her a buss that sounded louder than a musket. So her spunk was all gone, and she took my arm as tame as a pigeon, and we cut out for her father's house. She complained that i hung too heavy on her arm, for I was enermost used up after laying so long between the branches. So she took up a stone that would weigh about fifty pound and put it in her pocket on the other side to balance agin my weight, and so she moved along as upright as a steamboat. She told me that her Sunday bonnet was a hornet's nest garnished with wolves' tails and eagles' feathers, and that she wore a bran new goun made of a whole bear's hide, the tail serving for a train. She said she could drink of the branch without a cup, could shoot a wild goose flying, and wade the Mississippi without wetting herself. She said she could not play on the piane nor sing like a nightingale, but she could outscream a catamount and jump over her own shadow; she had good strong horse sense and knew a woodchuck from a skunk. So I was pleased with her, and offered her all my plunder if she would let me split the difference and call her Mrs. Crockett.

She kinder said she must insult her father before she went so fur as to marry. So she took me into another room to introduce me to another beau that she had. He was setting on the edge of a grindstone at the back part of the room with his heels on the mantel-piece! He had the skull bone of a catamount for a snuff-box, and he was dressed like he had been used to seeing hard times. I got a side squint into one of his pockets, and saw it was full of eyes that had been gouged from people of my acquaintance. I knew my jig was up, for such a feller could outcourt me, and I thort the gal brot me in on proppus to have a fight. So i turned off, and threatened to call agin; and I cut through the bushes like a pint of whiskey among forty men.

1839

Days mo.	Days of the week.	Sun rises,	Sun sets.	Days increase	Sun slow.	☉ declin. North.	Length of Days.
1	Monday.	5 43	6 26	3 40	4 6	4° 23′	12 32
2	Tuesday.	5 42	6 27	3 42	3 48	4 46	12 36
3	Wednesday.	5 40	6 28	3 45	3 30	5 9	12 38
4	Thursday.	5 38	6 29	3 47	3 12	5 32	12 42
5	Friday.	5 36	6 30	3 50	2 54	5 55	12 44
6	Saturday.	5 34	6 31	3 53	2 37	6 17	12 46
7	**Sunday.**	5 32	6 32	3 55	2 19	6 40	12 50
8	Monday.	5 31	6 33	3 58	2 2	7 2	12 52
9	Tuesday.	5 29	6 34	4 1	1 45	7 25	12 54
10	Wednesday.	5 27	6 35	4 3	1 28	7 47	12 58
11	Thursday.	5 26	6 36	4 6	1 11	8 9	13 0
12	Friday.	5 24	6 37	4 9	0 55	8 31	13 4
13	Saturday.	5 23	6 38	4 12	0 39	8 53	13 6
14	**Sunday.**	5 21	6 39	4 14	0 23	9 15	13 10
15	Monday.	5 19	6 40	4 17	0 8	9 37	13 12
16	Tuesday.	5 18	6 41	4 20	fast 7	9 58	13 14
17	Wednesday.	5 16	6 42	4 22	0 22	10 19	13 18
18	Thursday.	5 14	6 43	4 25	0 36	10 40	13 20
19	Friday.	5 13	6 44	4 28	0 50	11 1	13 22
20	Saturday.	5 11	6 45	4 30	1 3	11 22	13 26
21	**Sunday.**	5 10	6 47	4 33	1 16	11 42	13 28
22	Monday.	5 8	6 48	4 36	1 29	12 3	13 30
23	Tuesday.	5 6	6 49	4 39	1 41	12 23	13 32
24	Wednesday.	5 5	6 50	4 41	1 52	12 43	13 36
25	Thursday.	5 3	6 52	4 44	2 4	13 3	13 38
26	Friday.	5 2	6 53	4 47	2 14	13 22	13 40
27	Saturday.	5 1	6 54	4 50	2 24	13 42	13 44
28	**Sunday.**	4 59	6 55	4 52	2 34	14 1	13 46
29	Monday.	4 58	6 57	4 55	2 43	14 20	13 48
30	Tuesday.	4 56	6 58	4 58	2 52	14 38	13 50

A Wolfish Affair.

Zebulon Kitchen, a partiklar friend of mine from the Big Black Fork of Little White River in Missouri, came to my house one summer to get a little insight into the ways of the world and larn civilizashun. So I repeated over to him some of my speeches in Congress, and told him how they lived in the big clearings down East. My wife was a little vain and wanted to show off her breeding to Zebulon, as he was cum from the West, and so she combed out her new bearskin petticoat, and put on her crocodile-skin short-goun, and shoes made of buffalo hide, and smoothed down her hair with bear's grease. Then she looked right charming, and Zebulon was so much taken with her that I begun to feel jelus. Howsomever, he got his head so full of notions about what I told him that he intarmined to go down East himself, and thought he should then get a good deel of noledge about the world and other things and should carry home such a wonder of larning that his naburs would be astonished half out of their census. So he took his gun and his dog and went off alone. I knew Zeb was true pluck and a rail ring-tailed roarer, so I had no doubts he'd make his way where ever he went. So he giv my wife a smack that she has never forgot to this day, and off he went. Well, I thought no more about Zeb till about six weeks arterward, when I was out a hunting, and all of a sudden I cum across the bones of a dog. A little further on I seed the stump of a tree about ten foot high, and on the top eend of it stood a man's skiliton, with his gun in one hand and a piece of paper in the other. It looked rail frightful, and my hair stood straight on eend. I couldn't think how the skilliton could have got up there, and it was no use to ax it for its tongue had been

[Concluded on page 17.

A Pretty Predicament.

See Account of the Predicament, at Page 14.

1839

The Skeleton of Zebulon Kitchen.

eat out by the birds. Then I seed there was sum writing on the paper, though it was enymost washed out by the rain. I took it out of the skilliton's hand, and read as follows:—

"Deer Krokkit — i am surrounded by wolves. I had to run and got upon this old stump. I have shot away all my amminition and my dog is kilt. So I see no chance of my gitting away at all. If I go down the cussed varmints will ete me up, and if I stay here i shall git nothing to ete myself. So if you find me when ded, see me decently in turd, and i remane Yourn till deth, Zebulon Kitchen.

P. S. I rite this with blood from my finger."

I vow I was completely explunctificated when I red this, for it was as plain as preeching that the wolves had treed poor Zebulon, and he had stain on the stump the whole enduring six weeks. So I took down the bones of poor Zeb, and carried them home with the bones of his dog. I buried them both in one grave, and sent his gun and powder horn home to his family. My wife begged hard for one of the skilliton's hands which she said would make an excellent fan, but I would not let her have it, for fear she would be always thinking of Zeb, if she had something to put her in mind of him. I never forgave the wolves this deed, and whenever I met one arterward, I wasted my last charge of powder on his pesky hide, till I built a monniment to Zeb's memory with wolf bones.

1839

A Scentoriferous Fight with a Nigger.

I had just got afloat on the Great Bend, in my Alleghany skiff, and was about pushing off, when I seed the reeds bending most double, a trifle from the landing place. So I brought my rifle to bear and was just about getting a blizzard at the cretur, when it popped up its head, and I seed by the wool on the skull that it was a pesky great bull nigger.

'Blackey,' says I—for I wanted to talk civil to it,—'what may be your business jest now along shore and down among the reeds, with your two eyes sticking out like a panther's?'

With that he begun to look rail saucy and grinned like a log house on fire. So says I to him, 'it 's no use Mr. Nig, or whatever your name is, to come the possum over me. I'm jest from roaring river, wide awake and duly sober, and don't feel afeard of any nigger that ever stept between here, and the other side of the eend of the yearth. So cut dirt, or by gum, I'll bark you clean from the end of your nose to the tip of your tail.' With that he looked as dumb as a wooden clock, and I thought the feller was going to hang fire. But instead of that, he edged along, and give a spring into my skiff, and ketched the long pole, and give the skiff a reverend set right out toward the middle of the stream. This was too much to take from a nigger no how, so I raised my riflé and was jest going to drop him into the water, when I hearn a low growl behind me, and when I turned round, though I kept one leetle corner of my eye on the nigger all the time, I seed a great black bear coming up to take the nigger's part. So seeing they were birds of a feather, I thought best to let the nigger go a piece and try to kill the four-legged varmint, because if I didn't kill him he might kill me, and I thought that would be most ridiculous. I let strip, and the ball hit the bear on the eend of the nose. So he stood right up on his hind legs, like a Congress man when he ketches the speaker's eye, and I seed there was going to be a serious misunderstanding between us right off, for my rifle was fired off, and the nigger had gone with the skiff; so I was a sort of forced to stand up to my lick log, salt or no salt. Then when I seed his great nails that sprawled out like a lobster's claws sharpened to a point, I thought he might have all my old moccasins and welcome, if he would only put them on. I took my rifle by the barrel and intarmined to explunctify his seven senses by a rap on the head.

Well he jumped right at me with his mouth wide open. I happened to slip and didn't get a chance to take good aim. I hit him on the ribs and he squalled right out like an old woman at an awakening. But I pitched head foremost into the muss, and when that etarnal nigger seed me fall, he thought I was a gone sucker, so he come right back with the skiff to steal my rifle and powder horn, as soon as the bear should finish his breakfast off my ribs. The bear grew sort o' careless too when he saw that I was down, and this gave me a chance to haul out my knife which I whipped into his belly and deprived him of his bowels. The varmint could'nt do much arter he was fairly cleaned out inside, and he laid pretty still. So I cocked my eye at snow-ball then, and when he tried to give a set with the pole, he was in such a flustification that he fell into the water, and the skiff shot out into the stream about ten foot. So I was all ready for the pesky black thief, and stood close to the shore to tree him in good arnest when he landed. He seed me waiting for him and grinned like a steel trap. Up he came out of the water like a mad alligator, and I stood by as fierce as the latter eend of an 'arthquake. In the first place I ketched him by the wool and jerked out two hand's full, which made him feel quite unpleasant. He then run off and kum at me with his head. He got hold of my two ears and gave me a butt right in the front part of my head, that enermost blinded me, for the feller's skull was as hard as the two sides of an iron pot. So I got one of my ears out of his infarnal black paw, and then I got two good blows at him with my feet on his shins. That made him so mad that he run his fingers right up my nostrils. I didn't mind that much, for it shut out the enduring bad smell which the cretur had about him when he got fairly warm. So we wrassled and jerked and bit for a long time, till I got a chance at one of his eyes with my thum nail. Then when I begun to put on the rail Kentucky twist, he knew it was all day with him, and he fell on his knees and begged for mercy. His eye stood out about half an inch, and I felt the bottom of the socket with the eend of my thum. I telled him to confess everything or I would snap his eye right out. So he owned that he had been out all night on a stealing excursion, and was trying to find his way to the swamp. He agreed to let me tie him up with grape vines, and I made the varmint fast, and put him into the skiff and carried him home. I seed the nigger once more when I was on my way to Congress, and he squinted most ridiculous. This was the fust fight I ever had with a nigger, and I hope it will be the last, for the way I like to have got starved out with his cussed strong smell was a causion to a skunk. But if he hadn't confessed, I would have made him so near-sighted that he couldn't have seen a whip till he felt it.

1839

Davy Crockett's Dream.

One day when it was so cold that I was afeard to open my mouth, lest I should freeze my tongue, I took my little dog named Grizzle and cut out for Salt River Bay to kill something for dinner. I got a good ways from home afore I knowed where I was, and as I had swetted some before I left the house my hat froze fast to my head, and I like to have put my neck out of joint in trying to pull it off. When I sneezed the icicles crackled all up and down the inside of my nose, like when you walk over a bog in winter time. The varmints was so scarce that I couldn't find one, and so when I come to an old log hut that had belonged to some squatter that had ben reformed out by the nabors, I stood my rifle up agin one of the door posts and went in. I kindled up a little fire and told Grizzle I was going to take a nap. I piled up a heap of chesnut burs for a pillow and straitened myself out on the ground, for I can curl closer than a rattle-snake and lay straiter than a log. I laid with the back of my head agin the hearth, and my eyes looking up chimney so that I could see when it was noon by the sun, for Mrs. Crockett was always rantankerous when I staid out over the time. I got to sleep before Grizzle had done warming the eend of his nose, and I had swallowed so much cold wind that it laid hard on my stomach, and as I laid gulping and belching the wind went out of me and roared up chimney like a young whirlwind. So I had a pesky dream, and kinder thought, till I waked up, that I was floating down the Massassippy in a holler tree, and I hadn't room to stir my legs and arms no more than they were withed together with young saplings. While I was there and want able to help myself a feller called Oak Wing that lived about twenty miles off, and that I had give a most almighty licking once, cum and looked in with his blind eye that I had gouged out five years before, and I saw him looking in one end of the hollow log, and he axed me if I wanted to get out. I telled him to tie a rope to one of my legs and draw me out as soon as God would let him and as much sooner as he was a mind to. But he said he wouln't do it that way, he would ram me out with a pole. So he took a long pole and rammed it down agin my head as if he was ramming home the cattridge in a cannon. This didn't make me budge an inch, but it pounded my head down in between my shoulders till I look'd like a turcle with his head drawn in. This started my temper a trifle, and I ript and swore till the breath boiled out of the end of the log like the steam out of the funnel pipe of a steemboat. Jest then I woke up, and seed my wife pulling my leg, for it was enermost sundown and she had cum arter me. There was a long icicle hanging to her nose, and when she tried to kiss me, she run it right into my eye. I telled her my dreem, and sed I would have revenge on Oak Wing for pounding my head. She said it was all a dreem and that Oak was not to blame; but I had a very diffrent idee of the matter. So I went and talked to him, and telled him what he had done to me in a dreem, and it was settled that he should make me an apology in his next dreem, and that wood make us square, for I don't like to be run upon when I'm asleep, any more than I do when I'm awake.

Buying a Horse.

There was a feller from down East, to a town called Varmount, that come into our parts to sell his hosses. He squinted with one eye, and the other kept looking up for rain. So my wife keered about him, and she was in a great flustification to go a shopping at the place where he was, and buy her a saddle hoss. So she went and got one. She paid forty dollars for it and brought it home, for I'm sure it couldn't bring her. My wife was never no judge of the article, though she could tell a bear from a panther by the feel of his bite, if it was so dark that she could n't hear herself talk. The hoss was lame in his fore legs and hind legs too, and he had a crook in his tail. He was blind of one eye and deaf of both ears. He couldn't stand up, he was so infirm, and he couldn't lay down becase his bowels were out of order. So the hoss-jockey was to come the next morning arter his money. I put a halter around the neck of the cretur and tied his head up to the limb of a tree. I put an old saddle on his back, and put a bridle on him. I fixed the bridle so that the least strain would break it off the bitts, by taking out the stitches. Then I went into the woods and got a hornets' neest, and stopped it up so that the creturs couldn't git out. In the morning the feller cum arter his pay. I begun to praise the hoss, and telled him the animal was so spirited, I did n't like for my wife to ride him. He said he was as gentle as a lamb. I axed him to get on and let me see how he would go. The jockey leeped up and got in the saddle. As soon as he had lighted on the beast, I beat in the hornets' neest, and flung it agin the hoss's backsides. The animal showed some spirit then, for the little varmints cum out, and spurred up the cretur most beautiful. He set out on the full run, and the bridle broke right off in the jockey's hand. The hoss then dug through the forest, without stopping to count the leaves, and the feller clung to the hoss's mane, like a chesnut burr to a bearskin. The last I heered of him, he was seen up by the fork of Duck River, going through the country like a runaway steamboat. He never cum back arter his money.

Col. Crockett and the Yankee Horse Jockey. See page 19.

The Pirates Head,

As drawn by Ben Harding. See Page 24.

1839

Days mo.	Days of the week.	Sun rises,	Sun sets.	Days increase.	Sun fast.	☉ declin. North.	Length of Days.
1	Wednesday.	4 54	6 59	5 0	3 0	14° 57′	13 54
2	Thursday.	4 53	7 0	5 2	3 7	15 15	13 56
3	Friday.	4 52	7 1	5 4	3 15	15 33	13 58
4	Saturday.	4 50	7 2	5 7	3 21	15 50	14 0
5	**Sunday.**	4 49	7 3	5 9	3 27	16 8	14 2
6	Monday.	4 48	7 4	5 11	3 32	16 25	14 6
7	Tuesday.	4 47	7 5	5 13	3 37	16 42	14 8
8	Wednesday.	4 46	7 6	5 15	3 42	16 58	14 10
9	Thursday.	4 45	7 7	5 17	3 46	17 14	14 12
10	Friday.	4 44	7 8	5 19	3 49	17 30	14 14
11	Saturday.	4 43	7 9	5 21	3 51	17 46	14 16
12	**Sunday.**	4 42	7 10	5 23	3 53	18 1	14 18
13	Monday.	4 41	7 11	5 25	3 55	18 16	14 20
14	Tuesday.	4 40	7 12	5 27	3 56	18 31	14 22
15	Wednesday.	4 39	7 13	5 29	3 56	18 46	14 24
16	Thursday.	4 38	7 14	5 31	3 56	19 0	14 26
17	Friday.	4 37	7 15	5 33	3 55	19 14	14 28
18	Saturday.	4 36	7 16	5 35	3 54	19 27	14 30
19	**Sunday.**	4 36	7 17	5 37	3 52	19 40	14 32
20	Monday.	4 35	7 18	5 39	3 49	19 53	14 34
21	Tuesday.	4 34	7 19	5 41	3 46	20 6	14 36
22	Wednesday.	4 33	7 20	5 43	3 42	20 18	14 38
23	Thursday.	4 32	7 21	5 45	3 38	20 30	14 40
24	Friday.	4 31	7 22	5 47	3 33	20 41	14 42
25	Saturday.	4 30	7 23	5 48	3 28	20 52	14 44
26	**Sunday.**	4 29	7 24	5 50	3 22	21 3	14 44
27	Monday.	4 28	7 25	5 52	3 16	21 14	14 46
28	Tuesday.	4 28	7 26	5 53	3 9	21 24	14 48
29	Wednesday.	4 27	7 27	5 55	3 2	21 33	14 50
30	Thursday.	4 26	7 27	5 57	2 54	21 43	14 52
31	Friday.	4 26	7 28	5 58	2 46	21 52	14 52

Adventure with a Tar.

I was laying asleep on the Massissippi one day, with a piece of river scum for a pillow, and floating down stream in rail free and easy style, when all at once I was waked up by something that cum agin my ribs like it was trying to feel for an opening into my bowels. So I just raised my head to see what kind of a varmint was sharpening his teeth agin my ribs, and seed it was something that lookt so much like a human cretur that I was half a mind to speek to it. But it had a tail to its head about as big around as my arm and as long as a hoss pistle. The cretur was floating on three kegs fastened to a log, and held a pole in his hand that he had punched me with in the ribs, when I fust woke up. His trowsers was made of white sail cloth, and they was so wide about the legs that I knowed he had stold 'em from some big fat feller, for they didn't fit him no more than my wife's raccoon skin shift would fit the fine ladies in Washington. He had on light thin shoes with big ribbons in 'em, and a painted hat with another big ribbon in that. So then I concluded rite off he had ben robbing a Yankee pedlar and got away all his flashy trumpery. Says I, 'Stranger, I take it you are a human by the looks of your face, but you are one of the greatest curosities I've seen in these parts. I do n't wonder you wake me up to look at ye.' 'By the devil!' says he, 'the thing has got the use of lingo like a Christian. I thought I had spoke a cat-fish. Where are you cruising, old rusty bottom? You are the queerest rigged sea craft that I ever saw on soundings or off.' 'You infarnal heathen,' says I, 'I don't understand all your stuff, and I spose you are fresh down this way. But I'll have you understand that I'm a snorter by birth and eddycation,

Days mo.	Days of the week.	Sun rises,	Sun sets.	Days increase	Sun fast.	☉ declin North.	Length of Days.
1	Saturday.	4 25	7 29	5 59	2 38	22° 0′	14 54
2	**Sunday.**	4 24	7 29	6 1	2 29	22 8	14 54
3	Monday.	4 24	7 30	6 2	2 19	22 16	14 56
4	Tuesday.	4 23	7 31	6 3	2 10	22 23	14 56
5	Wednesday.	4 23	7 32	6 4	2 0	22 30	14 58
6	Thursday.	4 23	7 33	6 5	1 49	22 37	14 58
7	Friday.	4 22	7 33	6 6	1 39	22 43	15 0
8	Saturday.	4 22	7 34	6 7	1 28	22 49	15 2
9	**Sunday.**	4 22	7 35	6 8	1 17	22 54	15 2
10	Monday.	4 22	7 35	6 9	1 5	22 59	15 2
11	Tuesday.	4 22	7 36	6 9	0 53	23 4	15 4
12	Wednesday.	4 22	7 37	6 10	0 41	23 8	15 4
13	Thursday.	4 22	7 37	6 10	0 29	23 12	15 4
14	Friday.	4 22	7 38	6 11	0 17	23 15	15 6
15	Saturday.	4 22	7 38	6 11	0 4	23 18	15 6
16	**Sunday.**	4 22	7 38	6 12	slow. 8	23 21	15 6
17	Monday.	4 22	7 38	6 12	0 21	23 23	15 6
18	Tuesday.	4 22	7 39	6 12	0 34	23 25	15 6
19	Wednesday.	4 23	7 39	6 13	0 47	23 26	15 6
20	Thursday.	4 23	7 39	6 13	1 0	23 27	15 6
21	Friday.	4 23	7 39	6 13	1 13	23 28	15 6
22	Saturday.	4 23	7 39	6 13	1 26	23 28	15 6
23	**Sunday.**	4 23	7 40	decre.	1 39	23 27	15 6
24	Monday.	4 24	7 40	0 0	1 52	23 27	15 6
25	Tuesday.	4 24	7 40	0 0	2 5	23 25	15 6
26	Wednesday.	4 24	7 40	0 1	2 18	23 24	15 6
27	Thursday.	4 25	7 40	0 1	2 30	23 22	15 6
28	Friday.	4 25	7 40	0 1	2 43	23 20	15 6
29	Saturday.	4 25	7 40	0 2	2 55	23 17	15 6
30	**Sunday.**	4 26	7 40	0 2	3 68	23 14	15 4

and if you don't go floating along, and leave me to finish my nap I'll give you a taste of my breed. I'll begin with the snapping turtle, and after I've chawed you up with that, I'll rub you down with a spice of the alligator.' With that he looked as mad as a shovel full of hot coals, and he took a long string of tobakkur out of his pocket, and arter he had bit off a piece long enough to hang a buffalo, he roared out, 'I'll shiver your mizen in less time than you can say Jack Robinson, you fresh water lubber! You rock crab! You deck sweeper! swab!' Says I then, for my steam begun to get rather obstropolous, 'I'll double you up like a spare shirt. My name is Crockett and I'll put my mark on your infarnal wolf-hide before you've gone the length of a panther's tail further.' With that he roared right out a laffing, and I was so astonished, I held my breath to see the cretur laff on the eve of a battle, but I soon seed the reeson of it, for he stooped down and reached out his hand, and says, 'tell me for God's sake, old fogy, are you the feller that makes them allmynacks about cruising after panthers and snakes and swimming over the Mississippi?' Says I, 'I'm a roarer at that bizness that you've mentioned, stranger. Going to Congress and making allmynacks is my trade.' 'Give us your flipper then, old chap,' says he, 'I wood n't hurt a hare of your head for the world. Is n't there a grog shop here on the coast, for by G— I'll treat you if I sell my jacket. I'd give two weeks allowance if our boson was here — Hurra! three cheers for old Crockett! He used to read your allmynack to us on the forecastle, for, d'ye see, I can't read. I got my larning under the lee of the long boat, and swear my prayers at a lee earing in a gale o' wind. But I can read pikturs to d———n, and I could spell out your crocodile's tails from their heads when I see 'em drawed out in your book.' I felt as good natured as a soaped eel when he praised up my book in this way, and I axed him how fur he was going. He sed he was going to New Orleens; and then I telled him if he would cum to my house, I wood give him a bear stake as quick as we got there, and as much whiskey as he could put into his skin. With that he pulled off his hat and swung it round his head like he was going to fly, and he says 'come aboard, old Neptune, and I'll see your passage paid, or throw us a line and I'll give you a tow.' But I swimmed ashore, and then we went up together through the forest as good friends as a tame hawk and blind rooster. The way he walked was a caution, for he swung about like a bear skin hung to the limb of a tree. When we got home my wife didn't know what to think on him, but my darters took a mighty shine to him, and he ketched hold of Nab and gave her such a smack on the lips that she couldn't breathe for about two minnits. 'He said she was a slick craft, and we didn't know what that meant, but Nab said arterwards it meant that she was as sweet as honey. So we got dinner reddy, and he pulled out his jacknife and the way the vittles went into him was like turning a hoss into a stable. Arter we got through, he filled a horn chock full of whiskey and didn't stop to swallow it, but it run into him jeest as nat'ral as if he war born so. Then I giv him a critter's head to set on, and he smoked a short pipe while I axed him about where he cum from and who he was, and what was going on in Congress. He said his name was Ben Harding, and then he telled such stories about what he had seed as made the gals dream o' nights for a fortnite arter he was gone; and as I spose the reader would like to hear some of 'em, I think I shall put 'em in print; but he had a voice that was so ruff, I can't rite it doun, but I will have a cut made to picktur it out. Here it is:

Picture of Ben Harding's Voice.

Ben Harding and the Pirates.

One day arter a wolf hunt with my friend Ben Harding, we cut out for home, to enjoy a fricasse made of bear's tongue and buffaloes' feet. My wife was very busy in doing up the mess, but she had got somewhat delayed, for she had kep time by a wooden clock that a pedlar left her. The clock had somehow held fire, and so she took it down and opened it, and tried to hammer up the spring with the tongs, but the more she tried to fix it, the more it wouldn't go; and when she laid it a one side she found she had been belated with her dinner. So Ben and me sot down by the fire-place and waited for the dinner to get ready. Ben laid one of his legs up on to a stool that was kivered by a buffalo's hide, took an old cut of tubbacker out of his vest pocket, and when the steam of the vittles come to his nostrils it made him curl up his nose like a boar's tail. He felt mighty sociable and clever on the strength of what would come when we got to eating. So I begun to ax him sum questions about the sea. Says I to Ben, and he lookt right at me, sez I 'Ben,' and he says 'Well, Kurnill.' 'What do you think,' says I, 'I've been thinking that all nations is infested with some sort of varmints or another, that desarves killing. Now hereabouts we have the cussed yaller skins to pleg us, and tortur our wives and children, and the Jews the bible tells us how they were chawed up by the Philistines and Frenchmen; and I larn that doun your way on the seas thar is a smart chance of creturs that they call pilots, who thinks no more of cutting a feller's throat than they would of cutting up a bear or treeing a painter. Now I spose you can give me some idee of them characturs, and I should railly like to know.' Ben tipped up the whiskey barrel and put about a quart under his jacket before he telled me anything about it. Then he hemmed and hawked and pulled up his britches and says he, 'You say right Kurnell, there's no craft in these woods of yourn that can hold a candle to a pirate in the way of breaking up human kind. I was running down the gulf in the schooner Susan out of New York, some ten or twenty years ago, and we spoke a clipper with the American flag at her mast head. We bore up and stood close to her as it was blowing fresh, to ax them if they could spare us some water. Then all at oncst about a hundred heads popped up from behind the bullworks, like Jack-in-the-box when you unship the kivver. They begun to jabber right away, like a flock of sea-gulls and Mother Carey's chickens when the cook flings his slush overboard. I seed what was a coming, for the death head and marrow bones went up to the peak quicker than you ever see one of the damned pirate lubbers run up by the neck on Gibbet Island. They lowered down a boat, and we laid our yards aback as that was the only way to save our bacon. Up they come over the side like a drove of bees settling on a dead horse. One devilish savage looking chap, with big black mustaches ordered me to hand him the man ropes as he cum up the gangway. I swore I'd never reach the man ropes to a pirate, for they were made for his master. The fire flew out of his eyes and he scrabbled up the side like one of your bears going up a tree; and as soon as he got on the deck, he hauled out his cutlass and gave me a crack with it over the starn that made me hop a rod. I've got the mark of it like a stripe of the American flag to this day, on my hind parts. So I stood a one side, and then they made the steward show 'em where the gold was stowed, and bekase he didn't move fast enuff for them, one of the bloody-minded ruffins caught a string of pig tail tubbacker out of his pocket and wound it around the darkey's neck, and hoisted him up to the main boom. The poor fellow's tongue stuck out half a fathom, but you see he couldn't say a word, seeing that he was choked. He kicked a little and sprawled out his arms and fingers; but he was soon dead and went to the sharks. Thay maid the captin go up aloft and set on the cross-trees for about two hours, and when he seed them overhauling his chist, and looked doun at 'em, they pointed their pistles at him, and told him if he didn't mind his eye they would drill a hole through his skull cap. One of the bloody sharks went to the caboose, and told the cook to give him a bite of soft tack; and bekase he had got none, d'ye see, they struck off his head with a cutlash and throwed it into the coppers and biled all the wool off his head.'

I telled Ben that if I had been there I should have treed some of the varmints up the masts. He said that was unpossible, as there was so many on 'em. But he said they sometimes got into a fix, with a smart chance of white rope.

So says Ben, 'I'll tell you what, I've had some cussed droll adventurs among them bloody devils, but some of the slickest yarns I ever heered of is telled in the Pirate's Own Book. They've got it to sell at the Bookshops, and it is chock full of such stories about pirates as made my hair stand up when I heerd it read, like a bunch of marlingspikes. It is the curousest thing I ever squinted at in the way of reading. There is one feller in it named Benavides that had his head cut off and stuck on a pole near the sea. The birds came and picked out one of his eyes, which would have been a great misfortin if he was alive.' I axed him if this was put into a picktur, and he said yes. He said there was a large picktur of the feller's head, with the eend of the pole coming out of his mouth. Then he took a piece of coal and drawed it out on the wall, and gave it a dab in the eye with his fist, to show how it looked when the eye was picked out. 'There is a plenty of pickturs,' says he, 'in the book, that shows what good fortin the scamps comes to at last, and I've seen, with my own eyes, as many as a dozen of 'em shaking the end of a white rope, and dancing above board.'

Col. Crockett and the Elk.

Perhaps you dont know, stranger, that a big mark is not always so easily hit as a little one; but it are a fact for all that, and I'll prove it to your entire satisfakshun. I war out hunting on the upper lower fork of Great Little Deep Shallow creek, and the day was hot enough to make it oncomfortable to stand to leeward of a nigger, and so, as I war delightfully tired, I lay down under a white oak and took a snooze and dreamed of the devil, and no mistake. I a sorter kinder thort I'd gone down to the suller, to draw a pitcher of right Monongahela, and when I looked up thar war his reverence, saving his presence, sitting astraddle on the head of the cask, with horns a yard longer than the moral law, and a tail like an alligator. No one can say I ever refused to meet any gentleman on his own terms, and so I hove the licker rite into his off eye, and was just a going to have dove into him, when I woke up. My eye! there

Days mo.	Days of the week.	Sun rises,		Sun sets.		Days decrease.		Sun slow.		☉ declin. North.		Length of Days.	
1	Monday.	4	26	7	40	0	3	3	19	23°	10′	15	4
2	Tuesday.	4	26	7	40	0	4	3	31	23	6	15	4
3	Wednesday.	4	27	7	40	0	4	3	42	23	1	15	2
4	Thursday.	4	27	7	39	0	5	3	53	22	57	15	2
5	Friday.	4	28	7	39	0	6	4	4	22	51	15	0
6	Saturday.	4	29	7	39	0	7	4	15	22	46	15	0
7	**Sunday.**	4	30	7	39	0	8	4	25	22	40	14	58
8	Monday.	4	30	7	38	0	9	4	34	22	33	14	58
9	Tuesday.	4	31	7	38	0	10	4	44	22	27	14	58
10	Wednesday.	4	32	7	38	0	11	4	53	22	19	14	56
11	Thursday.	4	33	7	37	0	12	5	1	22	12	14	56
12	Friday.	4	33	7	37	0	13	5	9	22	4	14	54
13	Saturday.	4	34	7	36	0	15	5	17	21	55	14	54
14	**Sunday.**	4	35	7	36	0	16	5	24	21	47	14	52
15	Monday.	4	36	7	35	0	17	5	30	21	38	14	50
16	Tuesday.	4	37	7	34	0	19	5	37	21	28	14	48
17	Wednesday.	4	38	7	34	0	20	5	42	21	18	14	46
18	Thursday.	4	39	7	33	0	21	5	48	21	8	14	44
19	Friday.	4	39	7	32	0	23	5	52	20	58	14	44
20	Saturday.	4	40	7	32	0	24	5	57	20	47	14	42
21	**Sunday.**	4	41	7	31	0	26	6	0	20	36	14	40
22	Monday.	4	42	7	30	0	28	6	3	20	24	14	38
23	Tuesday.	4	43	7	29	0	30	6	6	20	12	14	36
24	Wednesday.	4	44	7	28	0	32	6	8	20	0	14	34
25	Thursday.	4	45	7	27	0	34	6	9	19	47	14	32
26	Friday.	4	46	7	26	0	36	6	10	19	34	14	32
27	Saturday.	4	47	7	25	0	38	6	10	19	21	14	30
28	**Sunday.**	4	48	7	24	0	40	6	10	19	7	14	28
29	Monday.	4	49	7	23	0	42	6	9	18	53	14	26
30	Tuesday.	4	50	7	22	0	44	6	8	18	39	14	24
31	Wednesday.	4	51	7	21	0	46	6	5	18	25	14	22

stood his majesty in reel wide awake airnest, not ten steps off; but dont you come for to go for to think I was the leestest grain skeered, for I dont stand no such insinnivations. I up with my rifle and give him a thimble full of Dupont's best and half an ounce of lead slap between the two eyes, as I thort, but I was as much mistaken as if you'd burnt your shirt tail off. He was too near and I missed him intirely, which proves to me that if he war not the reel actual devil, he must have been his twin brother, or some other near relation. At any rate he pitched inter me like a streak of forked lightning, and though I've no objekshun to a horn of a hot day, the feeling of a pair of 'em, tickling a gentleman's ribs is by no meens agreeable. However, his horns stood eight foot apart to a circumstance, and I took a seat between em. I wish I may be shot if the way he carried me through the prairie war not a caution to steamboats and rail roads. I never had such a ride in my life. It war not long before I got out my butcher, to make an experiment on his jugular; but I war so ashamed of missing him that I couldn't use it. Now I'm not exactly a feather on a scruple of conscience, and my gentleman soon found that if he war a hoss I war a rough rider, and so he lay down with me and I got off. 'Stranger,' sez I, 'I never said the hard word yet, and so I wont give up whipt; but if you're satisfied so am I, and we wont say another word about it.' I thought this was doing the civil thing by him, but he gave a snort like a safety valve and streaked it with his tail up, as much as to say he didn't like my company; which in my mind was a kinder Natchez-under-the-hill spessimen of his broughten up. This was the only thing in my life I ever war ashamed of, for the critter war as big as a four year old colt. I might as well have missed the broadside of a barn.

Days mo.	Days of the week.	Sun rises,	Sun sets.	Days decrease.	Sun slow.	☉ declin. North.	Length of Days.
1	Thursday.	4 52	7 20	0 48	6 3	18° 10′	14 20
2	Friday.	4 53	7 19	0 50	5 59	17 55	14 18
3	Saturday.	4 54	7 18	0 52	5 55	17 39	14 14
4	**Sunday.**	4 55	7 16	0 54	5 50	17 24	14 12
5	Monday.	4 56	7 15	0 56	5 45	17 8	14 10
6	Tuesday.	4 57	7 14	0 58	5 39	16 52	14 8
7	Wednesday.	4 58	7 13	1 0	5 33	16 35	14 6
8	Thursday.	4 59	7 11	1 2	5 25	16 18	14 4
9	Friday.	5 0	7 10	1 4	5 18	16 1	14 2
10	Saturday.	5 1	7 9	1 7	5 9	15 44	13 0
11	**Sunday.**	5 2	7 8	1 9	5 1	15 26	13 56
12	Monday.	5 3	7 7	1 11	4 51	15 8	13 54
13	Tuesday.	5 4	7 5	1 14	4 41	14 50	13 52
14	Wednesday.	5 5	7 4	1 16	4 31	14 32	13 48
15	Thursday.	5 6	7 2	1 18	4 20	14 14	13 46
16	Friday.	5 7	7 1	1 21	4 8	13 55	13 44
17	Saturday.	5 8	6 59	1 23	3 56	13 36	13 42
18	**Sunday.**	5 9	6 58	1 26	3 44	13 17	13 38
19	Monday.	5 10	6 56	1 28	3 31	12 57	13 36
20	Tuesday.	5 11	6 55	1 31	3 17	12 38	13 34
21	Wednesday.	5 12	6 54	1 34	3 3	12 18	13 32
22	Thursday.	5 14	6 52	1 37	2 49	11 58	13 28
23	Friday.	5 15	6 51	1 39	2 34	11 38	13 26
24	Saturday.	5 16	6 49	1 42	2 19	11 17	13 24
25	**Sunday.**	5 17	6 48	1 45	2 3	10 57	13 20
26	Monday.	5 18	6 46	1 48	1 47	10 36	13 18
27	Tuesday.	5 19	6 44	1 50	1 30	10 15	13 16
28	Wednesday.	5 20	6 42	1 53	1 13	9 54	13 12
29	Thursday.	5 21	6 41	1 56	0 56	9 33	13 10
30	Friday.	5 22	6 39	1 59	0 38	9 11	13 8
31	Saturday.	5 23	6 37	2 2	0 20	8 50	13 4

Col. Crockett's Account of a Duel.

I once got an invite to a French gentleman's house in New Orleans; but I wish'd I'd staid away when I got there. There was but a lean chance of eating. All there war on the table would have been no part of a priming to a lump of bear meat and a hoe cake on board the flat I cum down in. There war nothing but soup after soup, and that war but small potatoes, for I felt such a pinching about the lower regions as if I could have eaten a horse and given the rider a hard chase. I wish I may be shot with a packsaddle if I couldn't have eaten a buffalo bull and picked my teeth with the horns. At last I got hold of something I took for the hind quarter of a possum; but when I called to the nigger behind me to hand me the grease, the way they stared at me wasn't slow. And the possum turned out to be nothing more than a skunk arter all. There's no counting for taste, and every body knows the French are as nasty christians as turkey buzzards. After dinner one of the niggers brought me a little cup full of water, about as big as an egg shell, and to others the same. I thort it was a toothful of the real Talley valley cord to top off with, and it went down my throat like a grease patch down a smooth rifle. Lord! It war warm water, and I kind of like to cast up my accounts right before all that mucilaginous company. I a kind of thort the nigger had been set on to put a trick on me, and I spit on my hands to use his master up as small as a mouse; but when I see all the others washing their fingers ends in the same kind of cups, I thort I would pass over their ignorance in silent contempt; for every one knows that a Frenchman don't know any better than to call a hat a chopper, and a horse a shovel.

Duel between an Englishman and a Frenchman.

Well, the poor Frenchman asked the company to sing, and I thort I should hear a hyme, or the Hunters of Kentucky, or Remember Sinful Youth; but they only sung such things as sot me asleep till it come to an Englishman's turn, and he only contrived to get out one werse, and it eended with "We'll look forward with hope to to-morrow." Then up jumped a Frenchman so lean you might have counted his ribs across the Mississippi, looking as savagarous as a painter. "What you go for insult me, that am stranger?" said he. "You look for General Moreau — begar, he be one traitre, and you insult my master the grand general first Consul Napoleon, when you speak of him. You are one john foutre, I will have one grand apologie." The more they told him that to-morrow didn't mean General Moreau, the more he said he understood them very well, and nothing would do him but a fight no how, no way you could fix it. O, by the etarnal, but he was a real screamer!

Next morning just as the crows woke from their first nap they met on the levee, with a whole crowd of people about them, for they don't mind cutting a man's throat there, no more than I would drawing my knife across the weasand of a buck. I didn't see as they had any pistols or bowie knives, and I settled it in my mind that it was only to be a knock down and drag out rough and tumble, or else fair play and no gouging; but presently they pulled out two swords about as thick as nail rods without edges, and too it they went without saying a word, like a black snake at a tree toad.

The first dive the Englishman made at the Frenchman, I thought would have been a sogdologer; but no, he only knocked his snuff box to pieces, and made him sneeze as if a steam boat blowed up; but the Frenchman was down on him like a duck upon a June bug, boring him right through the seat of his pantaloons, and tearing his shirt tail off. If he'd hit where he aimed as hard as he surged, the Englishman would'nt have been able to sit on a hard bench for four weaks. Then down comes Mr. Frog again on John Bull, and carrid away his watch seal as clean as I could do it with old kill devil at fifty yards. Johnny next spontenaciously poaked his iron through Johnny Crapper's left whisker, and he was so hot with madness, that it sizzled like a kurling tongs. Then they ran down on each other like Joe Barber, cotton or no cotton, and the Englishman tore off half a yard of gold lace from his waistcoat, and was through his coat like a streak of forked lightning; but the Frenchman took away his wig on the point of his toasting iron. I thort one war shot thro the belly and the other thro the brains, but it only made them more cantankerous than ever, and they would have ate each other up to the tips of the tales, if I had'nt rolled up my sleeves and dove in between em. "Gentlemen," said I, "my name's Joe Dowdle the ragman. In Kentuck, they call me roaring and scattering Davy Crockett; but on the levee a rale Bengal tiger. Fifteen feet from the tip of the tale to the eend of the nose, and fifteen feet from the eend of the nose to the tip of the tale, thirty feet altogether — a roarer by the etarnal. Fleas aint lobsters, and General Moreau aint tomorrow nor next day nither." So seeing me in airnest, after I'd examplified the rights of the text to 'em they shook hands and went and took a horn together.

1839

Adventure with the Indians and Mud Turtles. See Page 30.

30 SEPTEMBER, NINTH MONTH. 1839.

Days mo.	Days of the week.	Sun rises,	Sun sets.	Days decr'se.	Sun slow.	☉ declin. North.	Length of Days.
1	**Sunday.**	5 24	6 36	2 4	0 0	8° 28′	13 2
2	Monday.	5 26	6 35	2 7	0 18	8 6	13 0
3	Tuesday.	5 27	6 33	2 10	0 36	7 44	12 56
4	Wednesday.	5 28	6 31	2 12	0 55	7 22	12 54
5	Thursday.	5 29	6 30	2 15	1 15	7 0	12 52
6	Friday.	5 30	6 28	2 18	1 35	6 38	12 48
7	Saturday.	5 31	6 26	2 21	1 55	6 16	12 46
8	**Sunday.**	5 32	6 25	2 24	2 15	5 53	12 42
9	Monday.	5 33	6 23	2 26	2 36	5 30	12 40
10	Tuesday.	5 34	6 21	2 29	2 56	5 8	12 36
11	Wednesday.	5 35	6 19	2 32	3 17	4 45	12 34
12	Thursday.	5 36	6 17	2 35	3 38	4 22	12 32
13	Friday.	5 37	6 16	2 38	3 59	3 59	12 28
14	Saturday.	5 38	6 14	2 40	4 20	3 36	12 26
15	**Sunday.**	5 39	6 12	2 43	4 41	3 13	12 22
16	Monday.	5 40	6 11	2 46	5 2	2 50	12 20
17	Tuesday.	5 41	6 9	2 49	5 23	2 27	12 18
18	Wednesday.	5 42	6 7	2 52	5 44	2 4	12 14
19	Thursday.	5 43	6 5	2 54	6 5	1 40	12 12
20	Friday.	5 44	6 4	2 57	6 26	1 17	12 8
21	Saturday.	5 45	6 2	3 0	6 47	0 54	12 6
22	**Sunday.**	5 46	6 0	3 3	7 8	0 30	12 4
23	Monday.	5 47	5 58	3 6	7 29	North 7	12 0
24	Tuesday.	5 48	5 56	3 8	7 49	S'th 17	11 58
25	Wednesday.	5 49	5 54	3 11	8 10	0 40	11 56
26	Thursday.	5 50	5 52	3 14	8 30	1 4	11 52
27	Friday.	5 51	5 50	3 17	8 50	1 27	11 50
28	Saturday.	5 53	5 49	3 20	9 11	1 50	11 48
29	**Sunday.**	5 54	5 47	3 23	9 30	2 14	11 44
30	Monday.	5 55	5 45	3 26	9 50	2 37	11 42

Colonel Crockett and the Mud Turtles.

Folks talk very strange about courage. Some think there ar nothing so beautiful as to be always gouging one another's eyes out, biting off ears and noses and rollicking other folks with sockdologers; but I'll give up my claims to be called a sensible man if there ar any bravery in it at all. You'll never see a feller amorous of knocking down and dragging out, but what you'll find he's so much stouter than his neighbors that he's no call to be afeared of em, and if he meets a raal salt, that cock wont fight. That makes all the balance between a bully and a brave man. For my own part, my name ar Thunder and Lightning, and he that gets in my track may look out for a scorching. I call myself raal grit, and cut like a razor; but I'll cry coward to the first man that ever eat an oyster—and talking of oysters puts me in mind of snapping turkles.

I war coming down the Narrow Broadhorn in a canoe with a load of deer and bear meat, in the fall of 182— when all of a sudden I heerd such a screeching and hollering as if heaven and arthe war coming together. It put me in mind of Old Hickory and the battle of the Horse Shoe, and I kinder sorter suspicioned thar war something worse than gals in the bushes, and I put ashore to take my share of the fun that war going on. And what do you think it war, stranger? Ay, and what *do* you think it war? I wish I may be kicked to death by grasshoppers if it war anything at all. It war only a dozen loping Shawnees dancing about a neest of snapping turkles they'd just dug out. While I war looking at 'em, one of their dogs cum behind me and bit my leg, like an ugly, lantern-ribbed, onnateral son of a bitch as he was, and I hope it are nither skandalous, immoral nor ondacent to call him so. So sez I, 'If you don't find out that my teeth are stronger than your'n, you thin-gutted egg-sucker, thar ar no snakes in Virginny and my name ar not Davy Crockett.' Presently the Injun

Days mo.	Days of the week.	Sun rises,	Sun sets.	Days decr'se.	Sun fast.	☉ declin. South.	Length of Days.
1	Tuesday.	5 56	5 43	3 28	10 9	3° 0′	11 38
2	Wednesday.	5 57	5 42	3 31	10 28	3 24	11 34
3	Thursday.	5 58	5 40	3 34	10 47	3 47	11 32
4	Friday.	5 59	5 39	3 36	11 6	4 11	11 28
5	Saturday.	6 1	5 38	3 39	11 24	4 34	11 26
6	**Sunday.**	6 2	5 36	3 42	11 42	4 57	11 24
7	Monday.	6 3	5 34	3 45	11 59	5 20	11 20
8	Tuesday.	6 4	5 33	3 48	12 16	5 43	11 18
9	Wednesday.	6 5	5 31	3 50	12 33	6 6	11 14
10	Thursday.	6 6	5 29	3 53	12 49	6 29	11 12
11	Friday.	6 8	5 28	3 56	13 5	6 51	11 10
12	Saturday.	6 9	5 26	3 59	13 20	7 14	11 6
13	**Sunday.**	6 10	5 24	4 2	13 34	7 37	11 4
14	Monday.	6 11	5 22	4 4	13 49	7 59	11 0
15	Tuesday.	6 12	5 20	4 7	14 2	8 22	10 58
16	Wednesday.	6 13	5 19	4 10	14 15	8 44	10 56
17	Thursday.	6 14	5 17	4 13	14 28	9 6	10 52
18	Friday.	6 15	5 16	4 16	14 39	9 28	10 50
19	Saturday.	6 17	5 14	4 18	14 51	9 50	10 46
20	**Sunday.**	6 18	5 13	4 21	15 1	10 12	10 44
21	Monday.	6 19	5 11	4 24	15 11	10 33	10 42
22	Tuesday.	6 21	5 10	4 27	15 21	10 55	10 38
23	Wednesday.	6 22	5 8	4 30	15 29	11 16	10 36
24	Thursday.	6 23	5 7	4 32	15 37	11 37	10 34
25	Friday.	6 24	5 5	4 35	15 44	11 58	10 30
26	Saturday.	6 25	5 4	4 38	15 51	12 18	10 28
27	**Sunday.**	6 27	5 2	4 41	15 57	12 39	10 24
28	Monday.	6 28	5 1	4 44	16 2	12 59	10 22
29	Tuesday.	6 29	5 0	4 46	16 6	13 19	10 20
30	Wednesday.	6 31	4 58	4 49	16 10	13 39	10 18
31	Thursday.	6 32	4 57	4 52	16 13	13 59	10 14

savages cut off the turkles heads, and they didn't sort of kinder think themselves treated the most friendly; for they kept such a snapping as would have astonished anything hungry. So I picked up one of the biggest heads on the eend of my rammer and cum behind the dog and put it to his tail, and it cotched hold and hung on like grim death to a dead nigger. I ar not ashamed to own I took the advantage of him, for isn't turn about fair play? Didn't he cum behind and bite me? Howsever, he cleared out over the prairie faster than God's wrath, and it's my belief and considerate opinion that he ar running to this day, for nither I nor the Injun savages ever see no more of him.

The Shawnee that owned the dog give me such a tanyard grin as I thought nobody but Davy Crockett could equal; but he had heern tell of me before, and thought it war not best to aggrafy the matter, though it war plain his fingers itched to be at my topknot. But to work he went, and cut up the turkles and put all their harts into a wooden bowl, where they kept hopping about like so many live cricket balls made of Injee rubber. He took one up and swallowed it, and looked me rite in the face and sez he, 'No Big Knife do that! Big Knife soft heart too much!'—and the others all grunted like so many bacon pigs at corn time. Now I never took a stump in my life, and if anybody axes you who will, you may tell him it ar not Davy Crockett, especially from an Injun savage. So I swallered three of the turkles harts right off, and I'd done it if I'd knowed they'd been rank pisen. They didn't kill me, though I own I feel pretty considerable squawmish every time I think of a snapping turkle, and I felt as if all the Paddies in Murphy Land war dancing an Irish jig in my belly for three days arter.* But all the Injun savages allotted I war the greatest brave ever they seen.

* The heart of a snapping turtle will retain life, or at least muscular action, several days after it is separated from the body.

Ben Harding falling in with Col. Crockett. See Page 22.

1839

Colonel Crockett and the Methodizer. See Page 34.

Days mo.	Days of the week.	Sun rises,	Sun sets.	Days decr'se.	Sun fast.	☉ declin. South.	Length of Days.
1	Friday.	6 33	4 55	4 55	16 15	14° 19′	10 12
2	Saturday.	6 34	4 54	4 58	16 16	14 38	10 10
3	**Sunday.**	6 35	4 53	5 0	16 17	14 57	10 6
4	Monday.	6 36	4 51	5 3	16 17	15 16	10 4
5	Tuesday.	6 38	4 50	5 5	16 16	15 34	10 2
6	Wednesday.	6 39	4 49	5 7	16 14	15 52	10 0
7	Thursday.	6 40	4 48	5 10	16 11	16 10	9 56
8	Friday.	6 42	4 46	5 12	16 7	16 28	9 54
9	Saturday.	6 43	4 45	5 14	16 3	16 45	9 52
10	**Sunday.**	6 44	4 44	5 17	15 58	17 3	9 50
11	Monday.	6 46	4 43	5 19	15 51	17 19	9 48
12	Tuesday.	6 47	4 42	5 21	15 44	17 36	9 46
13	Wednesday.	6 48	4 41	5 24	15 37	17 52	9 42
14	Thursday.	6 50	4 40	5 26	15 28	18 8	9 40
15	Friday.	6 51	4 39	5 28	15 18	18 24	9 38
16	Saturday.	6 52	4 38	5 30	15 8	18 39	9 36
17	**Sunday.**	6 53	4 37	5 32	14 56	18 54	9 34
18	Monday.	6 54	4 36	5 34	14 44	19 9	9 32
19	Tuesday.	6 55	4 35	5 36	14 31	19 23	9 30
20	Wednesday.	6 57	4 35	5 38	14 17	19 37	9 28
21	Thursday.	6 58	4 34	5 40	14 3	19 51	9 26
22	Friday.	6 59	4 33	5 42	13 47	20 4	9 24
23	Saturday.	7 0	4 32	5 44	13 31	20 17	9 22
24	**Sunday.**	7 2	4 32	5 46	13 14	20 29	9 20
25	Monday.	7 3	4 31	5 48	12 56	20 41	9 18
26	Tuesday.	7 4	4 30	5 50	12 38	20 53	9 16
27	Wednesday.	7 5	4 30	5 52	12 18	21 4	9 14
28	Thursday.	7 6	4 29	5 53	11 58	21 15	9 14
29	Friday.	7 8	4 29	5 55	11 38	21 26	9 12
30	Saturday.	7 9	4 29	5 56	11 16	21 36	9 10

Colonel Crockett and the Methodizer.

I war riding to St. Louy one day in the year six, with a richus buck on each side of my hoss, for I 'd been bouncing deer on Tantivy prairie, and I kinder thort I 'd let my hoss have a mouthful out of the Mississip, when I heerd a most riproarions hollering, as if fifty thousand devils were having their tails chopped off clost to their butt eends all at once and then having the hoperation gone over agin closer. So thinking it war too painters fiteing, I looked sharp at my priming and rode that way, expecting to get a shot and maybe two. But when I got thar I wish I may shot if it war not a methody parson a whaling it into the natyves to kill. The brute war enticing em all to kingdom cum by a short cut he had found out, he said, and the way he explaterated to em war a causion. Tom Benton war no part of a priming to him. Thar war one feller streaking it up to the pulpit on his knees, enough to make his wife sneeze her nose off, if she had the mending on em. Then thar war a feller two foot longer than the moral law galravaging on a stump and trying to reach Heaven, he said. I told him he'd better go atop of the next bluff, but he took no notiss of me, and another feller told me to shut up my salt box for fear the flies should get down my throat. The gals war all a crying and that made me feel quite solumkolly. But what made me the maddest was to see as many as a hundred niggers turning up the whites of their eyes, jest as if they had soles to be saved. If I war to ketch you galliwanting so on my plantation, mister, sez I to myself, I 'd make an American flag of your back in the twinkling of a bed-post. However, he got done soon, and marched rite down into the Mississip, and hauled two or three niggers in after him, and ducked them so often that I thought the life was extinctified in 'em.

Days mo.	Days of the week.	Sun rises,		Sun sets.		Days decrease.		Sun fast.		☉ declin. South.		Length of Days	
1	**Sunday.**	7	10	4	29	5	57	10	54	21°	46	9	8
2	Monday.	7	11	4	29	5	59	10	32	21	55	9	8
3	Tuesday.	7	12	4	28	6	0	10	8	22	4	9	6
4	Wednesday.	7	13	4	28	6	1	9	45	22	12	9	4
5	Thursday.	7	14	4	28	6	2	9	20	22	20	9	4
6	Friday.	7	15	4	28	6	3	8	55	22	28	9	2
7	Saturday.	7	16	4	28	6	4	8	30	22	35	9	2
8	**Sunday.**	7	17	4	28	6	5	8	4	22	42	9	0
9	Monday.	7	18	4	28	6	6	7	37	22	48	9	0
10	Tuesday.	7	19	4	28	6	7	7	10	22	54	8	58
11	Wednesday.	7	20	4	28	6	8	6	43	22	59	8	58
12	Thursday.	7	21	4	28	6	9	6	15	23	4	8	56
13	Friday.	7	21	4	28	6	10	5	47	23	9	8	56
14	Saturday.	7	22	4	28	6	11	5	18	23	13	8	56
15	**Sunday.**	7	23	4	28	6	11	4	49	23	16	8	54
16	Monday.	7	24	4	28	6	12	4	20	23	19	8	54
17	Tuesday.	7	24	4	29	6	12	3	50	23	22	8	54
18	Wednesday.	7	25	4	29	6	12	3	21	23	24	8	54
19	Thursday.	7	25	4	29	6	12	2	51	23	26	8	54
20	Friday.	7	26	4	30	6	13	2	21	23	27	8	54
21	Saturday.	7	26	4	30	6	13	1	51	23	27	8	54
22	**Sunday.**	7	27	4	31	6	13	1	21	23	28	8	54
23	Monday.	7	27	4	31	incr'se.		0	51	23	27	8	54
24	Tuesday.	7	28	4	32	0	0	fast	21	23	27	8	54
25	Wednesday.	7	28	4	32	0	0	S.	9	23	26	8	54
26	Thursday.	7	29	4	33	0	0	0	39	23	24	8	54
27	Friday.	7	29	4	34	0	1	1	9	23	22	8	54
28	Saturday.	7	29	4	34	0	1	1	39	23	19	8	54
29	**Sunday.**	7	29	4	35	0	2	2	8	23	16	8	56
30	Monday.	7	30	4	36	0	2	2	37	23	13	8	56
31	Tuesday.	7	30	4	37	0	3	3	6	23	9	8	56

Bimeby up cums a puke from Wheatbush more than half and half absquottleated with licker, and sez he, 'I say, mister, what do you get apiece for washing them are niggers?' Well, if the methodizer war not mad then there 's no snakes in Virginny, and he as good as told him he war a wiper or a copperhead, I disremember which; but the feller wouldn't say the hard word for all that. 'You needn't come for to go to be so kantankerous about it, stranger,' sez he, 'for I meant to give you a job. I 've got a couple of little niggers at hum, and if you can wash 'em white I wouldn't mind paying you something hansum and a chaw of tobacco.' And he got so atrocious that if somebody hadn't held him he 'd have walked into the methodizer knee deep, and a foot deeper. I was so kyind of curous to see what war going on that I went down to the edge of the water jest as the methodizer laid his cornstealers on a wench blacker than the ace of spades, and fatter than a December bear, and led her up to the neck into the drink. Down he shoved her woolly calabash under water and up popped her starn, bekayse any fool mought know it 's natteral for grease to float. The methodizer was discomboborated a few and shoved her starn down agin, and then up shot her topknot. He coodent git her whole corporosity under no how he could fix it till he hauled her in whar she couldn't touch the bottom, and then the current took her bodily, and the methodizer would have gone down stream with her like a Pawnee with another man's hoss if he hadn't let her go, and she 'd swallowed so much water aready that she evaporated like steam. The methodizer didn't seem to mind it no more than if she didn't cost nothing. 'There 's one gone to thy kingdom!' sez he, 'fetch on another. Wont you cum to glory, mister, wont you cum?' 'No,' sez I, 'I thank you as kyindly as if I did, but I can't swim.'

A SCENTORIFEROUS FIGHT WITH A NIGGER. SEE P. 18.

1839

Vol. 2.] "GO AHEAD!!" [No. 2.

THE CROCKETT ALMANAC 1840.

Crockett scared by an Owl....See page 2.

Containing Adventures, Exploits, Sprees & Scrapes in the West, & Life and Manners in the Backwoods.

Nashville, Tennessee. Published by Ben Harding.

PREFACE——by Ben Harding.

Sense we got out the last Allmyneck, thar has been so mutch enkurridgment that i hav plucked up spunk to git out anuther. I hav been kruising about, and living on my pention, ever cents i got out the last one, and hav spent sum part of my time in New York and some in Bostown, and sum in Fillydelphy. When I goes limping up Broadway and Washington Street or Chessnut Street, fokes dont no as i am a litterrary karaktur. Prehaps one wreizon of that is that the printurs diddent send around the aulmynack to awl the noosepaypur fokes last yeer, and so it hasent got about that i am the chap what makes 'em.

My late frend Kurnell Krockitt sot a good deel by his Allmynack, and sed it shood never sink so long as he had his hed above water; and now he is ded and gone, I kalkulate to keep it up out o' respect to his memory.

My helth has ben pritty good for a old man, and thar is sum hopes that i shall wether my seventieth year. As I spose the publick wood like to no aul about me, as my aulmynaks is aul the tork, and as they has profiles took doun of aul the grate karakturs, i mean to get an ingraver to picktur me out.

I intend to cum out this yeer in rail skreeming style, and has engaged to have it printed so slick that slush woodent make it no slicker; and then the kalkulations will be made so that if a feller was blown up in a steambote he cood contrive to be blowed into enny direction he thort propper. The way the sigh-for-inn is done up this year is sumthing for them to grin at what has got know teeth, and cant chaw upon the matthewmattocks. I'll giv enny won leef to make me splice the main brace by proxy, who kan find any fault in the sums. So to cut short my yarn, I'll only say if ennybody thinks he kan make a better allmynack, let him try, That's aul.

Eclipses in the year 1840.

I spose the reeder has seed fokes when they had picked a pocket, or done sum other pokerish job, hide behind somebody else to get out of site. Well that is jist the way the Sun and Moon will do this year: and they will do it twice. The Sun will be non-committal twice, and kinder hide partly out o' sight, but he will be a leetle sly about it, so that you cant see how it is done, in America. Nobody on this continent will be able to say black is the white of his eye, only in them parts of the world where they can see, and that wont be here by a jugfull. As to the moon, she will dodge a little behind the curtain, and that you will see; but tother time it wont be wizzibull on this here continent, no how nor no howsomever.

The fust will be the Moon at the time when it is full in February—then you see it will operate like cutting a big slice out of a cheese, but then it will all be dun down below the horrizun out of site; jist as a grate turkle bit off Sal Sleek's toe under water, when she was swimming over the Massissippy.

The second will be the Sun, on Tuesday, March 3d. Then the Sun will be enermost hid out of sight, and it will look grand, and as big as a painter's head with one i nokt out, and tother i asquint. But it will happen at half past 11 o'clock in the night, so that yon cant see it without you could creep along to the edge of the yearth and look over. But the fokes in Asha will see it, and all the pesky Hottentots and wild Arabs what lives between the Injun otion and Beer-in-Straits.

The third will be the Moon, and that will happen on Thursday, August 13, in the morning. This will be a small elipse, and will be wizzibull. The man whot duz my mattummattocks has sifered it out, as follows:—

The fourth, and that's the last one, will be the Sun. It will happen on Thursday, August 27, at half past two o'clock in the morning; and then the sun will look grand, for it will be clipsed awl out of sight—but you can't see it bekase its out of sight in 2 ways. It's clipsed out of site, and it's in the night time too, jist as Zipporeth Wing's goose war out of site when a Yankee pedlar stole it, and war out of site agin arter he ett it up. But if it warn't out of site nary time, you couldn't see the clipse in North America, bekase of what the cipher-man calls the moon's south lattitude.

Morning and Evening Stars.

The star wot they call VENUS will show a leg arly every morning, till arter the 24th of July, bekase she belongs to the stars in the American flag, and wants to see the Fourth of July by day break. But arter the 24th, she will only be up of evenings, like Sam Flat's gal as lived near Possum Swamp, who washed her close every nite and lay abed all day for 'em to dry. So she could only be up of evenings. Another star as they call JUPITER, what I spose was named arter my grand'ther's dog Jupe, will be Morning Star till May 4th, a proppus to commodate the New York fokes what moves on May day in the morning. But arter the 4th, this here Jupiter will be evening star till November 21st: and arter that the nights will be so cold, it wont get up till morning. The star what they call MARS will shine of evenings, till May 4th, and arter that, it will be up every morning so as to see the New Year come in. Another star they call SATURN, will present itself also every morning till June 9th; and then it will come of evenings till Dec. 14th; and arter that, it will go down the back track, and play possum in the morning.

Crockett Scared by an Owl.

There ar one thing that happent to me one evening that sum fokes woodent tell for seventeen possum skins full of whiskee; but I never stood for trifles, and aint got no need of kivvering over the truth, for to giv fokes a high notion of my kurridge. Thar never war a race horse that didn't git beet sum time in his life; and thar never was a rifle that didn't hang fire sum time or other. For all that the peeple will stair when they learn how Davy Crockett got skeered wunst, and they will stair a grate deel wuss when they larn what it war that skeered him.

It war on one foggy evening that I had ben out haff the day in sarch of a big painter as had been poking fun at me awl night and squalling most ridikilous under my winder. I got site of him wonst, as he war swimming over a rivver, and so I kepp on his trale for three ours arterward, till it got too dark to see, and the fog cum down at the same time as if the ... away and turnin to ... dead stop, and leaned a... tree, ... kill-devil under ...y chin; and war konsidering whether the p...nter wood cum back agin in the nite, when s...thing made a little noise amungst the dry twig... over my head, and then sung out, in a strange ...ung, like the tree war alive, or I had been l...ning agin a krok... war standing on the eend of his ... on I jumpt about ...even foot, tho I didn't stop to mezure the dist...ce, and then the cretur bawled out again as ...f he war tryin to split my head open with his noise. I cant say that I run so fast as I hav run afore now; but it coodn't hardly be said that I wauked, for I stradled so wide that I tore my trowses. The ground was miry and I slipt about like I war skating, and then the feller in the tree kept up his hollering. But at last I got used to it, and then I stopt, and drawed trigger tho I coodn't see nothing. But as soon as killdevil had spoke, I heered no more from the feller in the tree, and I konkluded he war dead. So I konsidered that a special intarposition of Providence, seeing it war likely it had saved my life. I crept softly back to the tree, and listened to heer the cretur strugling amongst the leeves; but I heered nothing. So I went up to the tree, with my arms spread out. I trod on sumthing jist about that time, and sposed it was some wadding I had dropt. So I stooped down and got hold on a bunch of fethers, and then I knowed it war a bird, and held it up. It war a ...sky grate owl, and then I noed that the cretur w...what had skeered me by his hooting, and I rem...ered the voice rite off. I spose awl the oaths ...wore then, if they war straitened out, wood re... clean acrost the Massissippi. It war the fust t...e that I had run from a cretur not so big as mys...; and I felt as stripid as a rainbow. I took up t... pesky owl, and shook him by one leg till I ... tired, and then put him into my pocket. A...r that I never allowed myself to be skeered at ...y cretur, without I war sartin it war not an ow...

1840. 1st Month, JANUARY, begins on Wednesday. Hath 31 Days, and is the 2d Winter Month.

Phases of the Moon.

● New Moon, 4th, 4h. 7m. Evening.
☽ First Quarter, 12th, 2h. 41m. Morning.
○ Full Moon, 18th, 7h. 15m. Evening.
☾ Last Quarter, 26th, 8h. 13m. Morning.

D W	ASPECTS, &c.	Sun's Dec.	Sun Slow	Moon South	☽ S
W	*Beware of little ex-*	23 4	3 37	9 17	♐
T	☌ ☽ ☿ & ♄. *penses;*	22 59	4 5	10 7	♐
F	*a small leak will sink*	22 54	4 33	10 59	♐
S	*a great ship. Be*	22 48	5 1	11 52	♑
E	2d Sun. af. Ch'mas.	22 42	5 29	aft 44	♑
M	Epiphany. High Tid	22 35	5 56	1 34	♒
T	☌ ☽ & ♂. *not too*	22 28	6 22	2 21	♒
W	☿ greatest elon. W.	22 20	6 48	3 7	♒
T	♂ in Perihelion. ☌	22 12	7 14	3 52	♓
F	*brief in con-* [☽ & ♅.	22 3	7 39	4 36	♓
S	*versation, lest you*	21 55	8 3	5 22	♈
E	1st Sun. af. Epiph.	21 45	8 27	6 12	♈
M	Low Tides. *be not*	21 35	8 50	7 5	♉
T	☌ ☽ & 7 ✱s. *under-*	21 25	9 12	8 3	♉
W	*stood; nor too dif-*	21 15	9 34	9 5	♊
T	☽ Perigee. *fuse,*	21 4	9 55	10 10	♊
F	*lest you be trouble-*	20 52	10 16	11 14	♋
S	*some. Ask a kite for*	20 40	10 35	morn	♋
E	2d Sund. af. Epiph.	20 28	10 54	0 13	♌
M	High Tides. *a fea-*	20 16	11 13	1 8	♌
T	*ther, and she'll say*	20 3	11 30	1 56	♍
W	☌ ♀ & ♄. *she has*	19 49	11 47	2 42	♍
T	*but just enough to*	19 36	12 3	3 25	♍
F	*fly with. That man*	19 21	12 18	4 6	♎
S	*hath no sense of mer-*	19 7	12 33	4 47	♎
E	3d Sund. af. Epiph.	18 52	12 46	5 30	♏
M	☽ Apogee. Very L.	18 37	12 59	6 14	♏
T	*cy, that* [Tides.	18 22	13 11	7 1	♏
W	☿ in Aphelion.	18 6	13 23	7 50	♐
T	☌ ☽ ♀ & ♄. *wants*	17 50	13 33	8 42	♐
F	*a sense of duty.*	17 33	13 43	9 34	♑

Astronomical Calculations, embracing the whole Union, and the Canadas, beginning at the following points:

Boston. D. M.	Sun Rises	Sun Sets	Days' L'gth	Moon Rises.	High water.	New York. D. M.	Sun Rises	Sun Sets	Days' L'gth	Moon Rises.	High water.
1	7 32	4 28	8 56	4 52	8 48	1	7 26	4 34	9 8	4 46	6 18
2	7 31	4 29	8 58	5 52	9 36	2	7 26	4 34	9 8	5 45	7 6
3	7 30	4 30	9 0	6 48	10 16	3	7 25	4 35	9 10	6 41	7 46
4	7 30	4 30	9 0	sets.	11 0	4	7 25	4 35	9 10	sets.	8 30
E	7 29	4 31	9 2	5 16	11 38	E	7 24	4 36	9 12	5 21	9 8
6	7 29	4 31	9 2	6 24	aft 14	6	7 24	4 36	9 12	6 27	9 44
7	7 28	4 32	9 4	7 34	0 51	7	7 23	4 37	9 14	7 36	10 21
8	7 28	4 32	9 4	8 44	1 19	8	7 23	4 37	9 14	8 44	10 49
9	7 27	4 33	9 6	9 54	2 6	9	7 22	4 38	9 16	9 54	11 36
10	7 27	4 33	9 6	11 3	2 43	10	7 21	4 39	9 18	11 2	aft 13
11	7 26	4 34	9 8	morn	3 26	11	7 21	4 39	9 18	morn	0 56
E	7 25	4 35	9 10	0 15	4 31	E	7 20	4 40	9 20	0 12	2 7
13	7 25	4 35	9 10	1 31	5 40	13	7 20	4 40	9 20	1 28	3 10
14	7 24	4 36	9 12	2 50	7 9	14	7 19	4 41	9 22	2 45	4 39
15	7 23	4 37	9 14	4 10	8 29	15	7 18	4 42	9 24	4 4	5 59
16	7 22	4 38	9 16	5 23	9 36	16	7 17	4 43	9 26	5 17	7 6
17	7 21	4 39	9 18	6 28	10 31	17	7 17	4 43	9 26	6 22	8 1
18	7 20	4 40	9 20	rises	11 13	18	7 16	4 44	9 28	rises	8 43
E	7 19	4 41	9 22	5 35	11 52	E	7 15	4 45	9 30	5 39	9 22
20	7 19	4 41	9 22	6 48	morn	20	7 14	4 46	9 32	6 51	10 0
21	7 18	4 42	9 24	8 0	0 30	21	7 13	4 47	9 34	8 20	10 37
22	7 17	4 43	9 26	9 8	1 7	22	7 12	4 48	9 36	9 8	11 19
23	7 16	4 44	9 28	10 13	1 49	23	7 11	4 49	9 38	10 12	11 50
24	7 15	4 45	9 30	11 18	2 20	24	7 10	4 50	9 40	11 15	morn
25	7 14	4 46	9 32	morn	2 58	25	7 9	4 51	9 42	morn	0 28
E	7 13	4 47	9 34	0 22	3 42	E	7 8	4 52	9 44	0 18	1 12
27	7 12	4 48	9 36	1 26	4 29	27	7 7	4 53	9 46	1 22	1 59
28	7 11	4 49	9 38	2 30	5 34	28	7 6	4 54	9 48	2 25	3 4
29	7 9	4 51	9 42	3 33	6 59	29	7 5	4 55	9 50	3 26	4 29
30	7 8	4 52	9 44	4 31	8 7	30	7 4	4 56	9 52	4 25	5 37
31	7 7	4 53	9 46	5 22	9 3	31	7 3	4 57	9 54	5 15	6 33

Washington. Sun Rises	Sun Sets.	Days' L'gth	Moon Rises	Charleston. D M.	Sun Rises	Sun Sets.	Days' L'gth	Moon Rises	High water	New Orleans. Sun Rises	Sun Sets	Days' L'gth.	Moon Rises.
7 20	4 40	9 20	4 41	1	7 4	4 56	9 52	4 26	4 48	6 57	5 3	10 6	4 20
7 20	4 40	9 20	5 39	2	7 4	4 56	9 52	5 22	5 36	6 57	5 3	10 6	5 15
7 20	4 40	9 20	6 35	3	7 3	4 57	9 54	6 19	6 16	6 56	5 4	10 8	6 12
7 19	4 41	9 22	sets.	4	7 3	4 57	9 54	sets.	7 0	6 56	5 4	10 8	sets.
7 19	4 41	9 22	5 24	E	7 3	4 57	9 54	5 32	7 38	6 55	5 5	10 10	5 37
7 18	4 42	9 24	6 28	6	7 2	4 58	9 56	6 31	8 14	6 55	5 5	10 10	6 34
7 18	4 42	9 24	7 37	7	7 2	4 58	9 56	7 38	8 51	6 55	5 5	10 10	7 40
7 17	4 43	9 26	8 45	8	7 1	4 59	9 58	8 48	9 19	6 55	5 5	10 10	8 48
7 17	4 43	9 26	9 54	9	7 1	4 59	9 58	9 54	10 6	6 54	5 6	10 12	9 54
7 16	4 44	9 28	11 1	10	7 0	5 0	10 0	10 58	10 43	6 54	5 6	10 12	10 57
7 16	4 44	9 28	morn	11	7 0	5 0	10 0	morn	11 26	6 54	5 6	10 12	morn
7 15	4 45	9 30	0 10	E	6 59	5 1	10 2	0 4	aft 37	6 53	5 7	10 14	0 0
7 15	4 45	9 30	1 25	13	6 59	5 1	10 2	1 16	1 40	6 52	5 8	10 16	1 12
7 14	4 46	9 32	2 41	14	6 59	5 1	10 4	2 28	3 9	6 52	5 8	10 16	2 23
7 13	4 47	9 34	3 59	15	6 58	5 2	10 4	3 44	4 29	6 52	5 8	10 16	3 37
7 12	4 48	9 36	5 10	16	6 57	5 3	10 6	4 51	5 36	6 51	5 9	10 18	4 45
7 12	4 48	9 36	6 15	17	6 57	5 3	10 6	5 54	6 31	6 51	5 9	10 18	5 48
7 11	4 49	9 38	rises	18	6 56	5 4	10 8	rises	7 13	6 50	5 10	10 20	rises
7 10	4 50	9 40	5 43	E	6 56	5 4	10 8	5 55	7 52	6 49	5 11	10 22	6 0
7 9	4 51	9 42	6 54	20	6 55	5 5	10 10	7 2	8 30	6 49	5 11	10 22	7 5
7 8	4 52	9 44	8 3	21	6 54	5 6	10 12	8 6	9 7	6 48	5 12	10 24	8 8
7 8	4 52	9 44	9 8	22	6 54	5 6	10 12	9 8	9 49	6 48	5 12	10 24	9 8
7 7	4 53	9 46	10 11	23	6 53	5 7	10 14	10 7	10 20	6 47	5 13	10 26	10 6
7 6	4 54	9 48	11 12	24	6 52	5 8	10 16	11 3	10 58	6 47	5 13	10 26	11 0
7 5	4 55	9 50	morn	25	6 51	5 9	10 18	11 58	11 42	6 46	5 14	10 28	11 54
7 4	4 56	9 52	0 13	E	6 51	5 9	10 18	morn	morn	6 45	5 15	10 30	morn
7 3	4 57	9 54	1 17	27	6 50	5 10	10 20	1 0	0 39	6 45	5 15	10 30	0 56
7 2	4 58	9 56	2 18	28	6 49	5 11	10 22	1 58	1 34	6 44	5 16	10 32	1 53
7 1	4 59	9 58	3 18	29	6 48	5 12	10 24	2 56	2 59	6 43	5 17	10 34	2 49
7 0	5 0	10 0	4 17	30	6 48	5 12	10 24	3 56	4 7	6 42	5 18	10 36	3 50
6 59	5 1	10 2	5 9	31	6 47	5 13	10 26	4 47	5 3	6 42	5 18	10 36	4 41

4

Ben Harding's Courtship.....See Page 10.

1840

Col. Crockett Beat at a Shooting Match.....See Page 11.

1840

1840. 2d Month, FEBRUARY, begins on Saturday. Hath 29 Days, and is the 3d Winter Month.

Phases of the Moon.

- ● New Moon, 3d, 8h. 37m. Morning.
- ☽ First Quarter, 10th, 10h. 41m. Morning.
- ○ Full Moon, 17th, 8h. 31m. Morning.
- ☾ Last Quarter, 25th, 5h. 29m. Morning.

Astronomical Calculations, embracing the whole Union, and the Canadas, beginning at the following points:

D. W.	ASPECTS, &c.	Sun's Dec.	Sun Slow	Moon South	☽ S
S	*Safe is he* [☌ ☽ & ☿.	17 16	13 52	10 27	♑
■	4th Sun. af. Epiph.	16 59	14 6	11 19	♑
M	*who serves a good*	16 42	14 7	aft. 9	♒
T	High Tides. *con-*	16 24	14 13	0 56	♒
W	☌ ☽ ♅ & ♂. *science.*	16 6	14 19	1 43	♓
T	*Seek not after the*	15 48	14 24	2 28	♓
F	□ ☉ & ♃. *failings*	15 30	14 28	3 15	♈
S	*of others. Sell not*	15 11	14 31	4 4	♈
■	5th Sun. af. Epiph.	14 52	14 33	4 54	♉
M	☌ ☽ & 7 ✱ s. *thy*	14 33	14 34	5 50	♉
T	☽ Perigee. *con-*	14 13	14 35	6 49	♊
W	*sciencewiththygoods*	13 54	14 35	7 52	♊
T	*A burden which one*	13 34	14 34	8 55	♋
F	*chooses is not felt.*	13 13	14 32	9 55	♋
S	☌ ♂ & ♅. *Do good*	12 53	14 30	10 52	♋
■	SeptuagessimaSun.	12 32	14 27	11 44	♌
M	☽ eclipsed invisible	12 12	14 23	morn	♌
T	High Tides. *if you*	11 51	14 18	0 31	♍
W	*expect to receive any.*	11 30	14 18	1 15	♍
T	*Do what you ought,*	11 8	14 7	1 57	♎
F	*come what may. It*	10 47	14 0	2 39	♎
S	*is better to* [☌ ☽ & ♃	10 25	13 53	3 21	♏
■	Sexagesima Sund.	10 3	13 45	4 6	♏
M	☽ apo. ☿ in Su. ☌ ☉	9 41	13 37	4 51	♏
T	*do well, than to say*	9 19	13 28	5 40	♐
W	Very L. T. ☌ ☽ & ♄	8 57	13 18	6 32	♐
T	*well. Be just, but*	8 34	13 8	7 24	♑
F	*trust not every one.*	8 12	12 57	8 17	♑
S	☌ ♀ & ☽. ☌ ♅ & ☿.	7 49	12 45	9 9	♑

Boston.

D. M.	Sun Rises	Sun Sets.	Days' L'gth	Moon Rises.	High water.
1	7 6	4 54	9 48	5 5	9 52
■	7 5	4 55	9 50	6 42	10 34
3	7 3	4 57	9 54	sets.	11 9
4	7 2	4 58	9 56	6 25	11 45
5	7 1	4 59	9 58	7 36	aft23
6	7 0	5 0	10 0	8 48	0 55
7	6 59	5 1	10 2	10 1	1 32
8	6 57	5 3	10 6	11 15	2 11
■	6 56	5 4	10 8	morn	2 52
10	6 55	5 5	10 10	0 31	3 53
11	6 54	5 6	10 12	1 50	5 13
12	6 52	5 8	10 16	3 4	6 32
13	6 51	5 9	10 18	4 10	8 20
14	6 50	5 10	10 20	5 5	9 23
15	6 49	5 11	10 22	5 47	10 12
■	6 47	5 13	10 26	6 21	10 53
17	6 45	5 15	10 30	rises	11 29
18	6 44	5 16	10 32	6 48	morn
19	6 42	5 18	10 36	7 53	0 3
20	6 41	5 19	10 38	8 59	0 33
21	6 40	5 20	10 40	10 5	1 4
22	6 39	5 21	10 42	11 10	1 38
■	6 37	5 23	10 46	morn	2 16
24	6 36	5 24	10 48	0 15	2 57
25	6 34	5 26	10 52	1 19	3 45
26	6 33	5 27	10 54	2 19	4 53
27	6 32	5 28	10 56	3 13	6 11
28	6 30	5 30	11 0	4 1	7 32
29	6 29	5 31	11 2	4 42	8 39

New York.

D. M.	Sun Rises	Sun Sets.	Days' L'gth	Moon Rises.	High water.
1	7 2	4 58	9 56	5 59	7 22
■	7 1	4 59	9 58	6 35	8 4
3	7 0	5 0	10 0	sets.	8 39
4	6 59	5 1	10 2	6 27	9 15
5	6 57	5 3	10 6	7 37	9 53
6	6 56	5 4	10 8	8 48	10 25
7	6 55	5 5	10 10	9 59	11 2
8	6 54	5 6	10 12	11 12	11 41
■	6 53	5 7	10 14	morn	aft22
10	6 52	5 8	10 16	0 26	1 23
11	6 50	5 10	10 20	1 44	2 43
12	6 49	5 11	10 22	2 57	4 28
13	6 48	5 12	10 24	4 3	5 50
14	6 47	5 13	10 26	4 58	6 53
15	6 45	5 15	10 30	5 41	7 42
■	6 44	5 16	10 32	6 16	8 23
17	6 43	5 17	10 34	rises	8 59
18	6 42	5 18	10 36	6 49	9 33
19	6 40	5 20	10 40	7 53	10 3
20	6 39	5 21	10 42	8 57	10 34
21	6 38	5 22	10 44	10 2	11 8
22	6 36	5 24	10 48	11 6	11 46
■	6 35	5 25	10 50	morn	morn
24	6 34	5 26	10 52	0 9	0 27
25	6 32	5 28	10 56	1 12	1 15
26	6 31	5 29	10 58	2 12	2 23
27	6 30	5 30	11 0	3 6	3 41
28	6 28	5 32	11 4	3 54	5 2
29	6 27	5 33	11 6	4 36	6 9

Washington.

D. M.	Sun Rises	Sun Sets.	Days' L'gth	Moon Rises.
1	6 58	5 2	10 4	5 53
■	6 57	5 3	10 6	6 28
3	6 56	5 4	10 8	sets.
4	6 55	5 5	10 10	6 29
5	6 54	5 6	10 12	7 38
6	6 53	5 7	10 14	8 48
7	6 52	5 8	10 16	9 57
8	6 50	5 10	10 20	11 9
■	6 49	5 11	10 22	morn
10	6 48	5 12	10 24	0 21
11	6 47	5 13	10 26	1 38
12	6 46	5 14	10 28	2 50
13	6 45	5 15	10 30	3 56
14	6 44	5 16	10 32	4 51
15	6 42	5 18	10 36	5 35
■	6 41	5 19	10 38	6 11
17	6 40	5 20	10 40	rises
18	6 39	5 21	10 42	6 50
19	6 38	5 22	10 44	7 53
20	6 36	5 24	10 48	8 55
21	6 35	5 25	10 50	9 59
22	6 34	5 26	10 52	11 2
■	6 33	5 27	10 54	morn
24	6 32	5 28	10 56	0 3
25	6 30	5 30	11 0	1 5
26	6 29	5 31	11 2	2 5
27	6 28	5 32	11 4	3 0
28	6 26	5 34	11 8	3 47
29	6 25	5 35	11 10	4 30

Charleston.

D. M.	Sun Rises	Sun Sets.	Days' L'gth	Moon Rises.	High water
1	6 46	5 14	10 28	5 34	5 52
■	6 45	5 15	10 30	6 8	6 34
3	6 45	5 15	10 30	sets.	7 9
4	6 44	5 16	10 32	6 35	7 45
5	6 43	5 17	10 34	7 41	8 23
6	6 42	5 18	10 36	8 48	8 55
7	6 41	5 19	10 38	9 52	9 32
8	6 40	5 20	10 40	11 0	10 11
■	6 40	5 20	10 40	morn	10 52
10	6 39	5 21	10 42	0 6	11 53
11	6 38	5 22	10 44	1 20	1 13
12	6 37	5 23	10 46	2 30	2 52
13	6 36	5 24	10 48	3 36	4 20
14	6 35	5 25	10 50	4 31	5 23
15	6 34	5 26	10 52	5 17	6 12
■	6 33	5 27	10 54	5 56	6 53
17	6 32	5 28	10 56	rises.	7 29
18	6 31	5 29	10 58	6 53	8 3
19	6 30	5 30	11 0	7 53	8 33
20	6 29	5 31	11 2	8 50	9 4
21	6 28	5 32	11 4	9 50	9 38
22	6 27	5 33	11 6	10 50	10 16
■	6 26	5 34	11 8	11 45	10 57
24	6 25	5 35	11 10	morn	11 45
25	6 24	5 36	11 12	0 45	morn
26	6 23	5 37	11 14	1 45	0 53
27	6 22	5 38	11 16	2 42	2 11
28	6 22	5 38	11 16	3 28	3 32
29	6 21	5 39	11 18	4 12	4 39

New Orleans.

D. M.	Sun Rises	Sun Sets	Days' Lg'th	Moon Rises.
1	6 41	5 19	10 38	5 26
■	6 40	5 20	10 40	6 2
3	6 40	5 20	10 40	sets.
4	6 39	5 21	10 42	6 37
5	6 38	5 22	10 44	7 42
6	6 37	5 23	10 46	8 48
7	6 37	5 23	10 46	9 49
8	6 36	5 24	10 48	10 57
■	6 35	5 25	10 50	morn
10	6 34	5 26	10 52	0 0
11	6 33	5 27	10 54	1 14
12	6 33	5 27	10 54	2 22
13	6 32	5 28	10 56	3 28
14	6 31	5 29	10 58	4 23
15	6 30	5 30	11 0	5 14
■	6 29	5 31	11 2	5 51
17	6 28	5 32	11 4	rises
18	6 28	5 32	11 4	6 54
19	6 27	5 33	11 6	7 53
20	6 26	5 34	11 8	8 47
21	6 25	5 35	11 10	9 47
22	6 24	5 36	11 12	10 46
■	6 23	5 37	11 14	11 39
24	6 22	5 38	11 16	morn
25	6 22	5 38	11 16	0 37
26	6 21	5 39	11 18	1 37
27	6 20	5 40	11 20	2 36
28	6 19	5 41	11 22	3 20
29	6 18	5 42	11 24	4 6

1840. 3d Month, MARCH, begins on Sunday. Hath 31 Days, and is the 1st Spring Month.

Phases of the Moon.

● New Moon, 3d, 10h. 45m. Evening.
☽ First Quarter, 10th, 5h. 50m. Evening.
○ Full Moon, 17th, 11h. 15m. Evening.
☾ Last Quarter, 26th, 1h. 27m. Morning.

D W	ASPECTS, &c.	Sun's Dec.	Sun Fast.	Moon South	☽ S
D	Shrove Sunday. *De-*	7 26	12 34	10 0	♒
M	*serve* [eclip. invis.	7 3	12 21	10 50	♒
T	Shrove Tuesday. ☉	6 40	12 9	11 38	♓
W	Ash Wed. 1st d. Lt.	6 17	11 55	aft25	♓
T	Very H. T. ☌ ☽ ♂.	5 54	11 42	1 13	♈
F	♃ station. ☌ ♅ & ☉.	5 31	11 27	2 3	♈
S	☽ Perigee. [& 7 ✱ s.	5 8	11 13	2 55	♉
D	1st S. in Lent. ☌ ☽	4 44	10 58	3 50	♉
M	☌ ☿ & ♂. *success, &*	4 21	10 43	4 49	♉
T	*you shall command it*	3 57	10 27	5 52	□
W	□ ♄ & ☉. *Equity is*	3 34	10 11	6 53	□
T	Low Tides. *the bond*	3 10	9 54	7 53	♋
F	☿ in Perihelion. *of*	2 46	9 38	8 49	♋
S	*human society. Bet-*	2 23	9 21	9 41	♌
D	2d Sunday in Lent.	1 59	9 3	10 29	♌
M	*ter to slip with the*	1 35	8 46	11 14	♍
T	*foot than the tongue.*	1 12	8 28	11 58	♍
W	*Praise without profit*	0 48	8 10	morn	♎
T	High Tides. *puts*	0 24	7 52	0 40	♎
F	☉ ent. ♈. V. Equi.	0 1	7 34	1 23	♎
S	*little in the pocket.*	0 23	7 16	2 8	♏
D	3d Su. in Lt. ☌ ☽ ♃	47	6 58	2 53	♏
M	☽ Apogee. *Solid*	1 10	6 39	3 40	♐
T	☌ ☽ & ♄. *sense is*	1 34	6 21	4 30	♐
W	*ever preferable to*	1 57	6 2	5 22	♐
T	*wit. Such as boast*	2 21	5 43	6 14	♑
F	Low Tides. *much,*	2 45	5 25	7 6	♑
S	☿ stationary. *usu-*	3 8	5 6	7 57	♒
D	4th S. in Lt. mid Lt	3 31	4 48	8 46	♒
M	*ally fail much.*	3 55	4 30	9 34	♒
T	☌ ☽ ♀ & ♅.	4 18	4 11	10 21	♓

Astronomical Calculations, embracing the whole Union, and the Canadas, beginning at the following points:

Boston. D. M.	Sun Rises	Sun Sets.	Days' L'gth	Moon Rises.	High water.	New York. D. M.	Sun Rises	Sun Sets.	Days' L'gth	Moon Rises.	High water.
D	6 27	5 33	11 6	5 15	9 30	D	6 26	5 34	11 8	5 10	7 0
2	6 26	5 34	11 8	5 42	10 13	2	6 24	5 36	11 12	5 38	7 43
3	6 25	5 35	11 10	sets.	10 48	3	6 23	5 37	11 14	sets.	8 18
4	6 23	5 37	11 14	6 36	11 22	4	6 22	5 38	11 16	6 36	8 52
5	6 21	5 39	11 18	7 51	11 58	5	6 20	5 40	11 20	7 50	9 28
6	6 20	5 40	11 20	9 10	aft35	6	6 19	5 41	11 22	9 10	10 5
7	6 19	5 41	11 22	10 27	1 10	7	6 18	5 42	11 24	10 23	10 40
D	6 17	5 43	11 26	11 46	1 55	D	6 16	5 44	11 28	11 40	11 25
9	6 16	5 44	11 28	morn	2 47	9	6 15	5 45	11 30	morn	aft17
10	6 14	5 46	11 32	1 2	3 57	10	6 14	5 46	11 32	0 54	1 27
11	6 13	5 47	11 34	2 9	5 34	11	6 12	5 48	11 36	2 1	3 4
12	6 11	5 49	11 38	3 2	6 58	12	6 11	5 49	11 38	2 56	4 28
13	6 10	5 50	11 40	3 48	8 15	13	6 9	5 51	11 42	3 43	5 45
14	6 9	5 51	11 42	4 22	9 10	14	6 8	5 52	11 44	4 19	6 40
D	6 8	5 52	11 44	4 52	9 55	D	6 7	5 53	11 46	4 50	7 25
16	6 6	5 54	11 48	5 16	10 33	16	6 5	5 55	11 50	5 15	8 3
17	6 4	5 56	11 52	rises	11 3	17	6 4	5 56	11 52	rises	8 33
18	6 3	5 57	11 54	6 50	11 35	18	6 3	5 57	11 54	6 49	9 5
19	6 1	5 59	11 58	7 55	morn	19	6 1	5 59	11 58	7 52	9 38
20	6 0	6 0	12 0	9 2	0 8	20	6 0	6 0	12 0	8 58	10 12
21	5 59	6 1	12 2	10 8	0 42	21	5 59	6 1	12 2	10 3	10 45
D	5 57	6 3	12 6	11 12	1 15	D	5 57	6 3	12 6	11 6	11 26
23	5 56	6 4	12 8	morn	1 56	23	5 56	6 4	12 8	morn	morn
24	5 54	6 6	12 12	0 14	2 42	24	5 55	6 5	12 10	0 6	0 12
25	5 52	6 8	12 16	1 11	3 33	25	5 53	6 7	12 14	1 3	1 3
26	5 51	6 9	12 18	2 2	4 34	26	5 52	6 8	12 16	1 56	2 4
27	5 50	6 10	12 20	2 43	5 41	27	5 50	6 10	12 20	2 38	3 11
28	5 49	6 11	12 22	3 19	7 5	28	5 49	6 11	12 22	3 15	4 35
D	5 47	6 13	12 26	3 47	8 12	D	5 48	6 12	12 24	3 44	5 42
30	5 45	6 15	12 30	4 14	9 3	30	5 47	6 13	12 26	4 12	6 33
31	5 44	6 16	12 32	4 37	9 48	31	5 45	6 15	12 30	4 37	7 18

Washington. Sun Rises	Sun Sets.	Days' L'gth	Moon Sets.	Charleston. D M.	Sun Rises	Sun Sets.	Days' L'gth	Moon Sets.	High water	New Orleans. Sun Rises	Sun Sets	Days' L'gth	Moon Sets.
6 24	5 36	11 12	5 5	D	6 19	5 41	11 22	4 49	5 30	6 17	5 43	11 26	4 40
6 23	5 37	11 14	5 34	2	6 18	5 42	11 24	5 21	6 13	6 16	5 44	11 28	5 14
6 21	5 39	11 18	sets.	3	6 17	5 43	11 26	sets.	6 48	6 15	5 45	11 30	sets.
6 20	5 40	11 20	6 36	4	6 16	5 44	11 28	6 36	7 22	6 14	5 46	11 32	6 36
6 19	5 41	11 22	7 49	5	6 15	5 45	11 30	7 46	7 58	6 13	5 47	11 34	7 44
6 18	5 42	11 24	9 4	6	6 14	5 46	11 32	8 56	8 35	6 13	5 47	11 34	8 50
6 17	5 43	11 26	10 19	7	6 13	5 47	11 34	10 6	9 10	6 12	5 48	11 36	10 0
6 15	5 45	11 30	11 34	D	6 12	5 48	11 36	11 16	9 55	6 11	5 49	11 38	11 4
6 14	5 46	11 32	morn	9	6 11	5 49	11 38	morn	10 47	6 10	5 50	11 40	morn
6 12	5 48	11 36	0 46	10	6 10	5 50	11 40	0 23	11 57	6 9	5 51	11 42	0 6
6 11	5 49	11 38	1 53	11	6 9	5 51	11 42	1 29	1 34	6 8	5 52	11 44	1 13
6 10	5 50	11 40	2 50	12	6 8	5 52	11 44	2 31	2 58	6 7	5 53	11 46	2 17
6 9	5 51	11 42	3 38	13	6 7	5 53	11 46	3 23	4 15	6 6	5 54	11 48	3 15
6 8	5 52	11 44	4 16	14	6 6	5 54	11 48	4 7	5 10	6 5	5 55	11 50	4 3
6 6	5 54	11 48	4 48	D	6 5	5 55	11 50	4 42	5 55	6 4	5 56	11 52	4 39
6 5	5 55	11 50	5 14	16	6 4	5 56	11 52	5 11	6 33	6 3	5 57	11 54	5 9
6 4	5 56	11 52	rises	17	6 3	5 57	11 54	rises	7 3	6 3	5 57	11 54	rises
6 2	5 58	11 56	6 48	18	6 2	5 58	11 56	6 45	7 35	6 2	5 58	11 56	6 43
6 1	5 59	11 58	7 49	19	6 1	5 59	11 58	7 39	8 8	6 1	5 59	11 58	7 36
6 0	6 0	12 0	8 54	20	6 0	6 0	12 0	8 41	8 42	6 0	6 0	12 0	8 33
5 59	6 1	12 2	9 58	21	5 59	6 1	12 2	9 43	9 15	5 59	6 1	12 2	9 33
5 58	6 2	12 4	11 0	D	5 58	6 2	12 4	10 43	9 56	5 58	6 2	12 4	10 30
5 57	6 3	12 6	11 58	23	5 57	6 3	12 6	11 36	10 42	5 57	6 3	12 6	11 21
5 55	6 5	12 10	morn	24	5 56	6 4	12 8	morn	11 33	5 56	6 4	12 8	morn
5 54	6 6	12 12	0 55	25	5 55	6 5	12 10	0 33	morn	5 55	6 5	12 10	0 15
5 52	6 8	12 16	1 50	26	5 54	6 6	12 12	1 30	0 34	5 54	6 6	12 12	1 12
5 51	6 9	12 18	2 33	27	5 53	6 7	12 14	2 19	1 41	5 54	6 6	12 12	2 8
5 50	6 10	12 20	3 11	28	5 52	6 8	12 16	2 58	3 5	5 53	6 7	12 14	2 52
5 49	6 11	12 22	3 41	D	5 51	6 9	12 18	3 22	4 12	5 52	6 8	12 16	3 26
5 47	6 13	12 26	4 10	30	5 50	6 10	12 20	4 4	5 3	5 51	6 9	12 18	4 0
5 46	6 14	12 28	4 37	31	5 49	6 11	12 22	4 37	5 48	5 50	6 10	12 20	4 37

An Evening Visiter.

I bleeve i never telled the reeder about a little affair that cum about shortly arter i got married and went to settle on the north side of the big Muddy. Thar war a kuzzin of my wife's that took his plunder and went with me. He had ben to Cincinnati and had got a grate eddication for them days. He could grammarize and geografize and fillossofize, and would wear out a slate a siferin in one weak. Then he had his square roots and his round roots, and I bleeve he had the root of all evil, for he war jist sich a pesky feller as it wood take five hundred like him to make an honest man. But i dont want to explicitrize him too hard seeing that he is dead, and when one is in his grave he cant harm nobody, for he is a quiet citizen then, if he never war befour. I sed when i fust begun this story that he war a kuzzin to my wife, but that war a lie, for he only maid me bleeve he war, but i found him out arterward. He wanted to go and settle with me in the cleering, and we packed up and went. When we got to the big Muddy, i begun to make a hole in the forest, and i built a log house as fast as i could, tho i wos obleeged to hav killdevil at my side all the time, as the painters had a grate deel of curosity to see how a white man's flesh tasted. Them varmints had got tired of Indian meet, for their red skins war so tuff it sot their teeth on edge, and so they war very dainty arter a peece of my bacon. But i couldn't obleege them in that way no how, tho i war willing to do ennything in my line that war reesonable seeing i war a stranger in them parts and didn't want to be on bad tarms with the inhabitants. They put me to grate expence for amminition, and i sent some of them to the divil without benefit of clargy, and sum of them i shot in the starn and they went off shaking their tales as if they felt ridiculous. All this time the feller that war with me kept poring over his books, for he sed he intended to open a skool as

[See page 10.]

Indian Notions.....See Page 12.

1840

 An Evening Visiter...continued from page 8.

soon as our clearing had got peepled, and he looked to me and my wife to supply him with a smart chance of skollars.

Arter i had got my log house rigged up in pritty good style, we all moved into it. It war rite enuff all but one winder that war not finished. One dark evening I sot in one corner and the skoolmaster sot in tother, befour a roaring fire. My wife had gone to bed and war fast asleep in a crib i had bilt up on one side of the room. Well, while we sot there talking about nothing at all, i heerd a sort of scratching noise outside of the house, and I looked up to where killdevil hung; but before i could git up to take it down, a monstropolus grate wild cat bounced in at the winder, and in a minnit she war in the middle of the floor, and crouched down and wagged her tale, and kept her eyes rolling in her head fust at me and then at the skoolmaster. He looked obflisticated, and i seed he could not sifer himself out of the scrape. The varmint was the most saverageous beast that i ever sot my 2 eyes on, and her teeth looked as white as if she had cleaned 'em every mornin. But her eyes grew bigger and wilder every minnit. We sot as still as two rotten stumps in a fog. I did not dare to move my head to look at killdevil, for i couldn't hav time to take it down befour the varmint would have her teeth in my carkass. So we didn't stir, and the wild cretur kept squinting fust at me and then at my frend, not knowing which to choose, and she lookt mighty proud to think she could have the pick between us. I felt so mad i kood have bit through a five inch plank. The skoolmaster nor i didn't nary one of us want to be ete up, for i had dun a hard day's wurk, and war too tired to go through with sich a job befour i had a good night's rest. The skoolmaster war hugaceously oneasy, and i seed he thort it war a very ridiculous peece of bizziness; so he speeks to me, and sed, "What do you think we had best to do, Crockett?" I telled him that depended mostly on the varmint who seemed to have the casting vote on this okkasion, but it war most likely one of us wood be chawed up befour we war a minnit older, and as he had good larning, i spose he knowed how to make his peece with God in real book fashion; but as to me i had no purtensions to larning, but bleeved i war never guilty of desarting a frend or turning my back to a hungry feller-critter, and must trust to God's mercy to make it up to me where i war lacking. Then he begun to blubber rite out, and sed if we could only direct the varmint's eyes to the place where my wife laid, he might ete her up, and so our lives would be saved! When i heered that, i forgot all about the danger and jumped rite up on eend like a ramping alligator. I war going to ketch the mean-spirited infarnal coward, that wanted to turn off the danger on a woman, rite by the throat, but i seed the wild cat war making his spring at me. So i jumpt towards killdevil and war reeching out my hand to take it down, when i seed it war gone. I felt as streaked as a bushel basket for haff a second; but jist as the varmint touched me with her teeth, i heered killdevil speak and the wildcat tumbled doun dead at my feet! I war amazed at fust, but in the next minnit my wife had her arms around my neck. Killdevil had hung close to her crib, and when i jumped up it woke her, and she had ketched the rifle like a flash and fired it in time to save my life. Then i seed she war worthy to be the wife of Davy Crockett.

Ben Harding's Courtship.

When me and Ben war out in the forest one day, he got to torking pretty free, and at last he got upon the fare sect. He telled me he had been in luv; and when we cum to a plaice called Cold Spring, we sot our rifles up agin a tree, and mixed whisky in our horn, and maid sociable for an our and a haff. Arter Ben had wrenced out his mouth, he put a big eud in one sighed of his cheek and sot his tung upon the wild trot:—

"D'ye see, Kornill Krockitt, I wos niver very much given to overhaul a she craft till I got on the lee side of twenty one. But about that time ther wos one Bets Undergrove who come athwart my hawse so often that, at last, I begun to fix my blinkers upon her. I wos jist on the point of taking a viage to see, or I should have got spliced to her without benefit of klarjee, as they say when a thing is to be done in a hurry. So I give Bets a rousing buss, and told her I must go aboard, for the wind wos fare, and the capsun was going round like grinding coffee. The poor gal bawled rite out and stuck her nales into my close like a cat, and she shed teers out of one eye like spray going out of a lee skupper. Her tother eye, you must no, wos as blind as a skupper nale. I jumped into the jolly bote, and my messmates pulled me off to the ship; but we left poor Bets standing on the cliff till the ship got clean out-o-sight-o-land. There she stood in her white gown like Eddystone light-house. She wos a good gal, and I never seed her drunk more than three times in the whole two year that I wos acquainted with her.

We kreuced awf the coast awhile, and then went up the strates, and wile I wos there a thing happuned that let me into the fare sect very clear; and it wos more than I had ever heern on be 4. We kum to an ankur under an ileand called Yvica. There wos a big black bilding stood on the hill where gals is kept to larn religion. They call it a nunnery. I was ashore on liberty one day, with haff a duzzen other chaps; and we were pretty well corned be 4 night. So we agreed to go on a lark up to the nunnery. We found we koodent get in when we got there. An old woman cum to the door with a bunch of keeze hanging to her waiste, and she acted as bosun over the establishment. Ther wos no gitting aboard without her consent. But jist as I wos turning off like a sick munky, a poor raggamuffin priest cum up softly, and offered to hire me his dress, for a glass of auguadent. I took up with his offer, and was soon rigged out in the friar's gear. He help rig me out; and the rascal shaved off my whiskers and all the hare from the top of my head. I didn't hardly know myself, when I wos finished, and had a grate notion that I war the ship's chaplin who had cum ashore instead of me by mistake. As soon as I was rigged all-a-tanto, I went up to the gate of the nunnery, and the old woman let me in mighty quick. It war dark in the hall, and she didn't know me from the friar. So she begun to tell me about one of the novisses; that, I take it, wos a gal who hadn't got broke into the fashions. She wanted I should see this gal, and give her sum good sperituel advise. I begun to groan, and hold up my hands, and then she took me to a little sort of locker, where the poor gal was kept. As soon as I seed her I forgot all about Betz; for she wos as pritty as a dolphin, and had an i that cut rite into a feller's hart, like a jack-knife going through a bit of salt junk. As soon as I found myself shot up in this place with the gal, I begun to try to tork to her, but somehow I coodent bring my guns to bear, and git hold of the real Scripter lingo; and when I tried to say something of that sort, she laffed rite out in my face. Be 4 I cood get over that and look her in the countenance agin, I got fast asleep, for I had been poring the aguadent and cheechee into me like the whale swallowed Jonah. I spose I slept about three hours, and when I waked up, the gal was gone, and I arterwards heered that she had made her escape from the house, and gone back to her friends. I felt as streeked as a mackarel, and put my hand in my boozum to feel for black Betty; but jist then I heered a whisperin in the next cell to mine and so I hauled my carkase up and looked through the skylite, and there I seed an old feller that called himself a friar, and there wos a a pritty gal with him who had come to sell oranges. I seed this old rip giv her two or three smacks on the lips, and put his arm around her waste. Then I lay down on a bench close by the skylite, and cood heer every word they sed. The gal agreed to cum the nixt day at 9 o'clock in the mornin, and she axed him how she shood tell his cell from the rest, so that she could find it without any trubble. The old porpus told her he wood put a long nail in the keyhole of the door, and she cood feal the end of it with her fingers. So I laid still till morning, when I got up, and went out of my cell, and found the nail in the keyhole of the old feller's door. I pulled it out softly, and took it into my den, and stuck it through my keyhole. Pritty soon the gal come feeling along at the dores, and she felt the end of the nail. Then she popped into my cell, and I cotch'd her in my arms. She begun to kiss me rite off, and I thort I wos up to my ize in clover, but all at wunce she took a lurch leeward and jumpt back, and lookt at my face—then she seed I war not the man, and she squalled rite out, and shook like a leef. So the tother monk heered the gal skreem and cum running into my cell, and when he seed me and the gal, his holiness wos so kut up that he begun to rore like a bull—for he thort she had took a fansy to me. The gal jumpt into his arms, and begged him to save her from me, and while she was hanging to his neck, all the monks and nuns, and the old woman cum running up. So the monk tride to shake off the gal, but she hung to him like a turcle to a nigger's heel, and called him her own true love. I hauled my karkass out of the skrape, and left 'em to settle the bizziness for the old friar, their own way.

Col. Crockett beat at a Shooting Match.

I expect, stranger, you think old Davy Crockett war never beat at the long rifle; but he war tho. I expect there's no man so strong, but what he will find some one stronger. If you havent heerd tell of one Mike Fink, I'll tell you something about him, for he war a helliferocious fellow, and made an almighty fine shot. Mike was a boatman on the Mississip, but he had a little cabbin on the head of the Cumberland, and a horrid handsome wife, that loved him the wickedest that ever you see. Mike only worked enough to find his wife in rags, and himself in powder, and lead, and whiskey, and the rest of the time he spent in nocking over bar and turkeys, and bouncing deer, and sometimes drawing a lead on an injun. So one night I fell in with him in the woods, where him and his wife shook down a blanket for me in his wigwam. In the morning sez Mike to me, 'I've got the handsomest wife, and the fastest horse, and the sharpest shooting iron in all Kentuck, and if any man dare doubt it, I'll be in his hair quicker than hell could scorch a feather.' This put my dander up, and sez I, 'I've nothing to say agin your wife, Mike, for it cant be denied she's a shocking handsome woman, and Mrs. Crockett's in Tennessee, and I've got no horses. Now, Mike, I dont exactly like to tell you you lie about what you say about your rifle, but I'm d——d if you speak the truth, and I'll prove it. Do you see that are cat sitting on the top rail of your potato patch, about a hundred and fifty yards off? If she ever hears agin, I'll be shot if it shant be without ears.' So I blazed away, and I'll bet you a horse, the ball cut off both the old tom cat's ears close to his head, and shaved the hair off clean across the skull, as slick as if I'd done it with a razor, and the critter never stirred, nor knew he'd lost his ears till he tried to scratch 'em. 'Talk about your rifle after that, Mike!' sez I. 'Do you see that are sow away off furder than the eend of the world,' sez Mike, 'with a litter of pigs round her?' and he lets fly. The old sow give a grunt, but never stirred in her tracks, and Mike falls to loading and firing for dear life, till he hadn't left one of them are pigs enough tail to make a toothpick on. 'Now,' sez he, 'Col. Crockett, I'll be pretticularly obleedged to you if you'll put them are pig's tails on again,' sez he. 'That's onpossible, Mike,' sez I, 'but you've left one of 'em about an inch to steer by, and if it had a-been my work, I wouldn't have done it so wasteful. I'll mend your shot,' and so I lets fly, and cuts off the apology he'd left the poor cretur for decency. I wish I may drink the whole of Old Mississip, without a drop of the rale stuff in it, if you wouldn't have thort the tail had been drove in with a hammer. That made Mike a kinder sorter wrothy, and he sends a ball after his wife as she was going to the spring after a gourd full of water, and nocked half her coom out of her head, without stirring a hair, and calls out to her to stop for me to take a blizzard at what was left on it. The angeliferous critter stood still as a scarecrow in a cornfield, for she'd got used to Mike's tricks by long practiss. 'No, no, Mike,' sez I, 'Davy Crockett's hand would be sure to shake, if his iron war pointed within a hundred mile of a shemale, and I give up beat, Mike, and as we've had our eye-openers a-ready, we'll now take a flem-cutter, by way of an anti-fogmatic, and then we'll disperse.'

Account of a Goose Pulling.

As related by Col. Crockett to a Yankee, who did not know what the thing was.

My eyes, stranger, how illiterate some people is! Whar in the universal world war you broughten up, not to know what a goosepulling ar? No wonder you Yankees is despised all over the world. Howsever, you seem to be a clever sort of a feller, quite a conception to the gineral rule, and I dont care if I waste a few words in instructing you. You see thar war a little dust of a jollification at Luke Logroller's improvement in Rumsquattle Bottom, for Luke had got married to one of them cornfed Connecticut Hooshur gals, that you'll see sot a-straddle on every fence in Ohio. Luke's wife war a complement to her broughten up, for she war a lady every inch of her, six feet high in her stocking feet, that is she would have been, ony she'd got no stockings. Her hair war the color of raw flax, and hung round her neck and sholeders like Spanish baird on a magnoly. The parson war not come wen I lit down, and Luke and his wife war divartin themselves and the company with a ressle on the grass afore the door, and I wish I may be flung myself if she didn't fling him three times hand running. When will you find one of your Yankee gals that would do that, Stranger? I cant say tho I think it war altogether rite, for the husband ort always to be uppermost in the family—that ar a fact, and Mrs. Logroller tore her best gingham, and the seat of Luke's onmentionables in the tussell. When the parson cum and put the yoke on Luke and his lady, thar war scrub races and dancing that beat cockfiting. And then thar war rassling and shooting at a mark, and I suppose it's enough to say Davy Crockett war on hand—and you needn't ax whose ball cut the cross the most oftenest. Thar war not a gentleman thar that war a sarcumstance to Davy Crockett at rassling, and I'm the man what sez it. Howsever, when the whiskey begun to fly round, the boys begun to look at each other like so many wild cats, and if Luke hadn't have thort of something to keep 'em quiet, his lady would have had a bushell of eyes to sweep up off the floor, thar'd have been such gougeing. So he axes the gentlemen if they wouldn't like a goosepulling, and they all hurrahed for the goose as I've since heered 'em hurrah for Jackson.

But it war not a goose pulling after all, for it war a gander pulling. Mrs. Logroller picked out a gander that didn't lay eggs before Adam war a little boy; but he mought have done it if he'd been a goose. It was as much as she could do to hold him between her knees while she pulled the feathers clean off his neck and smeered it with soft sope as beautifull as Jinerall Jackson did the people. The way he squawked war a caution—you'd raly have thort that something war the matter with him; but what can you expect from a goose. I've seen a feller lay still and have his sculp taken off and make less noise. But Luke tied him by the legs to the eend of a long branch of a scrub oke, and those gentlemen what had horses got on to 'em. 'Look out! for I'm a cummin!' sez Hugh Horsefoot, and dashed at the gander as if the devil had kicked him on eend. But goosey wasn't to be had that time, for he dodged as if an Injun had been taking a squint at him, and the way he run his nose agin a bough war ridiculous. He fell off and bled like a stuck pig. And thar war a good many more what tried it; but goosey dodged, and the limb surged backward and forward, and up and down, and his neck war well soped and so tough it mought have sarved to cordell a keel boat of two hundred ton. So thar war few that got hold on it, and them that did couldn't hold on. At last a feller, not knee high to a chaw of tobacco got hold and wouldn't let go, but hung on to goosey like death to a dead nigger, and his horse went from under him, and left him hanging like Absalom in the midst of the oke. But the bough wouldn't bear him and the goose too, and down he come and barked his shins, and the goose played away about his head with his wings, so that he almost rumsquattled him. By this time he was as wolfy and savagerous as a rattlesnake in a circle of ash

1840

leaves and fire, and he got goosey between his feet and pulled away at his head with both hands. But he sot his teeth to no righteous purpose—the head wouldn't cum off. Then he tried to ring it off, but he mite as well have tried to twist off a cotton wood a hundred year old, and some of the boys offered to bet that goosey would whip him after all. That made him as rothy as a meat axe, and he swore that he could whip every goose that ever was hatched, and he got a hatchet and tried to chop off the poor cretur's mazzard, but it war dull, and the ground war soft, and all he could do war to drive the beast's neck into the mud. But I begun to take pity on goosey, for his sufferings was intolerable, and so I lent the feller a nife, and he sawed his head off with it, and put the animal out of his pain. And now, stranger, I expect you'll be able to tell what a goose pulling is when enny body axes you.

When the gander war dead some of the boys begun to cavail again, and crow for a fite; but the dancing put a stop to that. The whiskey war turned out of an arthen jug and handed round in a mussel shell, for Luke war poor, and hadn't got all his fixins about him. The gentlemen pulled off their coats to it, for it war in July, and it war warm work. Mrs. Logroller's mother gave out the tune, as she sot knitting her stocking in the chimbly corner, for we hadn't no fiddle, and I can tell you, her darter didn't spare shoe leather. The old woman didn't know me, and she had to call out the figgers as well as sing 'em, for the dancers to navigate by. It war somehow so. 'Dance up to that gal with a hole in the heel of her stocking.' 'Down in the middle with the blue check apron.' 'Now chassez with slim Sal Dowdy.' 'Now dance up to the entire stranger.' We danced till Luke begun to git pritty considerably oneasy, and about midnite, 'Gentlemen and Ladies,' sez he, 'I'm a man that wouldn't cum for to go for to be onperlite on enny account whatsomever, and I always expect to do the thing what's rite; but gentlemen and ladies, suppose my case and Molly's war your own, and you'll not take the stud if I tell you that if you live enny whar its time to go hum.' So we took pity on Luke and bid him good night. I expect stranger, if you knew the sport of a wedding in the back woods, you'd want to go there and be married once a week.

Indian Notions.

If the reeder never lived in the west, I spose he dont no that the injuns ar all a pesky set of hethens, and has notions that never war set down in the bible. They beleeve that a rakkoon or a painter, or a rok has a sole, and are to be found in tother world, like a kristian what worships God and fites for his cuntry.

One day when I had been for 24 hours on the trale of a bare, and war as hungry as seven wolves tied together by the tale, I lost my way, and cum upon a injun wigwam before I knowed what I had got to. I thort I wood go in and rest myself. So I went and looked in, and seed a very hansum yung injun thar; but it war the only injun that ever lookt hansum to me. He war thinking very serious, and a little she pappoose, about 3 yeer old were setting on the ground klose to his feet and looking up into his face. They lookt more like human creturs with human feelings, than any of the breed that I ever noed before. The injun got up and telled me to cum in. So when I had sot down and war eeting a bowl of sowp that the little gal had give me, I notissed that the red skin war very still; and he didn't seem to no as I war pressent; and the gal sot down agin by his feet and lookt up in his face. Then I konkluded to make em tork, and artur a wile I got the injun to speek of his own affares, and he telled me his story so strate that if he had had a white skin instead of a red one I might ha' kinder half beleeved what he sed.

He telled me that his wife and him war married bekase they both had loved one anuther from a child; and that when she died it war like the sun had gone down into the big lake, and ben put out like a wad falling into the Massasippy. He sed he had gone to the place whar she war berried and sot thar all nite, and had prayed the Good Spirit to take him away to the land of ghosts, so that he mite see his wife, for he sed he loved her like the small lake what receeves the streem which cums down from the mountain; and when the streem is dried up, the lake must dry up too, bekase no more water would cum into it. A little while arterward 2 of his children died, and he had none left but the little gal I telled of. He sed how things went on this way for a hole yeer, when one evening that he war goin home to his wigwam, a high wind lifted him off his feet, and carried him over some kuntries what he had never seed before, till he cum to a grate lake, and thar he fell with his own wait, and sunk down for about a mile, when he cum out upon a butiful green plane. The grass war all about two inches high, but lookt more fresh and green than any grass he had ever seed before. He walked along till he cum to a high wall that war made of a sort of rich glass, of a dark blue cullor, and he thort he must stop here; but when he went up to feel of it, he found it war only a apperrition, and that he could walk rite threw it! Then he knowed he war in tother world, and he felt half afeared and half glad. Two painters cum along jist as he got thro' the wall and showed there teeth, but they war only ghosts and coodent bite his solid flesh—but hear he seed beautiful trees and groves, and such blessed perfumes cum up into his nose, that he war made as happy as a lark. Thar war streems of cleer water what run among silver sands, and thar war fruit what war streeked with red and gold colors, and sich birds, and sich music they maid that it war more nor he cood do, to remember his own name. He seed two or three good Indian kings thar who war hunting on beautiful white hosses, and sum of the happy soles war a fishing and leeping, and as happy as a rainbow when the sun shines upon it! He was jist coming out from a whole bed of pretty roses, when he found he war on the side of a cleer and deliteful river. He was looking up and down the river, and seeing the happy soles ketch fish, when all at once, he saw a most glorious woman on tother side of the river who was looking rite at him, and she war droppin teers, and ringing her hands, and holding out her arms to him, as if she wanted to fly rite over the river, but coodent get akross. He lookt at her and seed it was his own wife what he had mourned so long, and had sot on her grave all night, so often. So he jumped into the river, and went rite down to the bottom, as it war only the gost of a river; and he worked over and they run into each others arms, but she war only a spirit, and he coodn't feel her till he war dead too. But they cood tork, and she axed a thousand questions, and so did he, and they put there arms around each other and tried to kiss; and then she led him to a most illigant bower what she had built of boughs and grate roses, and sweet things what he had never smelt till then; and he found his two little dead children in the bower; for their mother had found 'em and took 'em with her. She telled him she had built this bower for him, as she new he war honest and always prayed to the good sperrit, and would cum to that happy place when he died, with the other little one.

Davy Krockitt is none of your whimperers, but if I didn't drop tears as big as a bullet, I hope I may be shot. For the injun telled it so like the truth that I beleved every word of it—and the little gal too sed she wanted to go thar and see her mother. I bleeve the injun thort it war all true himself. I never seed him agin.

Severe Courtship.

I have had sum experunce in love matters, tho I dont pretend to be much smoother than a chesnut burr in November.

Severe Courtship.

I wonst had an old flame that I took sumthin of a shine to, bekase I had nothing else to do, and bekase other game war skarse at that seeson of the year. And she lived rite alongside of the path where I used to go to look for bears. When I coodent find nothing else that war worth sending to, I got upon the trail of Zipporina. She war a most partikeler skreemer, and I named her the wild cat of the forrest. She noed how to taik good keer of number one, and never cook a peece of meet that she hadn't kilt with her own hand. She cood jump up and strike her heels together twice, while a rifle war taking time to flash, and cood grin a nigger white. She cood ride a krokodile till he swet, and her hare war alive. She was a most butiful peece of woman flesh, and when I lookt at her I used to feel as if sumbuddy war running off with my rifle, and I didn't ker nothin about it. But sumhow it so fell out or fell in, that I found out a new hunting ground whar the bears war as thick as mull-asses, and so sum how I didn't go that weigh, where the gal lived. May be I got the bag, but if enny pesky he that wauks on two legs war to tell me so, I would put his rite i in my poket. Shawtly arter I shifted my tracks, thar war a feller cum down into them parts to chawlk down figgers and keep akkounts at the Wisskonsin mines. The way he didn't no nothing was most butiful, and he poked snuff into his knows, like he war a going to charge it and fire it off. He got a squint at Zipporina, and lookt at her thro his green spektakles, and so I spose he took her to be *green*, jist bekase she lookt so, when he seed her threw the green glass. But Zipporina squatted low, and pricked up her eers like a squirrel when he sees a rifle lookin at him endways. One nite he went to her father's door and rapt, and the dore opened of itself, as all the dores in old Kaintuck is tort to do when a stranger kalls. Zippy sort of had a notion what he war cum arter, and she put up her hair with a iron comb which I had guv her, and put on her bear-skin shawl to look as grashus as she cood, but he lookt at her as if he war going to the gallus, and her ize war like two koles of fire, and when she lookt at him, she grinned like a red hot gridiron. But he pulled off his hat, and made his obedience to her, like a long sapling when the wind blows it over like a rainbow. Then he sot down and begun to tork to her about the sun and the moon and about her eyes that he sed were like the seven stars. She noed that war a lye, bekase her eyes were like her muther's. Then he went off; but he kept kolling all the time, and stuck to her like a buzz to a sheep's wool. At last he grew as furce as a bear with his tale chopt off, and swore he wood put his arm round her neck if she would taik off that ruff bare-skin that she wore. This was a leetle too much for Zipporina, and she intarmined not to bare it.

One day he axed her to take a walk with him. She shouldered her rifle and slung her powder horn, and went out with him. He was pesky polite, and he offered to carry her rifle for her which she thought was a great affront, and so she war intarmined to pay him for it. She seed he was a green one and didn't know nothing, but her eddication, as I said before, had been most beautiful. She took him to a place where there was a bear's nest, and by this time it had got to be darkish. She pretended she wanted to go a little ways off, and telled him to wait till she come back. So she went down to the bear's nest and begun to stir up the bears with a branch. They made a terrible noise, and the young spark run for his life. He wandered about in the woods all night, and the next day, he found the house. He telled Zipporina that he heard a noise as of wild beasts, shortly after she left him, and that he thought she was in danger, and hunted after her, but that he got lost in the dark. She knew how much of this to believe, but squatted low, and did not say a word. He went on courting, and she pretended to be mighty tickled with his fine speeches. At last he got rail saucy, and was as obstropolous as a Yankee pedlar. He proposed to Zippy to meet him in the dark one evening and make him happy. She was as mad as a buffalo, but she hung fire and sung dumb. She agreed to meet him; and as soon as it was dark he sneaked out of the house and went to the place to be made happy. He waited about half an hour, and then he heard a rustling among the leaves. Zippy had telled him she should wear her bear skin cloak, and he thought he seed her coming. It was alfired dark, and so he couldn't tell a great black bear that Zippy had driven along before her from Zippy herself. So he went up to the bear, and the feller put his arms around the varmint's neck, and it stood right up on its hind legs, and give him a most beautiful hug. So he begun to talk to it, and thought all the time, it was Zippy. She heard him say, "Don't hug me quite so hard, dear Zipporina! Oh! Oh! Zippy—Zip—Zip, you will choke me with your love!" At last the bear begun to scratch, and he bawled right out like a calf that has lost its mother. Then Zippy went up behind the bear, and stuck her knife into his side, and the varmint tumbled down, but the young spark didn't see her, and he run off with a bloody shirt, and his coat torn off him. He went back to the mines, and never came near our place agin; but he told his acquaintances all along the Massissippy never to go up into our parts a courting, for the gals up that way loved so hard they would have squeezed his bowels out if he hadn't got away from them.

1840

1840. 4th Month, APRIL, begins on Wednesday. Hath 30 Days, and is the 2d Spring Month.

Phases of the Moon.

- ● New Moon, 2d, 9h. 45m. Morning.
- ☽ First Quarter, 9th, 0h. 58m. Morning.
- ○ Full Moon, 16th, 1h. 23m. Evening.
- ☾ Last Quarter, 24th, 6h. 17m. Evening.

Astronomical Calculations, embracing the whole Union, and the Canadas, beginning at the following points:

D. W.	ASPECTS, &c.	Sun's Dec.	Sun Slow.	Moon South	☽ S	Boston. D. M.	Sun Rises	Sun Sets	Days' L'gth	Moon Rises	High water.
W	*If you would be rich,*	4 41	3 53	11 9	♓	1	5 43	6 17	12 34	4 58	10 28
T	☌ ♂ & ☿. [☌ ☽ ☿.	5 4	3 35	aft 0	♈	2	5 41	6 19	12 36	sets.	11 5
F	Very High Tides.	5 27	3 17	0 52	♈	3	5 40	6 20	12 40	8 13	11 41
S	☽ Perigee. [☽ 7✱s.	5 50	2 59	1 48	♉	4	5 39	6 21	12 42	9 34	aft22
D	5th Sund. in Lent.	6 13	2 42	2 48	♉	D	5 37	6 23	12 46	10 56	1 7
M	☌ ♀ ♅. [Aphelion.	6 35	2 24	3 52	♊	6	5 36	6 24	12 48	morn	1 57
T	In. ☌ ☿ ☉. ♀ in	6 58	2 7	4 55	♊	7	5 34	6 26	12 52	0 5	2 53
W	*think of saving as*	7 20	1 50	5 56	♋	8	5 33	6 27	12 54	1 10	4 4
T	*well as getting. Use*	7 43	1 33	6 54	♋	9	5 31	6 29	12 58	1 57	5 25
F	Low Tides. *time as*	8 5	1 16	7 47	♌	10	5 30	6 30	13 0	2 36	6 47
S	*though you knew its*	8 27	1 0	8 35	♌	11	5 28	6 32	13 4	3 5	8 0
D	Palm Sund. *value.*	8 49	0 44	9 20	♍	D	5 27	6 33	13 6	3 30	8 50
M	*Of all studies study*	9 11	0 28	10 4	♍	13	5 26	6 34	13 8	3 52	9 35
T	*your own condition.*	9 32	0 13	10 46	♍	14	5 25	6 35	13 10	4 13	10 11
W	*Business makes a*	9 54	f 2	11 27	♎	15	5 23	6 37	13 14	4 33	10 41
T	Maundy Thursday.	10 15	0 17	morn	♎	16	5 22	6 38	13 16	rises	11 14
F	Good Friday. *man*	10 36	0 13	0 12	♏	17	5 21	6 39	13 18	8 2	11 47
S	Rather H. Tds. ☽ ♃	10 57	0 45	0 56	♏	18	5 19	6 41	13 22	9 6	morn
D	EASTER. *as well*	11 18	0 59	1 42	♏	D	5 18	6 42	13 24	10 13	0 22
M	☽ Apogee. ☿ sta.	11 38	1 12	2 32	♐	20	5 17	6 43	13 26	11 10	1 0
T	☌ ♄ & ☽. *as tries*	11 59	1 25	3 22	♐	21	5 15	6 45	13 30	morn	1 41
W	*him. Conversation*	12 19	1 37	4 14	♑	22	5 14	6 46	13 32	0 2	2 27
T	*teaches more than*	12 39	1 49	5 5	♑	23	5 13	6 47	13 34	0 46	3 12
F	*meditation. Credit*	12 59	2 0	5 55	♑	24	5 11	6 49	13 38	1 23	4 9
S	Low Tides. *lost is*	13 18	2 11	6 44	♒	25	5 10	6 50	13 40	1 53	5 12
D	Low Sund. ☌ ♀ ☿.	13 38	2 21	7 31	♒	D	5 9	6 51	13 42	2 20	6 22
M	*like a broken looking*	13 57	2 31	8 18	♓	27	5 8	6 52	13 44	2 43	7 33
T	☌ ☽ ♅. *glass*	14 16	2 40	9 4	♓	28	5 6	6 54	13 48	3 5	8 31
W	*Beauty is a bauble.*	14 34	2 49	9 51	♈	29	5 5	6 55	13 50	3 25	9 19
T	☌ ♀ ☽ & ☿.	14 53	2 57	10 41	♈	30	5 4	6 56	13 52	3 49	10 3

D. W.	New York. D. M.	Sun Rises	Sun Sets.	Days' L'gth	Moon Rises	High water.	Washington. Sun Rises	Sun Sets.	Days' L'gth	Moon Sets.
W	1	5 44	6 16	12 32	4 58	7 58	5 45	6 15	12 30	4 58
T	2	5 42	6 18	12 36	sets.	8 35	5 44	6 16	12 32	sets.
F	3	5 41	6 19	12 38	8 9	9 11	5 42	6 18	12 36	8 5
S	4	5 40	6 20	12 40	9 29	9 52	5 41	6 19	12 38	9 24
D	D	5 38	6 22	12 44	10 50	10 37	5 40	6 20	12 40	10 44
M	6	5 37	6 23	12 46	11 58	11 27	5 39	6 21	12 42	11 51
T	7	5 36	6 24	12 48	morn	aft23	5 37	6 23	12 46	morn
W	8	5 34	6 26	12 52	1 4	1 34	5 36	6 24	12 48	0 58
T	9	5 33	6 27	12 54	1 52	2 55	5 35	6 25	12 50	1 47
F	10	5 32	6 28	12 56	2 32	4 17	5 34	6 26	12 52	2 28
S	11	5 31	6 29	12 58	3 2	5 30	5 32	6 28	12 56	3 2
D	D	5 29	6 31	13 2	3 29	6 20	5 31	6 29	12 58	3 29
M	13	5 28	6 32	13 4	3 52	7 5	5 30	6 30	13 0	3 52
T	14	5 26	6 34	13 8	4 14	7 41	5 29	6 31	13 2	4 14
W	15	5 25	6 35	13 10	4 35	8 11	5 28	6 32	13 4	4 35
T	16	5 24	6 36	13 12	rises	8 44	5 26	6 34	13 8	rises
F	17	5 23	6 37	13 14	7 58	9 17	5 25	6 35	13 10	7 54
S	18	5 22	6 38	13 16	9 1	9 52	5 24	6 36	13 12	8 56
D	D	5 20	6 40	13 20	10 7	10 30	5 23	6 37	13 14	10 1
M	20	5 19	6 41	13 22	11 3	11 11	5 22	6 38	13 16	10 56
T	21	5 18	6 42	13 24	11 56	11 57	5 21	6 39	13 18	10 50
W	22	5 17	6 43	13 26	morn	morn	5 19	6 41	13 22	morn
T	23	5 16	6 44	13 28	0 41	0 42	5 18	6 42	13 24	0 36
F	24	5 14	6 46	13 32	1 19	1 39	5 17	6 43	13 26	1 15
S	25	5 13	6 47	13 34	1 50	2 42	5 16	6 44	13 28	1 47
D	D	5 12	6 48	13 36	2 18	3 52	5 15	6 45	13 30	2 16
M	27	5 11	6 49	13 38	2 42	5 3	5 14	6 46	13 32	2 41
T	28	5 9	6 51	13 42	3 5	6 1	5 13	6 47	13 34	3 5
W	29	5 8	6 52	13 44	3 26	6 49	5 12	6 48	13 36	3 28
T	30	5 7	6 53	13 46	3 52	7 33	5 10	6 50	13 40	3 55

D. W.	Charleston. D. M.	Sun Rises	Sun Sets.	Days' L'gth	Moon Sets.	High water	New Orleans. Sun Rises	Sun Sets	Days' L'gth	Moon Sets.
W	1	5 48	6 12	12 24	4 58	6 28	5 49	6 11	12 22	4 58
T	2	5 47	6 13	12 26	sets.	7 5	5 48	6 12	12 24	sets.
F	3	5 46	6 14	12 28	7 53	7 41	5 47	6 13	12 26	7 45
S	4	5 45	6 15	12 30	9 8	8 22	5 46	6 14	12 28	9 0
D	D	5 44	6 16	12 32	10 25	9 7	5 46	6 14	12 28	10 14
M	6	5 43	6 17	12 34	11 28	9 57	5 45	6 15	12 30	11 25
T	7	5 42	6 18	12 36	morn	10 53	5 44	6 16	12 32	morn
W	8	5 41	6 19	12 38	0 39	aft 4	5 43	6 17	12 34	0 28
T	9	5 40	6 20	12 40	1 31	1 25	5 42	6 18	12 36	1 21
F	10	5 39	6 21	12 42	2 15	2 47	5 41	6 19	12 38	2 12
S	11	5 38	6 22	12 44	2 50	4 0	5 40	6 20	12 40	2 46
D	D	5 37	6 23	12 46	3 23	4 50	5 39	6 21	12 42	3 20
M	13	5 36	6 24	12 48	3 52	5 35	5 39	6 21	12 42	3 52
T	14	5 35	6 25	12 50	4 18	6 11	5 38	6 22	12 44	4 18
W	15	5 34	6 26	12 52	4 43	6 41	5 37	6 23	12 46	4 47
T	16	5 33	6 27	12 54	rises	7 14	5 36	6 24	12 48	rises
F	17	5 32	6 28	12 56	7 42	7 47	5 35	6 25	12 50	7 34
S	18	5 31	6 29	12 58	8 40	8 22	5 34	6 26	12 52	8 31
D	D	5 30	6 30	13 0	9 42	9 0	5 33	6 27	12 54	9 30
M	20	5 29	6 31	13 2	10 35	9 41	5 33	6 27	12 54	10 21
T	21	5 28	6 32	13 4	11 31	10 27	5 32	6 28	12 56	11 19
W	22	5 27	6 33	13 6	morn	11 12	5 31	6 29	12 58	morn
T	23	5 27	6 33	13 6	0 20	morn	5 30	6 30	13 0	0 11
F	24	5 26	6 34	13 8	1 3	0 9	5 29	6 31	13 2	0 55
S	25	5 25	6 35	13 10	1 38	1 12	5 28	6 32	13 4	1 32
D	D	5 24	6 36	13 12	2 10	2 22	5 28	6 32	13 4	2 6
M	27	5 23	6 37	13 14	2 38	3 33	5 27	6 33	13 6	2 36
T	28	5 22	6 38	13 16	3 5	4 31	5 26	6 34	13 8	3 5
W	29	5 21	6 39	13 18	3 33	5 19	5 25	6 35	13 10	3 36
T	30	5 20	6 40	13 20	4 4	6 3	5 25	6 35	13 10	4 10

A Goose Pulling.....See Page 11.

A Land Cruise.

Torking of hoss-flesh one day with Ben Harding, he telled me of his doins off in forrin kuntrys:—

The anuimal kalled a hoss, Kornill Krockitt, never took my fansy exaktly, for i wunst tride one. He noed nothing about the rules of saling, and for that I dont think thar is a cretur upon arth that is kut out for a rail marine like a hoss.

When i was in Spain where they dont go 2 fathum from the house without riding on a hoss, i thort i wood jest take a turn with one, for the sake of being in the fashun. So i and a shipmate named Tom Fiferail, went to a feller that had hosses laying in dock, and axed him what he would charge to let us charter one of his hosses for the day. He telled us that we cood hav one for six rials: So we agreed to it, and swore we wood go aboard directly. Then he fell to rigging the craft. In the fust place he put on a couple of braces, and each end of 'em led to the cretur's cutwater. Them was for to steer by, and he sed they wood turn the hoss's head in a giffy. Then he clapped a poop deck made of lether rite on the beast about midships, and lether straps hung down to put your feet in. This place was rigged up for the steersman. So Tom and I disputed which of us should take his first trick at the hellum. Tom got on and I jumped up behind—he tried to steer, but it cum awkard to him to pull the wheel ropes facing the hellum; but as my bak was towards the head, I could do it to a charm. So I took the braces, and Tom kept a look out ahead for breakers with his spy-glass. I found it plagny easy steering, but the craft wouldn't mind the hellum. He went his own way, and so I had no trubble. At last, we hove in sight of a shantee, where was a plenty of brandy, and wine, and I axed Tom if we hadn't better heave to. He agreed to it, but then we didn't no how it was done. There was a grate cloth netting over the poop-deck and I thort if we cood git that up, we mite throw all aback, but we sot on it, and when I tried to pull it out, we both took a lurch and cum near going overboard. We seed we were going on in a heavy sea-way, and was leaving the shantee astern. Says I, "Tom this won't do." "Well," says Tom, "bring her head to the wind, and get starn-way on her." So I pulled on the weather-brace and Tom took hold and helped me, and at last we got the cretur's head in the wind's eye, but she fell off on tother tack and cum about; so that our heads war now towards the shantee, and then we cracked on, at the rate of ten knots. But when we got up abreast the shantee, we coodent come to a stand, but went rite by it. Then we hauled on the wether brace again and away we went as far the other way till we cum to a fence, and there we brought up all standing. I got off, and passed Tom up a big stone, and he seized it to the end of a piece of strong three-yarn spunyarn. So I got on agin and held the stone, which was our anchor, in my lap. Then we turned the head of our craft towards the shantee, and craked on all she could carry. As soon as we got abreast the shantee, we hauled on the weather brace and brought the head of our craft to the wind. Tom give the word—"Let go the anchor!" and I rolled the stone off the hoss's tale; but he kept on faster than ever, and as the cable was made fast around my body, I went off the hoss quicker than you could say Jack Robinson. I jumped up and seed por Tom going off at the rate of sixteen knots, while the craft was pitching up and down, like a brig's jibboom in a calm. Tom didn't know how to bring to, but he laid flat down, and put his arms around the hoss's neck, and held on like death to a dead nigger. At last he got hold of the long hair with his teeth and stuck like a louse in a beggar's cap. The hoss never stopt till he got to his owner's door—and I guess Tom wont try that sarvice agin. It's wuss than being in the Patriot sarvice.

Ben Harding's Account of a Shipwreck.

One day Ben went out with me to tree a bear; and he got clear of us arter a queer fashion that I won't say nothing about, because the reader wants to hear Ben's story fust. Me and Ben sot down on a stump back to back, as there want room for us to set side by side, and he took out his pipe and begun to smoke. So as the smoke went up his nose, it give his brains a glister and his idees come out like he was speechifying in Congress. He told this story which I spose must be true, or he wood have forgot all about it, it was so long sense it happened. Says he—When I was a little shaver about as big as the Cappin's dog, I took a great noshun to go to sea, because I thought, d'ye see, that there was no work to be done, and that the sailors had nothing to do, but to set still and let the wind blow 'em along. But I always had to work where I was brought up—but I wan't brought up at all, I was dragged up—and so I meant to top my boom and be off like a rigger. Well I slept in the cockloft, and the sarvant gal slept there too, and I couldn't get out of the place without crawling over her, and I must go in the night if I went at all, for there war as many eyes on the look out for me in the day time as ever peeped over a cathead when the port was in sight. So I didn't know exactly how to work it. I had got me a little snug tarpaulin hat, that looked as bright as a new guinea, and a blue jacket that had belonged to an old boatswain, and fitted me as a purser's shirt fits a handspike. I had 'em all done up in a bundle and stowed away snug under my pillow. I laid awake till I thought it was about eight bells, and then I got up softly as a soger sliding down the gangway when all hands is called. I put on my rigging and then felt my way to the door. I knew when I got close to the door for the sarvant gal always slept right across the passage, and the smell of her breath come up like the steem from an old slush tub. I knew if I waked her up it was all day with me; and so I stood still to see if she war hard and fast. I knew by her breathing that she slept as solid as a marine on post, and then put my hands on the floor and felt my way to her. I first touched her bed clothes, and then her flipper; but it didn't wake her, and so I begun to get over her. She laid still till I had fairly got over her, and I thought I was safe, but my toe happened to get tangled in her hair and as it was never combed, it was hard work to get my mudplanter loosed. She woke up and jumped like a struck dolphin. I spose the way she opened her throat was never matched since Captin Kid hailed the flying Dutchman off the Cape of Good Hope. She only stopped squalling to take breath, and the way she puffed it out might have set a good example to a typhoon. I spose her master heard her, but as good luck would have it, he run up aloft to her while I was running doun to the door. When I got to the door, I found it was locked and barred. I unshipped the bar with one hand and turned the key with the other, and let moonshine into the entry before the old porpus could get doun stairs. He chased me on horseback, but I got into the bush, and had the fun of larfing at him as he cum back. I then made tracks for the seaport. Early in the morning, I went doun on the wharf. There was a smack there just going out on a fishing cruise. I stepped up to the cappin and doused my peak, and asked him if he wanted to ship a hand. He was a long-sided Yankee that had been one voyage round Cape Horn in a Nantucket whaleman. He had a jaw as long as a sword-fish's sword, and his head bobbed at the end of his long neck when he spoke, like a ship's cat-head riding at anchor in a heavy sea-way. He said he wanted a boy about my size, and asked me if I knew how to cook. I thort the feller was soft in his garret, for I had always seen the women folks do the cooking when I lived in the country, and I larfed in his face, and went off. The next craft I hauled my little carcase aboard of was a brig going to Norfolk. The cappin was a little black looking fellow with an eye like a scoured pump-bolt, and his head was as round as a bullet. He asked me where I cum from. I told him I belonged to Norfolk, and I gave him a name—I forget now what the name was—but it was the first one I could think of. He agreed to take me. We hauled out of port in about two weeks afterwards. As soon as we got to sea, I felt

Ben Harding's Account of a Shipwreck.

rather qualmish, so to cure me, the mate sent me aloft to scrape doun the top-gallant-masts. I hadn't been up there long, when the wind begun to pipe. I hurried down, and it was well that I did, for the top-gallant-mast was hanging over the side, before my feet struck the deck. Here was the Devil to pay and no pitch hot. All hands was called to clear away the wreck; but it begun to blow like seven men. It would have done your heart good to hear the wind squalling amongst the rigging. It was worse than a camp-meeting. We laid aloft to take in sail. I got on the fore-top-sail yard close to the bunt, and the foot ropes was so long that my chin cum just up to the yard. All this time the wind was blowing so it took five men to hold the cappin's hair on. At last the ship cum up to the wind, and the sail flapped up and knocked me right off the yard. I went doun, head, neck, and shoulders, into the top, and went through the lubber holes, but I was brought up by the futtock shrouds, or I should have lost the number of my mess, as sure as the Devil's a nigger. The hands on the yard thought I had gone overboard, but they were in such a hurry they couldn't stop to see. They had got the sail almost furled, when the gale freshened, and it come down upon us like a rail harry-cane. Away went the sail out of the bolt-ropes, and the men hurried down from aloft. I laid still where I was, as I knew there would be more hard work to do. Pretty soon I heard the pumps a going. I thought the brig had sprung a leak, and so I didn't want to be drouned alone, and I went down on deck. As soon as the Cappin saw me he put his speaking trumpet to my ear, and asked me where I had come from. I told him I had been overboard, but that I had been washed aboard again by a sea. He said I ought to be thankful for my providential deliverance. When he said that I begun to look wild, for I knew we must be in a very dangerous condition or else the Cappin would n't have talked about Providence. The Cappin was of the religion of a louse, when he was ashore—he only went to meeting when he was carried; and I knew when he begun to be gracious that we had sprung a leak or something worse. In a minute, the mate jerked me along by the arm and told me to take my turn at the pump and be d——d to me. I felt encouraged when I heard him swear; but just then, the brig pitched over on her beam ends, and two men went overboard. The rest of the men fell down on their knees and begun to pray. That made the mate as mad as a pea in a hot skillet, and he ordered them to get up and cut away the mast. He said it was the most unseamanlike conduct he ever heard of. The mast was cut away and the brig righted. We went afoul of the pumps again, but it was of no use. The hold and cabin were soon all afloat, and the Cappin's arm-chair came bobbing out of the companionway without being sent for. All this time the sea made a clean sweep over us, and another man was carried overboard. The long and short of it is that we found it of no use to man the pumps without we could pump the ocean dry, and we considered ourselves sunk. It come on night, and a pretty night it was. There war no more star-light than there is in an earthern jug. The sea made a clear breach right over us, and we expected to go doun every minute. Besides all this, there was a great many fleas aboard that plagued us consoundedly.

About day-light the Cappin called all hands to prayers, and we knelt doun while he prayed. But when he war in about the middle of his prayer, he got sight of a large ship that was coming right down to us. He jumped up off his knees, flung the prayer book into the lee scuppers, and bawled out, "By G—d! there's a sail!" The way we bundled into the stranger's boat, and the way we swallowed the prime West India when we got aboard the ship was enough to give old folks the horse distemper.

The Heroine of Kaintuck.

Of all the ripsnorters I ever tutched upon, thar never war one that could pull her boat alongside of Grace Peabody, the horowine of Kaintuck. When she got her temper fairly up, she war more like seven thunder bolts, withed together with chain litening, than a human cretur. Her father war a squatter; but she ganed a residence as she war born in the plaice. I reckon that all the varmints in the state stood in fear of her, and would sooner stick their tales in a steal trap, than feel the gripe of her thum and 4 finger around their throttles. She had a most abstemious eye, and when she gave one look at a painter or a bear, he thought the sun had riz within rifle shot of his nose. She minded no sort of weather. She would go through a snow-bank without looking for the path, and would shed rain like a duck. It took seven women to hold her when she sneezed, and they said that when she was insulted by a Tennessee bully in the month of March, she jumped clean out of her close, she war so furce to cum at him. She cum pritty neer gitting discharged one onlucky morning in September. She war going to carry home some work, for she got her living by making Prarie pillows, which war bear-skins stuffed with buffalo horn scrapings, and they war made for two conveniences, to sleep on for one, and for the tother, when your head itched in the nite, you could skratch it by rubbing it agin the piller. So she did her arrant, and then sot out to cum home through the woods, as it war gitting late in the arternoon.

She hadn't got fur before she perseeved she was follored by something of the four-legged kind. She war not skared at all, and it would be a dangerous predicament for the bridge of a man's knows, who should tell her she war ever skared at enny thing. But she kepp one korner of her eye open, and wawked on. In a little while she kinder thort she saw about fifty wolves coming around her and jumping at her throat. As she coodent kill 'em all at once, she run up a tree that grew slanting, and when she got to the top of it she begun to break off pieces of the limbs and throw at 'em; and she killed two or three of the pesky creturs in this way; and made one of 'em gape for fourteen sekonds, as she hit him between the two ize with a twig as big round as her leg. But jist as she was killing them off by degrees, a bear cum up out of the tree, which war holler inside, and he bolted out so quick that he took her with him, and they cum doun together on the ground; but Grace hung on upon the bear and cum down astraddle of his back. The wolves got out of the way when they cum down, like when you throw a stone in the water; but they closed up as the bear begun to run. Grace had a bit of stick in her hand, about as long as my rifle, and as thick at one eend as a cat's body. The bear didn't like to have a rider, and the wolves tride to help him git her off; and as he cut through the dry leaves, with the wolves all around him, jumping at Grace, the leaves and twigs flew about, so that you couldn't see nothing but Grace's cudgel as she swung it over her head, to bring it down upon the profile of some infarnul wolf, that was left rolling in the forrest behind them, and spouting the bloody foam from his lips. But the wolves cum thicker and thicker, and Grace begun to git tired in the arms. She held on upon the bear's wool as well as she could; but he run and jumped and roared, bekase he knew it was all Grace's fault that the wolves rained around him like a snow-storm. Grace's cudgel begun to splinter, and the pesky varmints took advantage of that sarcumstance, for ther is no onor about 'em, and they care no more for fare play than an injun kares for the sarmont on the mountin. Grace begun to think her time had cum, for one wolf had tore off the soul of her shew, and another one had got the skirt of her gownd in his teeth. She was jist about letting go of the bear and dropping down among the wolves, when help cum. I had been out that arternoon with Grizzle a-hunting. Grizzle telled me as plane as he cood speak, that thar war something to pay in the bushes, and I run down that way; and sure enuff, I seed the twigs and leeves a-flying like thar war a small arthquake running along the ground. In a minnit the bear cum bolting out from a thicket, with wolves all around him, and I seed the cudgel agoing, but couldn't see Grace till I got close to her. I pulled trigger upon the varmints, and shot two. Then Grizzle and I went in among 'em like the wonderful workings of Providence in a thunder storm, and the wolves scattered jist as Grace cum to the ground. The bear got off clear, for I spozed he had done good sarviss, and tis not the fashun with Davy Crockett to do an ongrateful axeshun. Grace telled me I had saved her life, and a fortnite from that day, she sent me a pair of new stockings that she had gnit out of wolf-sinues.

Gum Swamp Breeding.

The most unpolite trick that ever was done up in Gum Swamp, tho that is the most unpolite place inside of the Massissippy, was done when I was playing possum for a gal in my young days, before i had ever heered of Congress. This gal was namod Jerusha Stubbs, and had only one eye, but that was pritty enough for two, and besides it had a grate advantage in our parts, where folks must rise arly, as she could wake up in haff the time that others could, as she had only one eye to open, while other folks had to open two. One of her legs was a little shorter than the other, but I telled her I shouldn't make no fuss about that as the road to my house laid all along on the side of a hill, so that the short leg seemed as if 'twas made a purpose for walking to my cabin. She had had two cancers cut out of her breast, so that she was as flat as a board up and down there, which I couldn't have got over no how, only she had a beautiful grate hump on her back, and that made up for having nothing of the kind in front. Enermost all her teeth had rotted out, but then she had a pesky grate swallow, so that she could take down her vittles without chawing. I forgot to say how she had a hare lip, but then she had a long nose, which almost covered the place from sight. There was a grate bunch on her left arm, but then she had a monstracious wen on the right side of her neck, that balanced that difficulty and made it all even agin. She was wonderful neat at pulling up parsenips, and could shake a dog by the ears, and they did tell how she chased one till his tale drew out and war left behind. She could lick two foxes, and make a wolf feel pesky unsartin. She once busted a pare of bellusses by blowing in at the nose of 'em, and smothered a chimney that war o' fire by settitg on the top of it. You may suppose such a gal as that would be scarce in courting, for she could put a hole through any man's hart at seventy pases distunce. Onluckily i warnt on very good tarms with her father, tho he war with me. So i got akquainted with the gal a leetle at a time. I knowed her pritty well from her shoulders and upwards, but she kept her mind to herself, and that made me feel as oneasy as a steemboat with one wheel. But i felt hugeously mad, when a feller from doun east cum into Gum Swamp, and put up at her father's house with all his plunder. He was a skool-master, and tho i say it myself he was kind of good looking, and as slick as an eel standing up on his tale. I sot and lookt on whilst he was talking to the gal, and didn't know what to do about it for a good while; but when i begun to git over not knowing what

[See page 28]

1840

1840. 5th Month, MAY, begins on Friday. Hath 31 Days, and is the 3d Spring Month.

Phases of the Moon.

● New Moon, 1st, 7h. 1m. Evening.
☽ First Quarter, 8th, 9h. 46m. Morning.
○ Full Moon, 16th, 6h. 26m. Morning.
☾ Last Quarter, 24th, 8h. 20m. Morning.
● New Moon, 31st, 2h. 11m. Morning.

Astronomical Calculations, embracing the whole Union, and the Canadas, beginning at the following points:

D W	ASPECTS, &c.	Sun's Dec.	Sun Fast.	Moon South	☽ S
F	☌♂&☽. *Thinking*	15 11	3 5	11 37	♉
S	☽7✶s. ☽ Per. H. T.	15 29	3 12	aft36	♉
D	2d Sun. af. Easter.	15 47	3 19	1 39	♊
M	☍♃&☉. ☌♂☉.	16 4	3 25	2 45	♊
T	☿ gr. elon. W. *is*	16 21	3 30	3 51	♋
W	*very far from know-*	16 38	3 35	4 54	♋
T	*ing. Expect nothing*	16 55	3 39	5 50	♌
F	*from him who prom-*	17 11	3 43	6 41	♌
S	Low Tides. *ises a*	17 27	3 47	7 27	♌
D	3d Sun. aft. Easter.	17 43	3 49	8 11	♍
M	*great deal. Hope is*	17 58	3 51	8 51	♍
T	*a good breakfast,*	18 14	3 53	9 32	♎
W	*but a bad supper.*	18 28	3 54	10 14	♎
T	*Good words cost*	18 43	3 55	10 58	♏
F	☌♃&☽ *nothing,*	18 57	3 54	11 43	♏
S	*but are worth much.*	19 11	3 54	morn	♏
D	4th S. af. E. ☽ Apo.	19 25	3 53	0 31	♐
M	High Tides. ☌♄☽	19 38	3 51	1 21	♐
T	*Draw not thy bow*	19 51	3 48	2 12	♑
W	*before thy arrow is*	20 3	3 46	3 3	♑
T	*fixed. Beware of*	20 16	3 42	3 54	♑
F	*him who regards not*	20 28	3 38	4 42	♒
S	*his reputation. Bet-*	20 39	3 34	5 29	♒
D	Rogation Sunday.	20 50	3 28	6 14	♓
M	Low Tides. ☌♅☽	21 1	3 23	6 58	♓
T	*ter be alone than in*	21 12	3 17	7 43	♓
W	☌♀☿. *bad com-*	21 22	3 10	8 30	♈
T	Ascen. Day. *pany.*	21 31	3 3	9 21	♈
F	*Be just and fear not.*	21 41	2 55	10 18	♉
S	☽ Perigee. ☌☽7✶s	21 50	2 47	11 19	♉
D	Sun. af. Ascension.	21 58	2 39	aft25	♊

Boston. D. M.	Sun Rises	Sun Sets	Days' L'gth	Moon Sets.	High water.	New York. D. M.	Sun Rises	Sun Sets.	Days' L'gth	Moon sets.	High water.
1	5 3	6 57	13 54	sets.	10 46	1	5 6	6 54	13 48	sets.	8 16
2	5 1	6 59	13 58	8 24	11 31	2	5 5	6 55	13 50	8 18	9 1
D	5 0	7 0	14 0	9 53	aft14	D	5 4	6 56	13 52	9 46	9 44
4	4 59	7 1	14 2	11 3	1 3	4	5 3	6 57	13 54	10 56	10 33
5	4 58	7 2	14 4	morn	1 55	5	5 2	6 58	13 56	11 55	11 25
6	4 57	7 3	14 6	0 1	2 57	6	5 0	7 0	14 0	morn	aft27
7	4 56	7 4	14 8	0 45	3 55	7	4 59	7 1	14 2	0 40	1 25
8	4 55	7 5	14 10	1 18	5 5	8	4 58	7 2	14 4	1 14	2 35
9	4 53	7 7	14 14	1 43	6 17	9	4 57	7 3	14 6	1 40	3 47
D	4 52	7 8	14 16	2 6	7 24	D	4 56	7 4	14 8	2 5	4 54
11	4 51	7 9	14 18	2 26	8 20	11	4 55	7 5	14 10	2 26	5 50
12	4 50	7 10	14 20	2 44	9 3	12	4 54	7 6	14 12	2 45	6 33
13	4 49	7 11	14 22	3 2	9 46	13	4 53	7 7	14 14	3 4	7 16
14	4 48	7 12	14 24	3 25	10 20	14	4 52	7 8	14 16	3 28	7 50
15	4 47	7 13	14 26	3 48	10 53	15	4 51	7 9	14 18	3 52	8 23
16	4 46	7 14	14 28	rises.	11 28	16	4 51	7 9	14 18	rises	8 58
D	4 45	7 15	14 30	9 6	morn	D	4 50	7 10	14 20	8 59	9 36
18	4 44	7 16	14 32	10 0	0 6	18	4 49	7 11	14 22	9 53	10 15
19	4 43	7 17	14 34	10 46	0 45	19	4 48	7 12	14 24	10 39	10 54
20	4 42	7 18	14 36	11 26	1 24	20	4 47	7 13	14 26	11 20	11 35
21	4 41	7 19	14 38	11 58	2 5	21	4 46	7 14	14 28	11 53	morn
22	4 40	7 20	14 40	morn	2 51	22	4 45	7 15	14 30	morn	0 21
23	4 39	7 21	14 42	0 26	3 37	23	4 44	7 16	14 32	0 22	1 7
D	4 39	7 21	14 42	0 48	4 29	D	4 43	7 17	14 34	0 45	1 59
25	4 38	7 22	14 44	1 9	5 31	25	4 43	7 17	14 34	1 8	3 1
26	4 37	7 23	14 46	1 30	6 40	26	4 42	7 18	14 36	1 30	4 10
27	4 36	7 24	14 48	1 50	7 50	27	4 41	7 19	14 38	1 52	5 20
28	4 36	7 24	14 48	2 14	8 47	28	4 41	7 19	14 38	2 17	6 17
29	4 35	7 25	14 50	2 47	9 43	29	4 40	7 20	14 40	2 51	7 13
30	4 34	7 26	14 52	3 24	10 52	30	4 39	7 21	14 42	3 30	8 22
D	4 33	7 27	14 54	sets.	11 23	D	4 39	7 21	14 42	sets.	8 53

Washington. Sun Rises	Sun Sets.	Days' L'gth	Moon Sets.	Charleston. D. M.	Sun Rises	Sun Sets.	Days' L'gth	Moon Sets.	High water	New Orleans. Sun Rises	Sun Sets	Days' L'gth	Moon Sets.
5 9	6 51	13 42	sets.	1	5 20	6 40	13 20	sets.	6 46	5 24	6 36	13 12	sets.
5 8	6 52	13 44	8 24	2	5 19	6 41	13 22	7 53	7 31	5 23	6 37	13 14	7 42
5 7	6 53	13 46	9 39	D	5 18	6 42	13 24	9 16	8 14	5 22	6 38	13 16	9 3
5 6	6 54	13 48	10 49	4	5 17	6 43	13 26	10 26	9 3	5 22	6 38	13 16	10 15
5 5	6 55	13 50	11 49	5	5 16	6 44	13 28	11 30	9 55	5 21	6 39	13 18	11 19
5 4	6 56	13 52	morn	6	5 15	6 45	13 30	morn	10 57	5 20	6 40	13 20	morn
5 3	6 57	13 54	0 35	7	5 14	6 46	13 32	0 21	11 55	5 20	6 40	13 20	0 10
5 2	6 58	13 56	1 10	8	5 14	6 46	13 32	1 0	1 5	5 19	6 41	13 22	0 51
5 1	6 59	13 58	1 37	9	5 13	6 47	13 34	1 28	2 17	5 18	6 42	13 24	1 22
5 0	7 0	14 0	2 4	D	5 12	6 48	13 36	2 1	3 24	5 18	6 42	13 24	1 56
4 59	7 1	14 2	2 26	11	5 12	6 48	13 36	2 26	4 20	5 17	6 43	13 26	2 26
4 58	7 2	14 4	2 46	12	5 11	6 49	13 38	2 49	5 3	5 16	6 44	13 28	2 51
4 57	7 3	14 6	3 6	13	5 10	6 50	13 40	3 12	5 46	5 16	6 44	13 28	3 16
4 56	7 4	14 8	3 31	14	5 9	6 51	13 42	3 40	6 20	5 15	6 45	13 30	3 46
4 55	7 5	14 10	3 56	15	5 9	6 51	13 42	4 8	6 53	5 14	6 46	13 32	4 16
4 55	7 5	14 10	rises	16	5 8	6 52	13 44	rises	7 28	5 14	6 46	13 32	rises
4 54	7 6	14 12	8 52	D	5 7	6 53	13 46	8 29	8 6	5 13	6 47	13 34	8 17
4 53	7 7	14 14	9 46	18	5 6	6 54	13 48	9 23	8 45	5 12	6 48	13 36	9 11
4 52	7 8	14 16	10 32	19	5 6	6 54	13 48	10 9	9 24	5 12	6 48	13 36	9 57
4 52	7 8	14 16	11 24	20	5 5	6 55	13 50	10 55	10 5	5 11	6 49	13 38	10 44
4 51	7 9	14 18	11 48	21	5 5	6 55	13 50	11 32	10 51	5 11	6 49	13 38	11 23
4 50	7 10	14 20	morn	22	5 4	6 56	13 52	morn	11 37	5 10	6 50	13 40	morn
4 49	7 11	14 22	0 18	23	5 4	6 56	13 52	0 6	morn	5 10	6 50	13 40	0 0
4 49	7 11	14 22	0 42	D	5 3	6 57	13 54	0 35	0 29	5 9	6 51	13 42	0 27
4 48	7 12	14 24	1 7	25	5 3	6 57	13 54	1 4	1 31	5 9	6 51	13 42	1 2
4 47	7 13	14 26	1 30	26	5 2	6 58	13 56	1 30	2 40	5 8	6 52	13 44	1 30
4 47	7 13	14 26	1 54	27	5 1	6 59	13 58	2 0	3 50	5 8	6 52	13 44	2 4
4 46	7 14	14 28	2 20	28	5 1	6 59	13 58	2 29	4 47	5 7	6 53	13 46	2 35
4 45	7 15	14 30	2 55	29	5 1	6 59	13 58	3 7	5 43	5 7	6 53	13 46	3 15
4 45	7 15	14 30	3 36	30	5 0	7 0	14 0	3 55	6 52	5 7	6 53	13 46	4 6
4 44	7 16	14 32	sets.	D	5 0	7 0	14 0	sets.	7 23	5 6	6 54	13 48	sets.

1840, 6th Month, JUNE, begins on Monday. Hath 30 Days, and is the 1st Summer Month.

Phases of the Moon.

☽ First Quarter, 6th, 8h. 11m. Evening.
○ Full Moon, 14th, 9h. 39m. Evening.
☾ Last Quarter, 22d, 6h. 21m. Evening.
● New Moon, 29th, 8h. 47m. Morning.

Astronomical Calculations, embracing the whole Union, and the Canadas, beginning at the following points:

D. W.	ASPECTS, &c.	Sun's Dec.	Sun Fast.	Moon South	☽ S.
M	Very High Tides.	22 7	2 30	1 33	□
T	*He that shows his*	22 15	2 21	2 38	♋
W	*passion, tells his en-*	22 22	2 11	3 37	♋
T	☌ ☿ & ♂. *emy*	22 29	2 1	4 29	♌
F	*where he may hit*	22 36	1 51	5 19	♌
S	*him.* [Low Tides.	22 42	1 40	6 3	♍
D	Pentecost, Whit Su	22 48	1 29	6 46	♍
M	Whit Monday. *Cru-*	22 53	1 18	7 27	♍
T	Whit Tues. ☍ ♄ ☉.	22 59	1 6	8 8	♎
W	Su. ☌ ☿ ☉. *elty to*	23 3	0 55	8 51	♎
T	☌ ♃ ☽. □ ♅ ☉.	23 7	0 43	9 36	♏
F	*females is the crime*	23 11	0 31	10 23	♏
S	☽ Apogee. *of a*	23 15	0 19	11 12	♐
D	Trin. Sun. ☌ ♄ ☽.	23 18	f 6	morn	♐
M	☌ ♀ & ♂. *monster.*	23 21	s 7	0 3	♐
T	High Tides. *Never*	23 23	0 19	0 55	♑
W	*sound the trumpet of*	23 25	0 32	1 45	♑
T	*your own fame. To*	23 26	0 45	2 35	♒
F	*believe a business*	23 27	0 58	3 20	♒
S	*impossible is the way*	23 28	1 11	4 6	♒
D	Summer Solstice.	23 28	1 24	4 48	♓
M	☌ ♅ & ☽. *to make it*	23 27	1 37	5 32	♓
T	Low Tides. *so.*	23 27	1 49	6 15	♈
W	*Judge not of men or*	23 26	2 2	7 3	♈
T	*things at first sight.*	23 24	2 15	7 55	♉
F	☌ ☽ 7 ✶s. *Never*	23 22	2 28	8 52	♉
S	*speak to deceive, nor*	23 20	2 40	9 56	□
D	2d S. af. T. ☽ Peri.	23 17	2 53	11 3	□
M	Very High Tides.	23 14	3 5	aft 11	♋
T	*listen to betray.*	23 11	3 17	1 15	♋

Boston.					
D. M.	Sun Rises	Sun Sets	Days' L'gth	Moon Sets.	High water.
1	4 33	7 27	14 54	9 49	aft 11
2	4 32	7 8	14 56	10 37	0 56
3	4 32	7 28	14 56	11 13	1 41
4	4 31	7 29	14 58	11 41	2 27
5	4 31	7 29	14 58	morn	3 19
6	4 30	7 30	15 0	0 7	4 13
D	4 30	7 30	15 0	0 27	5 15
8	4 29	7 31	15 2	0 46	6 18
9	4 29	7 31	15 2	1 5	7 20
10	4 28	7 32	15 4	1 24	8 19
11	4 28	7 32	15 4	1 48	9 9
12	4 28	7 32	15 4	2 15	9 53
13	4 28	7 32	15 4	2 48	10 31
D	4 28	7 32	15 4	rises	11 8
15	4 28	7 32	15 4	8 40	11 53
16	4 28	7 32	15 4	9 21	morn
17	4 28	7 32	15 4	9 55	0 24
18	4 28	7 32	15 4	10 21	1 2
19	4 28	7 32	15 4	10 47	1 37
20	4 28	7 32	15 4	11 7	2 16
D	4 28	7 32	15 4	11 28	2 52
22	4 28	7 32	15 4	11 46	3 37
23	4 28	7 32	15 4	morn	4 25
24	4 28	7 32	15 4	0 10	5 35
25	4 28	7 32	15 4	0 37	6 55
26	4 28	7 32	15 4	1 11	8 13
27	4 28	7 32	15 4	1 52	9 23
D	4 28	7 32	15 4	2 45	10 21
29	4 28	7 32	15 4	sets.	11 16
30	4 28	7 31	15 2	9 3	11 57

New York.						Washington.			
D. M.	Sun Rises	Sun Sets.	Days' L'gth	Moon Sets.	High water.	Sun Rises	Sun Sets.	Days' L'gth	Moon Sets.
1	4 38	7 22	14 44	9 42	9 41	4 43	7 17	14 34	9 35
2	4 37	7 23	14 46	10 31	10 26	4 43	7 17	14 34	10 25
3	4 37	7 23	14 46	11 8	11 11	4 42	7 18	14 36	11 4
4	4 36	7 24	14 48	11 38	11 57	4 42	7 18	14 36	11 35
5	4 36	7 24	14 48	morn	aft 49	4 42	7 18	14 36	morn
6	4 35	7 25	14 50	0 5	1 43	4 41	7 19	14 38	0 3
D	4 35	7 25	14 50	0 26	2 45	4 41	7 19	14 38	0 25
8	4 34	7 26	14 52	0 46	3 48	4 40	7 20	14 40	0 46
9	4 34	7 26	14 52	1 7	4 50	4 40	7 20	14 40	1 9
10	4 34	7 26	14 52	1 27	5 49	4 40	7 20	14 40	1 30
11	4 34	7 26	14 52	1 52	6 39	4 39	7 21	14 42	1 56
12	4 34	7 26	14 52	2 20	7 23	4 39	7 21	14 42	2 25
13	4 33	7 27	14 54	2 54	8 1	4 39	7 21	14 42	3 0
D	4 33	7 27	14 54	rises	8 38	4 39	7 21	14 42	rises.
15	4 33	7 27	14 54	8 33	9 23	4 39	7 21	14 42	8 26
16	4 33	7 27	14 54	9 15	9 54	4 39	7 21	14 42	9 9
17	4 33	7 27	14 54	9 45	10 32	4 39	7 21	14 42	9 45
18	4 33	7 27	14 54	10 17	11 7	4 39	7 21	14 42	10 13
19	4 33	7 27	14 54	10 44	11 46	4 38	7 22	14 44	10 41
20	4 33	7 27	14 54	11 5	morn	4 38	7 22	14 44	11 3
D	4 33	7 27	14 54	11 28	0 22	4 38	7 22	14 44	11 28
22	4 33	7 27	14 54	11 47	1 7	4 38	7 22	14 44	11 48
23	4 33	7 27	14 54	morn	1 55	4 38	7 22	14 44	morn
24	4 33	7 27	14 54	0 12	3 5	4 38	7 22	14 44	0 14
25	4 33	7 27	14 54	0 40	4 25	4 39	7 21	14 42	0 43
26	4 33	7 27	14 54	1 16	5 43	4 39	7 21	14 42	1 21
27	4 33	7 27	14 54	1 58	6 53	4 39	7 21	14 42	2 4
D	4 33	7 27	14 54	2 52	7 51	4 39	7 21	14 42	2 59
29	4 33	7 27	14 54	sets.	8 46	4 39	7 21	14 42	sets.
30	4 34	7 26	14 52	8 58	9 27	4 39	7 21	14 42	3 5

Charleston.						New Orleans.			
D. M.	Sun Rises	Sun Sets.	Days' L'gth	Moon Sets	High water	Sun Rises	Sun Sets	Days' L'gth.	Moon Sets.
1	4 59	7 1	14 2	9 12	8 11	5 6	6 54	13 48	9 0
2	4 59	7 1	14 2	10 6	8 56	5 5	6 55	13 50	9 55
3	4 58	7 2	14 4	10 48	9 41	5 5	6 55	13 50	10 38
4	4 58	7 2	14 4	11 25	10 27	5 5	6 55	13 50	11 17
5	4 58	7 2	14 4	11 57	11 19	5 5	6 55	13 50	11 53
6	4 57	7 3	14 6	morn	aft 13	5 4	6 56	13 52	morn
D	4 57	7 3	14 6	0 22	1 15	5 4	6 56	13 52	0 26
8	4 57	7 3	14 6	0 46	2 18	5 4	6 56	13 52	0 46
9	4 56	7 4	14 8	1 13	3 20	5 3	6 57	13 54	1 15
10	4 56	7 4	14 8	1 38	4 19	5 3	6 57	13 54	1 45
11	4 56	7 4	14 8	2 8	5 9	5 3	6 57	13 54	2 18
12	4 56	7 4	14 8	2 41	5 53	5 3	6 57	13 54	2 50
13	4 56	7 4	14 8	3 20	6 31	5 3	6 57	13 54	3 30
D	4 56	7 4	14 8	rises	7 8	5 3	6 57	13 54	rises
15	4 55	7 5	14 10	8 3	7 53	5 2	6 58	13 56	7 51
16	4 55	7 5	14 10	8 50	8 24	5 2	6 58	13 56	8 39
17	4 55	7 5	14 10	9 30	9 2	5 2	6 58	13 56	9 20
18	4 55	7 5	14 10	10 1	9 37	5 2	6 58	13 56	9 53
19	4 55	7 5	14 10	10 32	10 16	5 2	6 58	13 56	10 26
20	4 55	7 5	14 10	10 57	10 52	5 2	6 58	13 56	10 53
D	4 55	7 5	14 10	11 26	11 37	5 2	6 58	13 56	11 28
22	4 55	7 5	14 10	11 51	morn	5 2	6 58	13 56	11 53
23	4 55	7 5	14 10	morn	0 25	5 2	6 58	13 56	morn
24	4 55	7 5	14 10	0 20	1 35	5 2	6 58	13 56	0 24
25	4 55	7 5	14 10	0 52	2 55	5 2	6 58	13 56	0 58
26	4 55	7 5	14 10	1 35	4 13	5 2	6 58	13 56	1 46
27	4 55	7 5	14 10	2 23	5 23	5 2	6 58	13 56	2 34
D	4 55	7 5	14 10	3 22	6 21	5 3	6 57	13 54	3 26
29	4 55	7 5	14 10	sets.	7 16	5 3	6 57	13 54	sets.
30	4 56	7 4	14 8	8 39	7 57	5 3	6 57	13 54	8 28

24

Scrape with the Indians.....See Page 29.

1840

Col. Crockett and the Bear and the Swallows.

People tell a great many silly stories about swallows. Some say that if you kill one your cows will give bloody milk, and others tell as how they fly away in the fall and come back again in the spring, when the leaves of the white oaks are jest as big as a mowses ear. Agin, thar ar some that tell how they keep Christmas and New Year's among the little fishes, at the bottom of some pond; but you may tell all them that sea so they are dratted fools and dont know nothing about the matter. Swallows sleep all winter in the holler of some old rotten sycamore, and I'll tell you how I come to find it out.

I war out airly in the spring with my rifle on the banks of the Tennessee, making up my opinion about matters and things in general, when all of a sudden I heerd a clap of thunder, and that sot me a thinking "Now," sez I, "If I war to go home and tell of that the boys would think me a d—–d liar, if they didn't dare to call me so; for who ever heard of such a thing as thunder under a clear sky of a bright spring day." And with that I looked up, and agin I heerd the thunder, but it war not thunder any how I could fix it; for a hull swarm of swallors come bodily out of an old hollow sycamore, and it war the noise they made with the flapping of their wings. Now I thought to myself that them ar little varmints war doing some mischief in the tree, and that it war my duty to see into it; for you see just then I felt hugeously grandiferous; for

[See page 21.]

1840. 7th Month, JULY, begins on Wednesday. Hath 31 Days, and is the 2d Summer Month.

Phases of the Moon.

☽ First Quarter, 6th, 8h. 52m. Morning.
○ Full Moon, 14th, 0h. 17m. Evening.
☾ Last Quarter, 22d, 1h. 34m. Morning.
● New Moon, 28th, 4h. 14m. Evening.

Astronomical Calculations, embracing the whole Union, and the Canadas, beginning at the following points:

D W	ASPECTS, &c.	Sun's Dec.	Sun Slow.	Moon South	☽ S
W	☉ in Apogee. *A*	23 7	3 29	2 12	♌
T	*fool may ask more*	23 2	3 40	3 5	♌
F	*questions in an hour,*	22 58	3 51	3 51	♍
S	*than a wise man can*	22 53	4 2	4 35	♍
D	3d Sund. aft. Trin.	22 47	4 13	5 18	♎
M	♃ Stationary.	22 41	4 23	6 1	♎
T	Low Tides. *answer*	22 35	4 33	6 42	♎
W	☌ ☽ & ♃. *in*	22 28	4 42	7 29	♏
T	*seven years. All is*	22 21	4 51	8 14	♏
F	*but lip-wisdom that*	22 13	5 0	9 3	♐
S	☽ Apogee. ☌ ♄ ☽.	22 6	5 8	9 53	♐
D	4th Sund. aft. Trin.	21 57	5 15	10 45	♐
M	*wants experience. A*	21 49	5 23	11 37	♑
T	*man may talk like a*	21 40	5 29	morn	♑
W	High Tides. *wise*	21 30	5 36	0 26	♒
T	*man, and yet act like*	21 21	5 41	1 13	♒
F	☿ Greatest elonga.	21 10	5 47	1 59	♒
S	*a fool.* [☌ ☽ & ♅.	21 0	5 51	2 42	♓
D	5th Sund. aft. Trin	20 49	5 55	3 26	♓
M	*A man knows more*	20 38	5 59	4 10	♈
T	*to any purpose than*	20 26	6 2	4 56	♈
W	[Tides ☿ Aphe.	20 15	6 5	5 44	♉
T	☌ ☽ & 7 ✱ s. Low	20 2	6 7	6 38	♉
F	♀ in Su. ☌ ☉. *he*	19 50	6 8	7 37	□
S	*practices. The first*	19 37	6 9	8 40	□
D	6th S. af. T. ☽ Per.	19 24	6 10	9 47	♋
M	☌ ♂ & ☽. *step to*	19 10	6 9	10 52	♋
T	☌ ☽ & ♀. *great-*	18 56	6 9	11 53	♌
W	♀ in Perihelion.	18 42	6 7	aft 48	♌
T	Hig Tides. *ness*	18 28	6 5	1 39	♌
F	*is to be honest.*	18 13	6 2	2 25	♍

Boston.

D. M.	Sun Rises	Sun Sets	Days' L'gth	Moon Sets.	High water.
1	4 29	7 31	15 2	9 36	aft 44
2	4 29	7 31	15 2	10 1	1 20
3	4 29	7 31	15 2	10 24	1 58
4	4 30	7 30	15 0	10 43	2 40
D	4 30	7 30	15 0	11 3	3 35
6	4 31	7 29	14 58	11 24	4 26
7	4 31	7 29	14 58	11 45	5 9
8	4 31	7 29	14 58	morn	6 18
9	4 32	7 28	14 56	0 11	7 27
10	4 32	7 28	14 56	0 42	8 34
11	4 33	7 27	14 54	1 19	9 26
D	4 33	7 27	14 54	2 5	10 10
13	4 34	7 26	14 52	3 0	10 47
14	4 35	7 25	14 50	rises	11 24
15	4 36	7 24	14 48	8 20	morn
16	4 37	7 23	14 46	8 46	0 0
17	4 37	7 23	14 26	9 7	0 34
18	4 38	7 22	14 44	9 29	1 6
D	4 39	7 21	14 42	9 49	1 40
20	4 40	7 20	14 40	10 11	2 17
21	4 40	7 20	14 40	10 35	2 56
22	4 41	7 19	14 38	11 5	3 48
23	4 42	7 18	14 36	11 41	5 0
24	4 43	7 17	14 34	morn	6 33
25	4 44	7 16	14 32	0 27	8 4
D	4 45	7 15	14 30	1 29	9 14
27	4 46	7 14	14 28	2 43	10 13
28	4 47	7 13	14 26	sets.	11 0
29	4 48	7 12	14 24	4 56	11 40
30	4 49	7 11	14 22	8 22	aft 15
31	4 51	7 9	14 18	8 43	0 50

New York.

D. M.	Sun Rises	Sun Sets.	Days' L'gth	Moon Sets.	High water.
1	4 34	7 26	14 52	9 32	10 14
2	4 34	7 26	14 52	9 59	10 50
3	4 34	7 26	14 52	10 23	11 28
4	4 35	7 25	14 50	10 43	aft 10
D	4 35	7 25	14 50	11 4	1 5
6	4 36	7 24	14 48	11 27	1 56
7	4 36	7 24	14 48	11 49	2 39
8	4 37	7 23	14 46	morn	3 48
9	4 37	7 23	14 46	0 16	4 57
10	4 38	7 22	14 44	0 48	6 4
11	4 38	7 22	14 44	1 26	6 56
D	4 39	7 21	14 42	2 12	7 40
13	4 39	7 21	14 42	3 7	8 17
14	4 40	7 20	14 40	rises	8 54
15	4 41	7 19	14 38	8 15	9 30
16	4 41	7 19	14 38	8 43	10 4
17	4 42	7 18	14 36	9 5	10 36
18	4 43	7 17	14 34	9 28	11 10
D	4 44	7 16	14 32	9 49	11 47
20	4 44	7 16	14 32	10 13	morn
21	4 45	7 15	14 30	10 38	0 26
22	4 46	7 14	14 28	11 10	1 18
23	4 47	7 13	14 26	11 47	2 30
24	4 48	7 12	14 24	morn	4 3
25	4 49	7 11	14 22	0 34	5 34
D	4 50	7 10	14 20	1 36	6 44
27	4 51	7 9	14 18	2 50	7 43
28	4 51	7 9	14 18	sets.	8 30
29	4 52	7 8	14 16	7 53	9 10
30	4 53	7 7	14 14	8 20	9 45
31	4 54	7 6	14 12	8 43	10 20

Washington.

D. M.	Sun Rises	Sun Sets.	Days' L'gth	Moon Sets.
1	4 39	7 21	14 42	9 28
2	4 40	7 20	14 40	9 57
3	4 40	7 20	14 40	10 22
4	4 40	7 20	14 40	10 43
D	4 41	7 19	14 38	11 5
6	4 41	7 19	14 38	11 30
7	4 42	7 18	14 36	11 53
8	4 42	7 18	14 36	morn
9	4 43	7 17	14 34	0 21
10	4 43	7 17	14 34	0 54
11	4 44	7 16	14 32	1 33
D	4 45	7 15	14 30	2 19
13	4 45	7 15	14 30	3 14
14	4 45	7 15	14 30	rises
15	4 46	7 14	14 28	8 10
16	4 46	7 14	14 28	8 40
17	4 47	7 13	14 26	9 3
18	4 48	7 12	14 24	9 27
D	4 49	7 11	14 22	9 49
20	4 49	7 11	14 22	10 15
21	4 50	7 10	14 20	10 41
22	4 51	7 9	14 18	11 15
23	4 52	7 8	14 16	11 53
24	4 52	7 8	14 16	morn
25	4 53	7 7	14 14	0 41
D	4 54	7 6	14 12	1 43
27	4 55	7 5	14 10	2 57
28	4 56	7 4	14 8	sets.
29	4 57	7 3	14 6	7 46
30	4 58	7 2	14 4	8 18
31	4 59	7 1	14 2	8 43

Charleston.

D. M.	Sun Rises	Sun Sets.	Days' L'gth	Moon Sets	Higl. water
1	4 56	7 4	14 8	9 15	8 44
2	4 56	7 4	14 8	9 49	9 20
3	4 57	7 3	14 6	10 19	9 58
4	4 57	7 3	14 6	10 43	10 40
D	4 57	7 3	14 6	11 8	11 35
6	4 57	7 3	14 6	11 39	aft 26
7	4 58	7 2	14 4	morn	1 9
8	4 58	7 2	14 4	0 6	2 18
9	4 58	7 2	14 4	0 37	3 27
10	4 59	7 1	14 2	1 13	4 34
11	4 59	7 1	14 2	1 56	5 26
D	5 0	7 0	14 0	2 42	6 10
13	5 1	6 59	13 58	3 37	6 47
14	5 1	6 59	13 58	rises	7 24
15	5 1	9 59	13 58	7 54	8 0
16	5 2	6 58	13 56	8 31	8 34
17	5 2	6 58	13 56	8 57	9 6
18	5 3	6 57	13 54	9 24	9 40
D	5 3	6 57	13 54	9 49	10 17
20	5 4	6 56	13 52	10 19	10 56
21	5 4	6 56	13 52	10 50	11 48
22	5 5	6 55	13 50	11 31	morn
23	5 6	6 54	13 48	morn	1 0
24	5 6	6 54	13 48	0 12	2 33
25	5 7	6 53	13 46	1 4	4 4
D	5 8	6 52	13 44	2 6	5 14
27	5 8	6 52	13 44	3 20	6 13
28	5 9	6 51	13 42	sets.	7 0
29	5 10	6 50	13 40	7 40	7 40
30	5 10	6 50	13 40	8 13	8 15
31	5 11	6 49	13 38	8 43	8 50

New Orleans.

D. M.	Sun Rise	Sun Sets	Days' L'gth	Moon Sets.
1	5 3	6 57	13 54	9 8
2	5 3	6 57	13 54	9 47
3	5 4	6 56	13 52	10 17
4	5 4	6 56	13 52	10 43
D	5 4	6 56	13 52	11 10
6	5 4	6 56	13 52	11 45
7	5 5	6 55	13 50	morn
8	5 5	6 55	13 50	0 13
9	5 5	6 55	13 50	0 46
10	5 6	6 54	13 48	1 24
11	5 6	6 54	13 48	2 8
D	5 6	6 54	13 48	2 54
13	5 7	6 53	13 46	3 49
14	5 7	6 53	13 46	rises
15	5 8	6 52	13 44	7 45
16	5 8	6 52	13 44	8 25
17	5 9	6 51	13 42	8 53
18	5 9	6 51	13 42	9 22
D	5 9	6 51	13 42	9 49
20	5 10	6 50	13 40	10 23
21	5 10	6 50	13 40	10 56
22	5 11	6 49	13 38	11 40
23	5 12	6 48	13 36	morn
24	5 12	6 48	13 36	0 24
25	5 13	6 47	13 34	1 16
D	5 13	6 47	13 34	2 18
27	5 14	6 46	13 32	3 32
28	5 15	6 45	13 30	sets.
29	5 16	6 44	13 28	7 35
30	5 16	6 44	13 28	8 10
31	5 16	6 44	13 28	8 42

1840. 8th Month, AUGUST, begins on Saturday. Hath 31 Days, and is the 3d Summer Month.

Phases of the Moon.

☽ First Quarter, 5th, 0h. 0m. Morning.
○ Full Moon, 13th, 2h. 2m. Morning.
☾ Last Quarter, 20th, 7h. 8m. Morning.
● New Moon, 27th, 1h 35m. Morning.

Astronomical Calculations, embracing the whole Union, and the Canadas, beginning at the following points:

D W	ASPECTS, &c.	Sun's Dec.	Sun Slow.	Moon South	D S
S	□ ♃ & ☉. *A man*	17 58	5 59	3 9	♍
D	7th Sund. aft. Trin.	17 43	5 55	3 53	♎
M	*knows his companion*	17 27	5 51	4 36	♎
T	☌ ☽ & ♃. *in a long*	17 11	5 46	5 20	♏
W	*journey and a small*	16 55	5 40	6 8	♏
T	Very low Tides. *inn.*	16 38	5 34	6 56	♏
F	☽ Apogee. ☌ ☽ & ♄.	16 22	5 27	7 47	♐
S	*They who give will-*	16 5	5 19	8 38	♐
D	8th Sund. aft. Trin.	15 47	5 11	9 31	♑
M	*ingly, love to give*	15 30	5 2	10 22	♑
T	☌ ☿ & ♀. *quickly.*	15 12	4 53	11 10	♑
W	*Every fool can find*	14 54	4 43	11 57	♒
T	☽ eclipsed, visible.	14 36	4 33	morn	♒
F	High Tides. ☿ in	14 17	4 22	0 42	♓
S	☌ ☽ & ♅. [Inf. ☌ ☉.	13 59	4 10	1 26	♓
D	9th Sund. aft. Trin.	13 40	3 58	2 10	♈
M	*faults where a great*	13 21	3 46	2 56	♈
T	*many wise men can't*	13 1	3 33	3 44	♈
W	♄ stationary. *mend.*	12 42	3 19	4 36	♉
T	☌ ☽ & 7 ✶s. *Fair*	12 22	3 5	5 32	♉
F	Low Tides. *words*	12 2	2 51	6 33	♊
S	*break no*[☽ Perigee.	11 42	2 36	7 36	♊
D	10th Sun. aft. Trin.	11 22	2 21	8 40	♋
M	☌ ☽ ♂. ☿ stationary	11 1	2 5	9 42	♋
T	*bones, but foul words*	10 40	1 49	10 39	♌
W	*many a one*[☌ ☽ & ♀	10 19	1 32	11 31	♌
T	☉ eclipsed invisible	9 58	1 15	aft19	♍
F	High Tides. *Such as*	9 37	0 58	1 6	♍
S	*the tree is, such will*	9 16	0 41	1 51	♎
D	11th Sun. aft. Trin.	8 54	0 23	2 34	♎
M	*be the fruit.*	8 33	0 4	3 19	♎

Boston.

D. M.	Sun Rises	Sun Sets.	Days' L'gth	Moon Sets.	High water.
1	4 51	7 9	14 18	9 4	1 26
D	4 52	7 8	14 16	9 24	2 4
3	4 53	7 7	14 14	9 46	2 44
4	4 55	7 5	14 10	10 11	3 29
5	4 56	7 4	14 8	10 41	4 24
6	4 57	7 3	14 6	11 10	5 29
7	4 58	7 2	14 4	morn	6 47
8	4 59	7 1	14 2	0 0	8 5
D	5 0	7 0	14 0	0 51	9 4
10	5 1	6 59	13 58	1 52	9 52
11	5 2	6 58	13 56	2 57	10 28
12	5 4	6 56	13 52	3 55	11 2
13	5 5	6 55	13 50	rises	11 38
14	5 6	6 54	13 48	7 36	morn
15	5 7	6 53	13 46	7 56	0 9
D	5 9	6 51	13 42	8 19	0 40
17	5 10	6 50	13 40	8 42	1 14
18	5 11	6 49	13 38	9 9	1 53
19	5 13	6 47	13 34	9 43	2 39
20	5 14	6 46	13 32	10 25	3 34
21	5 15	6 45	13 30	11 19	4 51
22	5 17	6 43	13 26	morn	6 28
D	5 18	6 42	13 24	0 26	8 4
24	5 19	6 41	13 22	1 42	9 9
25	5 21	6 39	13 18	3 2	10 1
26	5 22	6 38	13 16	4 20	10 43
27	5 23	6 37	13 14	sets.	11 18
28	5 24	6 36	13 12	7 12	11 55
29	5 26	6 34	13 8	7 32	aft27
D	5 27	6 33	13 6	7 54	1 0
31	5 29	6 31	13 2	8 17	1 35

New York.

D. M.	Sun Rises	Sun Sets.	Days' L'gth	Moon Sets.	High water.
1	4 55	7 5	14 10	9 5	10 56
D	4 56	7 4	14 8	9 26	11 34
3	4 57	7 3	14 6	9 49	aft14
4	4 58	7 2	14 4	10 16	0 59
5	4 59	7 1	14 2	10 47	1 54
6	5 0	7 0	14 0	11 17	2 59
7	5 1	6 59	13 58	morn	4 17
8	5 3	6 57	13 54	0 7	5 35
D	5 4	6 56	13 52	0 58	6 34
10	5 5	6 55	13 50	1 59	7 22
11	5 6	6 54	13 48	3 3	7 58
12	5 7	6 53	13 46	4 0	8 32
13	5 8	6 52	13 44	rises	9 8
14	5 9	6 51	13 42	7 35	9 39
15	5 11	6 49	13 38	7 56	10 10
D	5 12	6 48	13 36	8 20	10 44
17	5 13	6 47	13 34	8 45	11 23
18	5 14	6 46	13 32	9 13	morn
19	5 15	6 45	13 30	9 48	0 9
20	5 17	6 43	13 26	10 31	1 4
21	5 18	6 42	13 24	11 26	2 21
22	5 19	6 41	13 22	morn	3 58
D	5 20	6 40	13 20	0 33	5 34
24	5 21	6 39	13 18	1 48	6 39
25	5 23	6 37	13 14	3 7	7 31
26	5 24	6 36	13 12	4 23	8 13
27	5 25	6 35	13 10	sets.	8 48
28	5 26	6 34	13 8	7 13	9 25
29	5 28	6 32	13 4	7 34	9 57
D	5 29	6 31	13 2	7 57	10 30
31	5 30	6 30	13 0	8 21	11 5

Washington.

D. M.	Sun Rises	Sun Sets.	Days' L'gth	Moon Sets.
1	4 59	7 1	14 2	9 6
D	5 0	7 0	14 0	9 28
3	5 1	6 59	13 58	9 52
4	5 2	6 58	13 56	10 21
5	5 3	6 57	13 54	10 53
6	5 4	6 56	13 52	11 24
7	5 5	6 55	13 50	morn
8	5 6	6 54	13 48	0 14
D	5 7	6 53	13 46	1 5
10	5 8	6 52	13 44	2 6
11	5 9	6 51	13 42	3 9
12	5 10	6 50	13 40	4 5
13	5 12	6 48	13 36	rises
14	5 13	6 47	13 34	7 34
15	5 14	6 46	13 32	7 56
D	5 15	6 45	13 30	8 21
17	5 16	6 44	13 28	8 48
18	5 17	6 43	13 26	9 17
19	5 18	6 42	13 24	9 53
20	5 19	6 41	13 22	10 37
21	5 21	6 39	13 18	11 33
22	5 22	6 38	13 16	morn
D	5 23	6 37	13 14	0 40
24	5 24	6 36	13 12	1 54
25	5 25	6 35	13 10	3 12
26	5 26	6 34	13 8	4 26
27	5 27	6 33	13 6	sets.
28	5 29	6 31	13 2	7 13
29	5 30	6 30	13 0	7 36
D	5 31	6 29	12 58	8 0
31	5 32	6 28	12 56	8 25

Charleston.

D. M.	Sun Rises	Sun Sets.	Days' L'gth	Moon Sets	High water
1	5 12	6 48	13 36	9 9	9 26
D	5 13	6 47	13 34	9 34	10 4
3	5 13	6 47	13 34	10 1	10 44
4	5 14	6 46	13 32	10 37	11 29
5	5 15	6 45	13 30	11 12	aft24
6	5 16	6 44	13 28	11 47	1 29
7	5 17	6 43	13 26	morn	2 47
8	5 17	6 43	13 26	0 37	4 5
D	5 18	6 42	13 24	1 28	5 4
10	5 19	6 41	13 22	2 29	5 52
11	5 20	6 40	13 20	3 28	6 28
12	5 21	6 39	13 18	4 21	7 2
13	5 22	6 38	13 16	rises	7 38
14	5 22	6 38	13 16	7 30	8 9
15	5 23	6 37	13 14	7 55	8 40
D	5 24	6 36	13 12	8 23	9 14
17	5 25	6 35	13 10	8 56	9 53
18	5 26	6 34	13 8	9 30	10 39
19	5 27	6 33	12 6	10 9	11 34
20	5 28	6 32	13 4	10 56	morn
21	5 29	6 31	13 2	11 56	0 51
22	5 30	6 30	13 0	morn	1 28
D	5 30	6 30	13 0	1 3	2 4
24	5 31	6 29	12 58	2 13	3 9
25	5 32	6 28	12 56	3 28	4 1
26	5 33	6 27	12 54	4 37	4 43
27	5 34	6 26	12 52	sets.	5 18
28	5 35	6 25	12 50	7 14	5 55
29	5 36	6 24	12 48		6 27
D	5 37	6 23	12 46		7 0
31	5 38	6 22	12 44		9 35

New Orleans.

D. M.	Sun Rises	Sun Sets	Days' L'gth	Moon Sets.
1	5 17	6 43	13 26	9 11
D	5 18	6 42	13 24	9 38
3	5 18	6 42	13 24	10 8
4	5 19	6 41	13 22	10 43
5	5 20	6 40	13 20	11 23
6	5 20	6 40	13 20	11 59
7	5 21	6 39	13 18	morn
8	5 22	6 38	13 16	0 49
D	5 23	6 37	13 14	1 40
10	5 23	6 37	13 14	2 41
11	5 24	6 36	13 12	3 39
12	5 25	6 35	13 12	4 30
13	5 26	6 34	13 8	rises
14	5 26	6 34	13 8	7 29
15	5 27	6 33	13 6	7 56
D	5 28	6 32	13 4	8 28
17	5 29	6 31	13 2	9 3
18	5 30	6 30	13 0	9 37
19	5 30	6 30	13 0	10 18
20	5 31	6 29	12 58	11 7
21	5 32	6 28	12 56	morn
22	5 33	6 27	12 54	0 8
D	5 34	6 26	12 52	1 15
24	5 34	6 26	12 52	2 24
25	5 35	6 25	12 50	3 37
26	5 36	6 24	12 48	4 41
27	5 37	6 23	12 46	sets.
28	5 38	6 22	12 44	7 12
29	5 38	6 22	12 44	7 44
D	5 39	6 21	12 42	8 15
31	5 40	6 20	12 40	8 45

Gum Swamp Breeding...continued from page 21.

to do about it, i felt an almighty notion to shove my thum nail into his left eye. Jerusha seed i was getting to be very odoriferous about it, tho a word from her would have laid my bristles in a minnit. At last she sot down to table one day, with her good eye next to the stranger, and her blind eye next to me. I took that for the most onrespectful thing that was ever done to me, and looked rite at the stranger, as if i war thinking whether it war best to swallow him or the dinner. You might as well try to play a game of cards on the back of a running deer, as to keep the run of how he looked. I cant ritely say how many colors he turned, but i know i seed three or four colors in his face that i never seed onnywhere else. I've heered tell of fellers that felt blue, but he felt all colors, besides a spot on the eend of his nose. So he axed me what i was grinning at, and i threw out one leg and scraped the heel of the other foot as i says, says i, "Stranger, I dont want to onsult you be 4 the gal, but if i had you in the forest i'd hang you on the limb of a tree by your onquestionable ugly nose.' He then axed his gal if it would be imperlite if he jist took the tip of my nose between his thum and finger and giv it a small pull. He telled her he would do nothing more, and would make no noize about it, and that he could do it all in haff a minnit. She telled him he might do that if he chooze, but she wouldn't allow onnything else to be done about it, only that; and so she leaned back in her cheer, to let him put his arm out before her, and do what he sed. That wos the fust time i wos so mad i couldn't stir, to think the kussed varmint shood tork of pulling my nose as if it was only snuffing a kandel that couldn't strike back agin. I wos thinking whether i shood eat him with salt, or take him in his boots jist as he wos, when i seed him lay down his nife and fork and reech out his hand. I sot as still as a clam till he got his hand close to my mouth, and then i opened shell and took his flipper between my teeth. He yelled like a nest of young wild cats struck with litening, and insinnivated it hurt him beautiful. The gal begun to bawl out and take the feller's part, and that astonished me so much that i forgot to let go the feller's hand till my teeth almost met through it. There was a smart chance of hot soup on the table, and that was kicked over rite off, for he floundered about like a speared sammun, without stopping this time, to ax the gal whether it would be imperlite or not. She ketched hold of his coat tail to haul him away from me, but that only hurt him wuss, and so to git cleer of her he kicked backwards, and put his heels into her bowels like he was going to walk over her. Pritty soon the hot soup begun to run down into his boots, and then he danced wuss than ever and upset the table, and all the dishes went to smash. At last he got on his nieze and axed my pardun, and then i let him go. Now i went home and thot it was all over, but what does the gal's father do but send me a bill of the crokkery, that the feller broke when he upsot the table. I thot this was the most unpolite thing that ever i heered on, and so i sent the munny bekase i thot 'twould be a disgrace to me for sich a mean feller to think i owed him any thing.

Col. Crockett, the Bear and the Swallows, from p. 25

the nabors had made me a justus pease. So I cut down a saplin with my knife and set it agin the tree and clim up like a squirrel; for you know a sycamore has a smooth bark. As I war bending over the edge of the holler to look down, the saplin broke under me, and trying to catch at something I lost my balance and fell down into the tree head foremust. When I got to the bottom I found myself a little the nastiest critter ever you saw, on account of the swallow's dung, and how to get out I didn't know; for the hole war deep, and when I looked up I could see the stars out of the top. Presently I put my hand into some thing as soft as a feather bed, and I heerd an awful growling, so that I thought it war the last trump sounding to fall in and dress to the right for the day of judgment. But it war only an old bar I woke out of his winter nap, and I out butcher to see which war the best man. But the kritter war clean amazed and seemed to like my room better than my company and made a bolt to get out of the scrape, most cowardly. "Hollo, stranger!" sez I; "we dont part company without having a fair shake for a fite;" and so saving your presence, I clinched hold both his posterities. But finding the hair war like to give way I got hold of his stump of a tail with my teeth, and then I had him fast enough. But still he kept on climing up the holler, and I begun to sorter like the idee; for you know he couldn't git up without pulling me up arter him. So when he begun to get tired, I quickened his pace with an awful fundamental poke with my butcher, jest by way of a gentle hint. Before long we got to the top of the tree, and then I got to the ground quicker than he did, seeing he come down tale foremust, I got my shooting iron to be ready for him. But he kinder seemed to got enough of my company, and went off squeeling as if something ailed his hinder parts, which I thought a kind of curious; for I've no opinion of a fellow that will take a kick; much less such usage as I give him. However, I let him go; for it would be onmanly to be onthankful for the sarvis he done me, and for all I know he's alive yet. And it war not the only thing I had to thank him for, I had a touch of the toothache before, and the bite I got at his tale cured me entirely. I've never had it since, and I can recommend it to all people that has the toothache to chew two inches of a bear's tale. I'ts a sartin cure. Thar ar a wicked sight of vartue in bear's grease, as I know by my own experience.

A Kentucky Team.

Thar is sum fokes that makes much of their figgers and larning and aul sorts of inventions, and I spose when they got their steembotes and rail roads a going they thort they war going to upset the world rite off and make the sun rise by steem, and contrive a new way to maik karves grow up to be oxen in one nite; but I'll be shot if I ever wanted to use any thing better than God's critters, which he has made with legs and fins to swim. As for your steembotes and rail-road whirligigs they ar only a sapling compared to what Bartholomew Grithard did last fall. I war going out with my dog Tiger to parsecute sum of the varmints in Little Creek near yellow-leg Swamp, when I seed the waters of the Massissippy in a wuss pother than the Pukes at the election. I knowed it warn't a steembote bekase thar war no smoke, but the spray war thick enuff to make up for it. I run down by the side of the river to smell out the muss, and then I seed a alligator's head, and then his tale whisking about like a sapling in a whirlwind. But I seed that Bartholomew was rite arter the varmint in his boat, and he war going at sich a rate I knowed he would tree him befour long. Then I seed another pesky grate alligator cuting out like awl possest rite along side of the tother one. So I up with my gun to shoot, and Bartholomew hauled out to me to hold fire, for the two varmints was tackled up and harnist to his bote, and he war driving 'em down streem. That war a settler and I stood and grinned at 'em till I loosened 2 of my front teeth, and as soon as they got out o' sight, I haw hawed rite out a laffing, and I laffed for about haff an our, so woilent that the trees shed all their leeves.

A day or two arterwards, I met Bartholomew in the woods, and he telled me he hoped I would be keerful not to draw a lead on any of his critters, as he had a number what he war trying to brake for the harness. I axed him if he thort any kristian cretur could use them pesky, unsarkumsized alligators. He sed he knowed it, and then he went on to say that he had one teem as war parfectly kind in harness, and that he should put in aul he new to git a chance for to carry the male with that teem. He sed how he had sent an invite to Amoss Kindle to kum and look at his beasts, and he shood lett Mister Kindle drive 'em out a few, round about the Great Bend if he want sattisfide without doin on it. Arter a while Bartholomew found it cost a pleggy site to keep 'em, and he turned 'em out to graze, and they aul cut dirt up streem and didn't cum back at nite, the ongrateful kritters; but Bartholomew sed he shouldn't keered nothing mutch about it only for one young one that war jist cum of age, which he war trying to brake in for the saddle, so as he cood go to meeting on Sunday without using his bote.

1840

Scrape with the Indians.

I war setting in my door waiting for dinner to cool, one hot day when I heered a rustling amongst some hop vines as growed at the eend of the house. I bawled out to my wife to bring killdevil, when I seed it war nothing but a pedlar, that cum steeling around the house as if he war jelus about being seen. So when he knowed I had seen him, he walked up to where I sot. He telled me he had cum all the way from 'yond the mountains with a bundle of spektakles to sell to the injuns. I didn't like his looks very well, but I never turned a feller cretur out into the forrest, when he war hungry.—So I telled him to walk in and he should have sumthing to put in his bowels. He sallied into the house like an eel crawling into a jug. I turned my head tother way when he begun to eat, for I never liked to look at a man what I give a dinner to till he had dun. Arter he war dun eating, he tride to sell me sum of his plunder, but I didn't know the use on 'em, for that war before I had been to Kongress. He telled me they would help fokes to see. He sed I must by a duzzin pare, for the more of them you put on your ize, the further you could see. I thort he were kinder lying and kinder telling the truth. But he torked me out of my munny, and I took a passle of his spektakles. The way he didn't clear out all that night and all the next day war a caution to squatters. He lay rite down along side of my provisions and whiskey barrel like he war a famine manufacturer. I heered a noise jist about day brake one mornin, and I lookt up and seed the pedlar war jist going out the dore. I telled my wife he war gone, and she sed it were like being cured of the fever and agee; but when I got up I seed that my powder horn and shot bag war gone too. That made me so mad that I split every button off my trowsers, and I swore so hard that it like to ha' lifted the roof of the house rite off. I sallied out arter the feller. I had a smart chance of small shot in my rifle, and ment to make his rump look like a huckkleberry pudding.

I had gone a good peace thro' the forrest before noon, when I heered a noise behind me. I lookt and seed a passel of Injuns. They war a good ways off, but they war cumin rite toward the place where I sot. At last they seed me, and gave a whoop and run to where I war like a whole herd of buffaloes. I cut dirt around amongst sum bushes, and then I seed that one eend of a log was open, and the open eend war hid in the bushes. But I found the hole war very small. So I stuck my finger down my throte and threw up all the vittles that war in my bowels. But I war not small enuff yet, and I tride to think of the meanest thing that I ever did, so as I might feel small. By them means I got in a proper fix for squeezing in, but arter all it war like spiking a cannon. The injuns cum up jist as I had got in. They flew around in a blusteriferous temper when they seed I war gone, and then they sot down on the log. Jist at that moment I felt I war going to sneeze, and I war afeared if I did it would split the log rite open. By good luck I had a little tract in my pockit put out by the Anti-snuff-taking Society. I stuffed one leef of it up my nose and that hindered me from sneezing.

At last the red skin varmints jumped up, and sed they must cross the river that war close by. "We'll roll this log down," says they, "and we'll cross over on the log." I war jist a goin to speak up and tell 'em that wood be very foolish, but I altered my mind and laid still. I felt the log begin to move, and my hair wood have stood strait up only thar want room enuff in the log for it to move. They snaked the log out from amongst the bushes, and begun to roll it down towards the river. I drawed up my feet all I could, for if the injuns had knowed what sort of bart thar war in that stick they wood hav bored it out without a skrew augur. When they got down enymost to the river I felt mighty pertiklar. I seed that if I got into the river, the log must do all the swimming, for thar war no room for me to strike out. Besides I knowed that when I and the log got wet, I should swell, so thar would be no gitting out for I war wedged pritty tight already. At last I konkluded to stand up to my lick log, salt or no salt, if it war only for to cheet the cussed varmints out of my scalp. So they rolled the log into the water. I held my breth till they had shoved off a little ways, and then begun to hitch out feet foremost. I got out and seed the injuns war all straddle of the log, and paddling as fast as they could, with their back towards me. I knowed if I struck out for the shore they would heer me and turn their heads, so I jist rolled the log over fust, and then swum for the land. As soon as I got up on the shore, I seed the injuns coming one arter the other. I put some dry powder into my pan, and telled them I wood shoot the fust injun as clapped his foot on the land. So they stopt and begun to dispute which should come ashore fust. They telled me if I wood cut off my skalp and fling it to them, thar should be no further harm done. That made me so mad I war afeared the shot in my rifle would melt and run out the muzzle. They didn't like to back out for fear of being called squaws when they got to their camp. At last one of 'em said he knowed me—that I wore a wig and hadn't got no skalp, and so the pesky cowards swam off.

The Yankee's Bar Room.

Come next September it's two year since a sawney chap named Nicholas Barney hauled his ugly corpse into our parts and set up a shop at the head of Musquash Swamp for to sell out liquor. Some fokes said that he used to go to see his neighbors and get well treated and carry off liquor to put into his bottles. Howsomever his horn tumblers war so little that when a hunter got hot with the chase and called on him for a glass, it would all vapurate with the heat of his breath before he could get it to his mouth. Such a varmint as that, war never seen in our clearing before. Nobody else had ever thought of selling whiskey, bekase it is the staff of life. Some of us wanted to clear him out, but he talked so fair about it, we couldn't find it no ways possible to give a reason, only we knew we hated the pesky cretur worse than a bed-blanket full of thunder bolts pickled down with three or four lengths of chain lightning. He war the queerest looking cretur that ever I seed. His face was so ugly that he never dast to look at any one for fear of losing their custom, and his ears was set so far back on his head that he could hear what war said behind his back better than what war said before his face. There war a squatter named Benjamin Kitchen that come into our parts, and he was haff a Yankee himself. So whenever he bought a glass of liquor, he got Nicholas to chalk it down till he had a score as long as a young saplin. The Yankee was most onscruplows amorous arter money, but somehow he trusted Ben from the top of the door clear down to the bottom of it. The chork marks war as thick as swallows in Spring. But when pay day come, all of a sudden the Yankee found the score gone. He ript and swore like a devil headed up and rolled down hill in a empty whiskey cask. Ben telled him to show him his account, and then he would pay it. But it was all rubbed off the board as clean as a licked platter, and so there was nothing to pay. No human cretur had been that way, and so the feller begun to conclude the chork had fell of itself. Mebby he thought the account had got to be so heavy that it's own weight made it fall off. Howsomever he thought he would watch next time. Ben's account begun to run up agin, and Barney kept an eye on the board. Ben had an old cow that used to feed about in them parts; and he seed her come straggling along one arternoon, and smelling about as if she had lost something. He had often seen her there before, and so he didn't take much notiss till she got up pritty close to his shantee. Then he looked rite at her: and what should the old cretur do but go strait up to the chork marks and begin licking them off with her tongue. Barney flew out of the winder and cotched her by the tale as rantankerous as a domestic sea sarpint; and then Ben Kitchen come staving up and axed him what he was doing with his cow. He then seed into it all, for the cow had ben driv up that way by Ben on proppus, and had been teached to lick down scores from a calf up. They had a hot dispute about it, that wouldn't hav ben settled till this day, only they agreed to leave it to two good men. As I had ben to Congress, Barney chose me, and Kitchen chose a puke named Ephraim Grizzel.

When the peeple heered that Ephraim and me

[See page 33.]

1840. 9th Month, SEPTEMBER, begins on Tuesday. Hath 30 Days, and is the 1st Fall Month.

Phases of the Moon.

☽ First Quarter, 3d, 5h. 31m. Evening.
○ Full Moon, 11th, 2h. 43m. Evening.
☾ Last Quarter, 18th, 0h. 30m. Evening.
● New Moon, 25th, 1h. 27m. Evening.

Astronomical Calculations, embracing the whole Union, and the Canadas, beginning at the following points:

D W	ASPECTS, &c.	Sun's Dec.	Sun Fast	Moon South	☽ S	Boston. D. M.	Sun Rises	Sun Sets.	Days' L'gth	Moon Sets.	High water.
T	☌ ☽ & ♃. ☿ greatest	8 11	0 14	4 6	♏	1	5 30	6 30	13 0	8 46	2 17
W	*Fetters* [elongation.	7 49	0 33	4 55	♏	2	5 31	6 29	12 58	9 20	3 3
T	*of gold are still fet-*	7 27	0 52	5 45	♐	3	5 32	6 28	12 56	10 1	3 59
F	☽ Apogee. ☌ ☽ & ♄	7 5	1 12	6 37	♐	4	5 34	6 26	12 52	10 49	5 4
S	Very l. tid. ☿ in per	6 42	1 32	7 29	♐	5	5 35	6 25	12 50	11 46	6 22
D	12th Sun. af. Trin.	6 20	1 52	8 19	♑	**D**	5 37	6 24	12 48	morn	7 38
M	□ ♄ & ☉. *ters, and*	5 58	2 12	9 9	♑	7	5 38	6 22	12 44	0 47	8 40
T	*silken cords pinch.*	5 35	2 32	10 0	♒	8	5 39	6 21	12 42	1 55	9 31
W	*Every man is the ar-*	5 12	2 53	10 44	♒	9	5 41	6 19	12 38	3 6	10 8
T	☍ ♅ & ☉. *chitect of*	4 50	3 13	11 29	♓	10	5 42	6 18	12 36	4 13	10 41
F	☌ ☽ & ♅. *his own*	4 27	3 34	morn	♓	11	5 44	6 16	12 32	rises	11 15
S	High Tides. *fortune.*	4 4	3 55	0 14	♓	12	5 45	6 15	12 30	6 31	11 51
D	13th Sun. aft. Trin.	3 41	4 16	1 1	♈	**D**	5 47	6 13	12 26	6 53	morn
M	*Every one basts the*	3 18	4 37	1 48	♈	14	5 48	6 12	12 24	7 20	0 23
T	*fat hog, while the*	2 55	4 58	2 40	♉	15	5 49	6 11	12 22	7 52	1 1
W	☌ ☽ & 7 ✶s. *lean*	2 32	5 20	3 35	♉	16	5 51	6 9	12 18	8 32	1 42
T	☽ Perigee. *one burns*	2 8	5 41	4 35	♊	17	5 52	6 8	12 16	9 24	2 35
F	*Speak well of your*	1 45	6 2	5 38	♊	18	5 54	6 6	12 12	10 26	3 42
S	Low Tides. *friend;*	1 22	6 23	6 42	♋	19	5 55	6 5	12 10	11 38	5 5
D	14th Sun. aft. Trin.	0 58	6 44	7 43	♋	**D**	5 56	6 4	12 8	morn	6 40
M	*of* [nal Equinox.	0 35	7 5	8 40	♋	21	5 58	6 2	12 4	0 56	8 4
T	☉ enters ♎. Autum-	0 12	7 26	9 32	♌	22	5 59	6 1	12 2	2 12	9 0
W	*your enemy say noth-*	0 12	7 46	10 20	♌	23	6 1	5 59	11 58	3 25	9 47
T	*ing. Set not too high*	0 35	8 7	11 8	♍	24	6 2	5 58	11 56	4 38	10 26
F	☌ ☽ & ☿. *a value on*	0 59	8 27	11 52	♍	25	6 4	5 56	11 52	sets.	10 58
S	H. Tid. ☿ in Su ☌ ☉	1 22	8 48	aft 36	♍	26	6 5	5 55	11 50	6 6	11 32
D	15th Sun. aft. Trin.	1 46	9 8	1 21	♎	**D**	6 7	5 53	11 46	6 26	aft 5
M	*your own* [☌ ☽ & ♀.	2 9	9 27	2 7	♎	28	6 8	5 52	11 44	6 55	0 41
T	☌ ☽ & ♃. *abilities.*	2 32	9 47	2 55	♏	29	6 9	5 51	11 42	7 26	1 17
W	*If you wish a thing*	2 56	10 6	3 45	♏	30	6 11	5 49	11 38	8 4	2 0
	done go: if not send.										

New York. D. M.	Sun Rises	Sun Sets.	Days' L'gth	Moon Sets.	High water.	Washington. Sun Rises	Sun Sets.	Days' L'gth	Moon Sets.
1	5 32	6 28	12 56	8 51	11 47	5 33	6 27	12 54	8 56
2	5 33	6 27	12 54	9 26	aft 33	5 34	6 26	12 52	9 32
3	5 34	6 26	12 52	10 8	1 29	5 36	6 24	12 48	10 15
4	5 36	6 24	12 48	10 56	2 34	5 37	6 23	12 46	11 3
5	5 37	6 23	12 46	11 53	3 52	5 38	6 22	12 44	morn
D	5 38	6 22	12 44	morn	5 8	5 39	6 21	12 42	0 0
7	5 40	6 20	12 40	0 53	6 10	5 41	6 19	12 38	0 59
8	5 41	6 19	12 38	2 0	7 1	5 42	6 18	12 36	2 5
9	5 42	6 18	12 36	3 10	7 38	5 43	6 17	12 34	3 14
10	5 43	6 17	12 34	4 15	8 11	5 44	6 16	12 32	4 17
11	5 45	6 15	12 30	rises	8 45	5 46	6 14	12 28	rises
12	5 46	6 14	12 28	6 32	9 21	5 47	6 13	12 26	6 33
D	5 47	6 13	12 26	6 55	9 53	5 48	6 12	12 24	6 57
14	5 49	6 11	12 22	24	10 31	5 50	6 10	12 20	7 28
15	5 50	6 10	12 20	57	11 12	5 51	6 9	12 18	8 2
16	5 51	6 9	12 18	38	morn	5 52	6 8	12 16	8 44
17	5 53	6 7	12 14	31	0 5	5 53	6 7	12 14	9 38
18	5 54	6 6	12 12	33	1 12	5 54	6 6	12 12	10 40
19	5 55	6 5	12 10	44	2 35	5 56	6 4	12 8	11 50
D	5 57	6 3	12 6	morn	4 10	5 57	6 3	12 6	morn
21	5 58	6 2	12 4	1 1	5 34	5 58	6 2	12 4	1 6
22	5 59	6 1	12 2	16	6 30	6 0	6 0	12 0	2 20
23	6 1	5 59	11 58	28	7 17	6 1	5 59	11 58	3 31
24	6 2	5 58	11 56	4 39	7 56	6 2	5 58	11 56	4 40
25	6 3	5 57	11 54	sets.	8 28	6 3	5 57	11 54	sets.
26	6 4	5 56	11 52	6 9	9 2	6 4	5 56	11 52	6 12
D	6 6	5 54	11 48	6 30	9 35	6 6	5 54	11 48	6 34
28	6 7	5 53	11 46	7 0	10 11	6 7	5 53	11 46	7 5
29	6 9	5 51	11 42	7 32	10 47	6 8	5 52	11 44	7 38
30	6 11	5 49	11 38	8 11	11 30	6 9	5 51	11 42	8 18

Charleston. D M.	Sun Rises	Sun Sets.	Days' L'gth	Moon Sets	High water	New Orleans. Sun Rises	Sun Sets	Days' L'gth	Moon Sets.
1	5 39	6 21	12 42	9 12	10 17	5 41	6 19	12 38	9 21
2	5 40	6 20	12 40	9 51	11 3	5 42	6 18	12 36	10 2
3	5 41	6 19	12 38	10 38	11 59	5 43	6 17	12 34	10 50
4	5 42	6 18	12 36	11 26	1 4	5 44	6 16	12 32	11 38
5	5 43	6 17	12 34	morn	2 22	5 45	6 15	12 30	morn
D	5 44	6 16	12 32	0 23	3 38	5 46	6 14	12 28	0 35
7	5 45	6 15	12 30	1 18	4 40	5 47	6 13	12 26	1 29
8	5 46	6 14	12 28	2 21	5 31	5 47	6 13	12 26	2 30
9	5 47	6 13	12 26	3 26	6 8	5 48	6 12	12 24	3 34
10	5 48	6 12	12 24	4 24	6 41	5 49	6 11	12 22	4 28
11	5 49	6 11	12 22	rises	7 15	5 50	6 10	12 20	rises.
12	5 50	6 10	12 20	6 36	7 51	5 51	6 9	12 18	6 38
D	5 51	6 9	12 18	7 3	8 23	5 52	6 8	12 16	7 7
14	5 52	6 8	12 16	7 41	9 1	5 53	6 7	12 14	7 48
15	5 53	6 7	12 14	8 18	9 42	5 53	6 7	12 14	8 27
16	5 54	6 6	12 12	9 3	10 35	5 54	6 6	12 12	9 14
17	5 55	6 5	12 10	19 1	11 42	5 55	6 5	12 10	10 13
18	5 56	6 4	12 8	11 3	morn	5 56	6 4	12 8	11 15
19	5 56	6 4	12 8	morn	1 5	5 57	6 3	12 6	morn
D	5 57	6 3	12 6	0 9	2 40	5 58	6 2	12 4	0 20
21	5 59	6 1	12 2	1 22	4 4	5 59	6 1	12 2	1 31
22	6 0	6 0	12 0	2 32	5 0	6 0	6 0	12 0	2 40
23	6 1	5 59	11 58	3 40	5 47	6 1	5 59	11 58	3 46
24	6 2	5 58	11 56	4 44	6 26	6 1	5 59	11 58	4 48
25	6 3	5 57	11 54	sets.	6 58	6 2	5 58	11 56	sets.
26	6 4	5 56	11 52	6 22	7 32	6 3	5 57	11 54	6 27
D	6 5	5 55	11 50	6 47	8 5	6 4	5 56	11 52	6 54
28	6 6	5 54	11 48	7 21	8 41	6 5	5 55	11 50	7 30
29	6 7	5 53	11 46	7 57	9 17	6 6	5 54	11 48	8 8
30	6 8	5 52	11 44	8 41	10 0	6 7	5 53	11 46	8 53

1840. Tenth Month, OCTOBER, begins on Thursday. Hath 31 Days, and is the 2d Fall Month.

Phases of the Moon.

☽ First Quarter, 3d. 11h. 41m. Morning.
○ Full Moon, 11th, 2h. 20m. Morning.
☾ Last Quarter, 17th, 7h. 5m. Evening.
● New Moon, 25th, 4h. 7m. Morning.

Astronomical Calculations, embracing the whole Union, and the Canadas, beginning at the following points:

D W	ASPECTS, &c.	Sun's Dec.	Sun Fast.	Moon South	☽ ♉
T	☌☽&♄. ☽ Apogee.	3 19	19 25	4 36	♐
F	*They that drive a-*	3 42	10 44	5 29	♐
S	*way time, spur a free*	4 6	11 3	6 20	♑
D	16th Sund.aft.Trin.	4 29	11 21	7 10	♑
M	Low Tides. *horse.*	4 52	11 39	7 58	♒
T	*Honesty is the best*	5 15	11 56	8 44	♒
W	*policy. Ask thy purse*	5 38	12 13	9 29	♒
T	☌ ☽ & ♅. *what*	6 1	12 30	10 14	♓
F	*thou shalt buy. Im-*	6 24	12 46	11 0	♓
S	*prove the wit you*	6 47	13 2	11 48	♈
D	17th Sund. aft.Trin.	7 9	13 17	mor.	♈
M	Very High Tides.	7 32	13 32	0 39	♉
T	☌☽&7✶s. ☽ Per.	7 54	13 46	1 35	♉
W	*have bought at a*	8 17	14 0	2 35	♊
T	♀ in ☋. *dear rate,*	8 39	14 13	3 39	♊
F	*and the wisdom you*	9 1	14 26	4 42	♋
S	*have gained by sad*	9 23	14 38	5 44	♋
D	18th Sund. aft. Trin.	9 45	14 49	6 44	♌
M	Low Tides. *expe-*	10 7	15 0	7 37	♌
T	☌ ☽ & ♂. *rience.*	10 28	15 10	8 25	♌
W	*Ignorance gives an*	10 50	15 20	9 11	♍
T	☌ ♀ & ♃. *eter-*	11 11	15 29	9 56	♍
F	*nity to prejudice, and*	11 32	15 37	10 39	♎
S	*a per-* [☌ ☽ & ☿.	11 53	15 44	11 23	♎
D	19th Sund.aft.Trin.	12 14	15 51	aft. 8	♏
M	☌ ☽ ☿ & ♃.	12 35	15 57	0 55	♏
T	Com. Tid. ☌♀&☽.	12 55	16 2	1 44	♏
W	*petuity* [☾ Apogee	13 15	16 6	2 34	♐
T	☌☽&♄. ☌☿&♃.	13 35	16 10	3 25	♐
F	*to error. Temperance*	13 55	16 13	4 16	♑
S	*is the best physic.*	14 14	16 15	5 6	♑

Boston.

D M.	Sun Rises	Sun Sets.	Days' L'gth	Moon Sets.	High water.
1	6 12	5 48	11 36	8 49	2 58
2	6 14	5 46	11 32	9 44	3 41
3	6 15	5 45	11 30	10 44	4 41
D	6 17	5 43	11 26	11 48	5 50
5	6 18	5 42	11 24	mor.	7 7
6	6 19	5 41	11 22	0 55	8 11
7	6 20	5 40	11 20	2 2	8 59
8	6 22	5 38	11 16	3 11	9 44
9	6 23	5 37	11 14	4 20	10 23
10	6 25	5 35	11 10	5 30	10 56
D	6 26	5 34	11 8	rise.	11 33
12	6 28	5 32	11 4	6 1	mor.
13	6 29	5 31	11 2	6 38	0 11
14	6 31	5 29	10 58	7 28	0 55
15	6 32	5 28	10 56	8 26	1 43
16	6 33	5 27	10 54	9 37	2 39
17	6 34	5 26	10 52	10 54	3 47
D	6 36	5 24	10 48	mor.	5 6
19	6 38	5 22	10 44	0 10	6 31
20	6 39	5 21	10 42	1 22	7 44
21	6 41	5 19	10 38	2 34	8 40
22	6 42	5 18	10 36	3 43	9 26
23	6 43	5 17	10 34	4 51	10 4
24	6 45	5 15	10 30	5 59	10 38
D	6 46	5 14	10 28	sets.	11 11
26	6 47	5 13	10 26	5 32	11 45
27	6 49	5 11	10 22	6 8	a 23
28	6 50	5 10	10 20	6 50	1 1
29	6 51	5 9	10 18	7 39	1 43
30	6 53	5 7	10 14	8 36	2 33
31	6 54	5 6	10 12	9 39	3 16

New York.

D. M.	Sun Rises	Sun Sets.	Days' L'gth	Moon Sets.	High water
1	6 12	5 48	11 36	8 56	a 28
2	6 13	5 47	11 34	9 51	1 11
3	6 14	5 46	11 32	10 50	2 11
D	6 16	5 44	11 28	11 53	3 20
5	6 17	5 43	11 26	morn	4 37
6	6 18	5 42	11 24	0 59	5 41
7	6 19	5 41	11 22	2 5	6 29
8	6 21	5 39	11 18	3 13	7 14
9	6 22	5 38	11 16	4 20	7 53
10	6 24	5 36	11 12	5 29	8 26
D	6 25	5 35	11 10	rises	9 3
12	6 26	5 34	11 8	6 6	9 41
13	6 28	5 32	11 4	6 44	10 25
14	6 29	5 31	11 2	7 35	11 13
15	6 30	5 30	11 0	8 33	morn
16	6 31	5 29	10 58	9 43	0 9
17	6 33	5 27	10 54	11 0	1 17
D	6 34	5 26	10 52	morn	2 36
19	6 35	5 25	10 50	0 14	4 1
20	6 37	5 23	10 46	1 25	5 14
21	6 38	5 22	10 44	2 36	6 10
22	6 39	5 21	10 42	3 43	6 56
23	6 40	5 20	10 40	4 50	7 34
24	6 42	5 18	10 36	5 56	8 8
D	6 43	5 17	10 34	sets.	8 41
26	6 44	5 16	10 32	5 37	9 15
27	6 46	5 14	10 28	6 14	9 53
28	6 47	5 13	10 26	6 57	10 31
29	6 48	5 12	10 24	7 46	11 13
30	6 49	5 11	10 22	8 42	aft. 3
31	6 51	5 9	10 18	9 45	0 46

Washington.

Sun Rises	Sun Sets.	Days' L'gth	Moon Sets.
6 11	5 49	11 38	9 3
6 12	5 48	11 36	9 58
6 13	5 47	11 34	10 56
6 15	5 45	11 30	11 58
6 16	5 44	11 28	morn
6 17	5 43	11 26	1 3
6 18	5 42	11 24	2 8
6 19	5 41	11 22	3 15
6 21	5 39	11 18	4 20
6 22	5 38	11 16	5 29
6 23	5 37	11 14	rises
6 25	5 35	11 10	6 11
6 26	5 34	11 8	6 50
6 27	5 33	11 6	7 42
6 28	5 32	11 4	8 40
6 29	5 31	11 2	9 49
6 31	5 29	10 58	11 4
6 32	5 28	10 56	morn
6 33	5 27	10 54	0 18
6 34	5 23	10 46	1 28
6 36	5 24	10 48	2 38
6 37	5 23	10 46	3 43
6 38	5 22	10 44	4 49
6 39	5 21	10 42	5 53
6 40	5 20	10 40	sets.
6 42	5 18	10 36	5 42
6 43	5 17	10 34	6 20
6 44	5 16	10 32	7 4
6 45	5 15	10 30	7 53
6 46	5 14	10 28	8 48
6 47	5 13	10 26	9 51

Charleston.

D M.	Sun Rises	Sun Sets.	Days' L'gth	Moon Sets	High water
1	6 9	5 51	11 42	9 26	10 58
2	6 10	5 50	11 40	10 21	11 41
3	6 11	5 49	11 38	11 15	aft 41
D	6 12	5 48	11 36	morn	1 50
5	6 13	5 47	11 34	0 13	3 7
6	6 14	5 46	11 32	1 15	4 11
7	6 15	5 45	11 30	2 17	4 59
8	6 16	5 44	11 28	3 21	5 44
9	6 17	5 43	11 26	4 20	6 23
10	6 18	5 42	11 24	5 25	6 56
D	6 19	5 41	11 22	rises	7 33
12	6 20	5 40	11 20	6 27	8 11
13	6 21	5 39	11 18	7 9	8 55
14	6 22	5 38	11 16	8 5	9 43
15	6 23	5 37	11 14	9 3	10 39
16	6 24	5 36	11 12	10 8	11 47
17	6 25	5 35	11 10	11 19	morn
D	6 26	5 34	11 8	morn	1 6
19	6 27	5 33	11 6	0 30	2 31
20	6 28	5 32	11 4	1 37	3 44
21	6 29	5 31	11 2	2 42	4 40
22	6 29	5 31	11 2	3 43	5 26
23	6 30	5 30	11 0	4 46	6 4
24	6 31	5 29	10 58	5 44	6 38
D	6 32	5 28	10 56	sets.	7 11
26	6 33	5 27	10 54	5 57	7 45
27	6 34	5 26	10 52	6 39	8 23
28	6 35	5 25	10 50	7 26	9 1
29	6 36	5 24	10 48	8 15	9 43
30	6 37	5 23	10 46	9 7	10 33
31	6 38	5 22	10 44	10 10	11 16

New Orleans.

Sun Rises	Sun Sets.	Days' L'gth	Moon Sets.
6 8	5 52	11 44	9 38
6 9	5 51	11 42	10 33
6 10	5 50	11 40	11 26
6 10	5 50	11 40	morn
6 11	5 49	11 38	0 23
6 12	5 48	11 36	1 23
6 13	5 47	11 34	2 23
6 14	5 46	11 32	3 21
6 15	5 45	11 30	4 20
6 16	5 44	11 28	5 20
6 17	5 43	11 26	rises
6 17	5 43	11 26	6 36
6 18	5 42	11 24	7 20
6 19	5 41	11 22	8 17
6 20	5 40	11 20	9 15
6 21	5 39	11 18	10 18
6 22	5 38	11 16	11 28
6 23	5 37	11 14	morn
6 24	5 36	11 12	0 38
6 25	5 35	11 10	1 43
6 25	5 35	11 10	2 46
6 26	5 34	11 8	3 43
6 27	5 33	11 6	4 42
6 28	5 32	11 4	5 38
6 28	5 32	11 4	sets.
6 30	5 30	11 0	6 7
6 30	5 30	11 0	6 50
6 31	5 29	10 58	7 39
6 32	5 28	10 56	8 29
6 33	5 27	10 54	9 18
6 34	5 26	10 52	10 21

The Heroine of Kaintuck.....See Page 20.

The Yankee's Bar Room....continued from page 29.

war to arbitrate the thing, there was a grate coming together of the naburs, to see which would hang fire fust. Not knowing what might happen I took my big knife and rifle with me, and cut out for the place where we war to have the talking match. It was on the top of a grate hill. I stood in the hollow of one stump, and Grizzle stood in another. Grizzle took a running start and begun, says he, "It's no use in talking. D'ye see, who ever heered of selling whisky in these parts before. I wouldn't do it to an injun. Mr. Kitchen's cow licked off the marks—well licking off them is not so bad as licking a man any how you can fix it. I've been licked myself, and never said a word about it except when I lost my left ear. I say that Mr. Barney desarves to be rode on a rail, for complaining agin a dumb beast. The cow was more reasonable than some human creturs, and knowed it want right to sell whiskey in the forrest."

Says I, "have you shut pan?" and he said how he was. So I took in breath and let down upon him. Says I, "Its worser to mislead a dumb cretur and larn it to do wrong, than it is to do it yourself. If your client had licked the varmint instead of teeching his cow to lick the chalk marks, I wouldn't have said a word. Fair play is fair play, and your friend is a skunk." He grit his teeth at me, and poked out his tongue about six inches. With that I telled him I was a pick-axe and would dig him out of his stump. He said he was a flint image cut out of a big rock. I telled him my gizzard was a wasp's nest and I breathed rifle balls. He said he could double up a streak o' lightening and thrash me with one eend of it. Then I was pesky oneasy and spit at him so hard that if he hadn't dodged it, he'd have had his nose knocked flat. He came to me feet foremost, and I caught his great toe in my mouth, but the nail came off very lucky for him, and he got his toe back again. But while he was bringing his foot to the ground, I caught the slack of his breeches in my teeth and lifted him up in the air, swinging like a scale beam, as if he didn't know which eend it was best to light on. But his trowsers tore through in a minnit, and he come doun sprawling. He jumped up speechless, and looked round as amazed as if he war just born into the world. He seed I war jist reddy to lay my paw on him agin, and his skin crawled. He turned as pale as a scalded nigger, and telled the peeple that was looking on how they had better interfere as he wus afraid he should be the death of me, if we cum to the scratch agin. I telled the lying sarpint to own he war chawed up, or I would make fiddle-strings of his tripe. So he squat low and felt mean. He sneaked off like an injun in a clearing. So the Yankee cum up and give me joy. Says I, "I tell you what stranger. I've got your case for you bekase I was axed to take up your cause, and I never refuses to do a favor to a man what aint able to stand up to his own lick log. But now I tell you as a friend, and my name is Davy Crockett, that you had better make tracks out of this clearing as fast as dry dust in a thunder squall, for I only pled your case bekase the other varmint was a streak or two meaner than you; but you are mean enough to put the sun in eclipse." That was the last that was seen of him in them parts

1840. Eleventh Month, NOVEMBER, begins on Sunday. Hath 30 Days, and is the 3d Fall Month.

Phases of the Moon.

☽ First Quarter, 2d. 8h. 12m. Morning.
○ Full Moon, 9th, 1h. 0m. Evening.
☾ Last Quarter, 16th, 3h. 59m. Morning.
● New Moon, 23d, 9h. 17m. Evening.

Astronomical Calculations, embracing the whole Union, and the Canadas, beginning at the following points:

						Boston.						New York.						Washington.				Charleston.						New Orleans.			
D W	ASPECTS, &c.	Sun's Dec.	Sun Fast.	Moon South	☽ S	D. M.	Sun Rises	Sun Sets.	Days' L'gth	Moon Sets.	High water.	D. M.	Sun Rises	Sun Sets.	Days' L'gth	Moon Sets.	High water.	Sun Rises	Sun Sets.	Days' L'gth	Moon Sets.	D. M.	Sun Rises	Sun Sets.	Days' L'gth	Moon Sets.	High water	Sun Rises	Sun Sets	Days' L'gth	Moon Sets.
D	20th Sund. aft. Trin	14 34	16 17	5 54	♑	D	6 55	5 5	10 10	10 46	4 9	D	6 52	5 8	10 16	10 51	1 39	6 48	5 12	10 24	10 56	D	6 39	5 21	10 42	11 12	aft. 9	6 35	5 25	10 50	11 21
M	*Consideration is due*	14 53	16 17	6 40	♒	2	6 57	5 3	10 6	11 50	5 7	2	6 53	5 7	10 14	11 54	2 37	6 49	5 11	10 22	11 58	2	6 40	5 20	10 40	morn	1 7	6 35	5 25	10 50	morn
T	Low Tides. *to all*	15 11	16 17	7 24	♒	3	6 58	5 2	10 4	morn	6 12	3	6 54	5 6	10 12	morn	3 42	6 50	5 10	10 20	morn	3	6 41	5 19	10 38	0 11	2 12	6 30	5 24	10 48	0 18
W	*things. No man ever*	15 30	16 16	8 8	♓	4	6 59	5 1	10 2	0 55	7 20	4	6 55	5 5	10 10	0 58	4 50	6 52	5 8	10 16	1 1	4	6 41	5 19	10 38	1 10	3 20	6 37	5 23	10 46	1 16
T	☌ ♅ & ☽. *offended*	15 48	16 14	8 52	♓	5	7 0	5 0	10 0	2 3	8 21	5	6 57	5 3	10 6	2 4	5 51	6 53	5 7	10 14	2 4	5	6 42	5 18	10 36	2 9	4 21	6 38	5 22	10 44	2 10
F	*his own conscience,*	16 6	16 12	9 38	♈	6	7 1	4 59	9 58	3 10	9 7	6	6 58	5 2	10 4	3 10	6 37	6 54	5 6	10 12	3 10	6	6 43	5 17	10 34	3 10	5 7	6 38	5 22	10 44	3 8
S	*but first or last it*	16 24	16 8	10 27	♈	7	7 3	4 57	9 54	4 22	9 52	7	6 59	5 1	10 2	4 20	7 22	6 55	5 5	10 10	4 18	7	6 44	5 16	10 32	4 12	5 52	6 39	5 21	10 42	4 8
D	21st Sund. aft. Trin	16 42	16 4	11 21	♈	D	7 4	4 56	9 52	5 38	10 35	D	7 0	5 0	10 0	5 35	8 5	6 56	5 4	10 8	5 32	D	6 45	5 15	10 30	5 22	6 35	6 40	5 20	10 40	5 13
M	☌ ☽ & 7 ✱ s.	16 59	15 59	morn	♉	9	7 5	4 55	9 50	rises	11 20	9	7 1	4 59	9 58	rises	8 50	6 57	5 3	10 6	rises	9	6 46	5 14	10 28	rises	7 20	6 41	5 19	10 38	rises
T	Very High Tides.	17 16	15 53	0 21	♉	10	7 6	4 54	9 48	5 19	morn	10	7 2	4 58	9 56	5 25	9 37	6 58	5 2	10 4	5 31	10	6 46	5 14	10 28	5 50	8 7	6 41	5 19	10 38	6 1
W	☽ Perigee. *was re-*	17 33	15 46	1 26	♊	11	7 7	4 53	9 46	6 17	0 7	11	7 3	4 57	9 54	6 24	10 24	6 59	5 1	10 2	6 31	11	6 47	5 13	10 26	6 54	8 54	6 42	5 18	10 36	7 6
T	☿ Gr. elongation.	17 49	15 38	2 32	♊	12	7 8	4 52	9 44	7 24	0 54	12	7 4	4 56	9 52	7 31	11 13	7 0	5 0	10 0	7 38	12	6 48	5 12	10 24	8 1	9 43	6 43	5 17	10 34	8 13
F	☌ ♀ & ♄. *venged*	18 5	15 30	3 37	♋	13	7 9	4 51	9 42	8 38	1 43	13	7 5	4 55	9 50	8 44	morn	7 1	4 59	9 58	8 50	13	6 49	5 11	10 22	9 9	10 35	6 43	5 17	10 34	9 20
S	*upon him. He that*	18 21	15 21	4 38	♋	14	7 10	4 50	9 40	9 56	2 37	14	7 6	4 54	9 48	10 1	0 5	7 2	4 58	9 56	10 6	14	6 50	5 10	10 20	10 22	11 35	6 44	5 16	10 32	10 31
D	22d Sund. aft. Trin.	18 36	15 10	5 33	♌	D	7 11	4 49	9 38	11 14	3 35	D	7 7	4 53	9 46	11 17	1 5	7 3	4 57	9 54	11 20	D	6 51	5 9	10 18	11 30	morn	6 45	5 15	10 30	11 39
M	*knows how to speak,*	18 51	14 59	6 24	♌	16	7 12	4 48	9 36	morn	4 42	16	7 8	4 52	9 44	morn	2 12	7 4	4 56	9 52	morn	16	6 52	5 8	10 16	morn	0 42	6 45	5 15	10 30	morn
T	Low Tides. *knows*	19 6	14 47	7 10	♍	17	7 13	4 47	9 34	0 26	5 49	17	7 9	4 51	9 42	0 28	3 19	7 5	4 55	9 50	0 30	17	6 52	5 8	10 16	0 36	1 49	6 46	5 14	10 28	0 40
W	☌ ♂ & ☽. *also*	19 20	14 34	7 54	♍	18	7 14	4 46	9 32	1 35	6 59	18	7 10	4 50	9 40	1 35	4 29	7 6	4 54	9 48	1 35	18	6 53	5 7	10 14	1 37	2 59	6 47	5 13	10 26	1 38
T	*when to be silent.*	19 34	14 21	8 37	♎	19	7 15	4 45	9 30	2 42	8 3	19	7 11	4 49	9 38	2 41	5 33	7 7	4 53	9 46	2 40	19	6 53	5 7	10 14	2 37	3 3	6 47	5 13	10 26	2 35
F	*Riches, like manure,*	19 48	14 6	9 19	♎	20	7 16	4 44	9 28	3 47	8 51	20	7 12	4 48	9 36	3 45	6 21	7 8	4 52	9 44	3 43	20	6 54	5 6	10 12	3 37	3 51	6 48	5 12	10 24	3 33
S	☌ ☉ & ♃. [station.	20 1	13 51	10 3	♏	21	7 17	4 43	9 26	4 51	9 35	21	7 13	4 47	9 34	4 48	7 5	7 8	4 52	9 44	4 45	21	6 54	5 6	10 12	4 36	4 35	6 48	5 12	10 24	4 30
D	23d S. aft. Trin. ☿	20 14	13 35	10 49	♏	D	7 18	4 42	9 24	5 56	10 12	D	7 14	4 46	9 32	5 51	7 42	7 9	4 51	9 42	5 46	D	6 55	5 5	10 10	5 31	5 12	6 49	5 11	10 22	5 22
M	☌ ☽ & ♃. *do no*	20 27	13 18	11 37	♐	23	7 19	4 41	9 22	sets.	10 49	23	7 15	4 45	9 30	sets.	8 19	7 10	4 50	9 40	sets.	23	6 56	5 4	10 8	sets.	6 49	6 50	5 10	10 20	sets.
T	Higher Tides. *good*	20 39	13 0	aft 26	♐	24	7 20	4 40	9 20	4 45	11 24	24	7 16	4 44	9 28	4 50	8 54	7 11	4 49	9 38	4 59	24	6 56	5 4	10 8	5 22	7 24	6 50	5 10	10 20	5 34
W	☌ ☽ ☿ & ♄ ♅ station	20 51	12 42	1 16	♑	25	7 21	4 39	9 18	5 31	aft 2	25	7 17	4 43	9 26	5 38	9 32	7 13	4 48	9 36	5 45	25	6 57	5 3	10 6	6 8	8 2	6 51	5 9	10 18	6 20
T	☽ Apogee ☌ ☽ & ♀.	21 2	12 23	2 7	♑	26	7 22	4 38	9 16	6 25	0 42	26	7 18	4 42	9 24	6 32	10 12	7 12	4 48	9 36	6 39	26	6 58	5 2	10 4	7 2	8 42	6 51	5 9	10 18	7 14
F	*till they are spread.*	21 13	12 3	2 57	♑	27	7 23	4 37	9 14	7 25	1 19	27	7 18	4 42	9 24	7 32	10 49	7 13	4 47	9 34	7 37	27	6 58	5 2	10 4	7 56	9 19	6 52	5 8	10 16	8 7
S	*Forget others' faults*	21 24	11 42	3 45	♒	28	7 24	4 36	9 12	8 28	2 0	28	7 19	4 41	9 22	8 33	11 30	7 14	4 46	9 32	8 38	28	6 59	5 1	10 2	8 53	10 0	6 52	5 8	10 16	9 3
D	Avent Sunday. *by*	21 34	11 21	4 30	♒	D	7 25	4 35	9 10	9 32	2 42	D	7 20	4 40	9 20	9 36	aft 12	7 14	4 46	9 32	9 40	D	6 59	5 1	10 2	9 52	10 42	6 53	5 7	10 14	10 0
M	*rememb'g your own.*	21 44	10 59	5 14	♓	30	7 26	4 34	9 8	10 36	3 25	30	7 21	4 39	9 18	10 39	0 55	7 15	4 45	9 30	10 42	30	7 0	5 0	10 0	10 51	11 25	6 53	5 7	10 14	10 57

1840. 12th Month, DECEMBER, begins on Tuesday. Hath 31 Days, and is the 1st Winter Month

Phases of the Moon.

☽ First Quarter, 2d. 2h. 21m. Morning.
○ Full Moon, 8th, 11h. 17m. Evening.
☾ Last Quarter, 15th, 4h. 0m. Evening.
● New Moon, 23d, 4h. 17m. Evening.
☽ First Quarter, 31st, 5h. 38 m. Evening.

Astronomical Calculations, embracing the whole Union, and the Canadas, beginning at the following points:

D W	ASPECTS, &c.	Sun's Dec.	Sun Fast	Moon South	☽ Sets	Boston. D M.	Sun Rises	Sun Sets.	Days' L'gth	Moon Sets.	High water.
T	[♅. ☿ Perihe.	21 53	10 36	5 56	♓	1	7 26	4 34	9 8	11 41	4 9
W	Inf. ☌ ☉ & ☿. ☌ ☽ &	22 2	10 13	6 38	♓	2	7 27	4 33	9 6	morn	5 3
T	Low Tides. *If you*	22 11	9 49	7 21	♈	3	7 28	4 32	9 4	0 46	6 6
F	*had fewer friends,*	22 19	9 36	8 7	♈	4	7 28	4 32	9 4	1 53	7 18
S	*and more enemies,*	22 26	9 0	8 56	♈	5	7 29	4 31	9 2	3 4	8 22
D	2nd Sunday in Adv	22 34	8 34	9 52	♉	D	7 29	4 31	9 2	4 19	9 20
M	☌ ☽ & 7 ✱ s.	22 41	8 8	10 53	♉	7	7 30	4 30	9 0	5 37	10 12
T	☉ & ♅ □. ☌ ☿ & ♃.	22 47	7 42	morn	♊	8	7 30	4 30	9 0	rises	11 5
W	☽ Perigee. *you had*	22 53	7 15	0 0	♊	9	7 30	4 30	9 0	4 52	11 53
T	Very High Tides.	22 58	6 48	1 8	♋	10	7 31	4 29	8 58	6 8	morn
F	☿ Stationary. *been*	23 3	6 20	2 14	♋	11	7 31	4 29	8 58	7 28	0 42
S	*a better man. Fools*	23 8	5 52	3 13	♌	12	7 31	4 29	8 58	8 49	1 23
D	3d Sunday in Adv.	23 12	5 23	4 8	♌	D	7 32	4 28	8 56	10 4	2 10
M	*make feasts and wise*	23 15	4 55	4 57	♍	14	7 32	4 28	8 56	11 15	2 58
T	☌ ♄ & ☉. *men*	23 19	4 26	5 42	♍	15	7 32	4 28	8 56	morn	3 48
W	L. Tides. ☌ ♂ & ☽.	23 21	3 56	6 24	♎	16	7 32	4 28	8 56	0 21	4 43
T	♂ Aphelion. *eat*	23 24	3 27	7 8	♎	17	7 32	4 28	8 56	1 27	5 47
F	☌ ☿ & ♃. *them.*	23 25	2 57	7 50	♎	18	7 32	4 28	8 56	2 33	6 53
S	*Resolution without*	23 27	2 27	8 35	♏	19	7 33	4 27	8 54	3 40	7 59
D	4th Sunday in Adv.	23 27	1 57	9 20	♏	D	7 33	4 27	8 54	4 43	8 52
M	☉ent. ♑. ☌ ☽ ♃ & ☿	23 28	1 27	10 11	♐	21	7 33	4 27	8 54	5 46	9 43
T	*action is a slothful*	23 28	0 57	11 0	♐	22	4 33	4 27	8 54	6 44	10 22
W	☽ Apogee ☌ ☽ & ♄.	23 27	F 27	11 52	♐	23	7 33	4 27	8 54	sets.	10 59
T	Higher Tides. *folly:*	23 26	S 3	a 41	♑	24	7 33	4 27	8 54	5 6	11 36
F	Christmas. *action*	23 24	0 33	1 30	♑	25	7 33	4 27	8 54	6 9	a 13
S	*without* [☌ ☽ & ♀.	23 22	1 3	2 16	♒	26	7 32	4 28	8 56	7 12	0 46
D	1st Sunday aft. Ch.	23 20	1 33	2 59	♒	D	7 32	4 28	8 56	8 15	1 21
M	*resolution is a fool-*	23 17	2 3	3 41	♒	28	7 32	4 28	8 56	9 19	2 26
T	*ish rashness. Ever*	23 13	2 32	4 23	♓	29	7 32	4 28	8 56	10 23	3 33
W	☌ ☽ & ♅. *drunk,*	23 10	3 1	5 4	♓	30	7 32	4 28	8 56	11 28	4 9
T	*ever dry.*	23 5	3 30	5 47	♈	31	7 32	4 28	8 56	morn	4 55

New York. D. M.	Sun Rises	Sun Sets.	Days' L'gth	Moon Sets.	High water	Washington. Sun Rises	Sun Sets.	Days' L'gth	Moon Sets.
1	7 21	4 39	9 18	11 42	1 39	7 15	4 45	9 30	11 43
2	7 22	4 38	9 16	morn	2 33	7 16	4 44	9 28	morn
3	7 22	4 38	9 16	0 45	3 36	7 17	4 43	9 26	0 46
4	7 23	4 37	9 14	1 50	4 48	7 17	4 43	9 26	1 51
5	7 23	4 37	9 14	3 0	5 52	7 18	4 42	9 24	2 58
D	7 24	4 36	9 12	4 14	6 50	7 18	4 42	9 24	4 11
7	7 24	4 36	9 12	5 32	7 42	7 19	4 41	9 22	5 27
8	7 25	4 35	9 10	rises	8 35	7 19	4 41	9 22	rises
9	7 25	4 35	9 10	5 0	9 23	7 20	4 40	9 20	5 6
10	7 26	4 34	9 8	6 14	10 12	7 20	4 40	9 20	6 20
11	7 26	4 34	9 8	7 33	10 53	7 20	4 40	9 20	7 38
12	7 26	4 34	9 8	8 53	11 40	7 21	4 39	9 18	8 57
D	7 26	4 34	9 8	10 7	morn	7 21	4 39	9 18	10 16
14	7 27	4 33	9 6	11 16	0 28	7 21	4 39	9 18	11 17
15	7 27	4 33	9 6	morn	1 18	7 21	4 39	9 18	morn
16	7 27	4 33	9 6	0 21	2 13	7 21	4 39	9 18	0 21
17	7 27	4 33	9 6	1 25	3 17	7 22	4 38	9 16	1 23
18	7 27	4 33	9 6	2 30	4 23	7 22	4 38	9 16	2 27
19	7 27	4 33	9 6	3 36	5 29	7 22	4 38	9 16	3 32
D	7 27	4 33	9 6	4 38	6 22	7 22	4 38	9 16	4 33
21	7 27	4 33	9 6	5 40	7 13	7 22	4 38	9 16	5 34
22	7 27	4 33	9 6	6 37	7 52	7 22	4 38	9 16	6 30
23	7 27	4 33	9 6	sets.	8 29	7 22	4 38	9 16	sets.
24	7 27	4 33	9 6	5 12	9 6	7 22	4 38	9 16	5 18
25	7 27	4 33	9 6	6 14	9 43	7 22	4 38	9 16	6 19
26	7 27	4 33	9 6	7 16	10 16	7 22	4 38	9 16	7 20
D	7 27	4 33	9 6	8 18	10 51	7 22	4 38	9 16	8 21
28	7 27	4 33	9 6	9 21	11 56	7 21	4 39	9 18	9 23
29	7 27	4 33	9 6	10 23	1 3	7 21	4 39	9 18	10 23
30	7 26	4 34	9 8	11 27	1 49	7 21	4 39	9 18	11 26
31	7 26	4 34	9 8	morn	2 25	7 21	4 39	9 18	morn

Charleston. D M.	Sun Rises	Sun Sets.	Days' L'gth	Moon Sets.	High water	New Orleans. Sun Rises	Sun Sets	Days' L'gth	Moon Sets.
1	7 0	5 0	10 0	11 46	aft. 9	6 54	5 6	10 12	11 48
2	7 1	4 59	9 58	morn	1 3	6 54	5 6	10 12	morn
3	7 1	4 59	9 58	0 46	2 6	6 55	5 5	10 10	0 46
4	7 1	4 59	9 58	1 48	3 18	6 55	5 5	10 10	1 45
5	7 2	4 58	9 56	2 50	4 22	6 55	5 5	10 10	2 45
D	7 2	4 58	9 56	4 0	5 20	6 56	5 4	10 8	3 51
7	7 2	4 58	9 56	5 12	6 12	6 56	5 4	10 8	5 2
8	7 3	4 57	9 54	rises	7 5	6 56	5 4	10 8	rises.
9	7 3	4 57	8 54	5 29	7 53	6 56	5 4	10 8	5 41
10	7 3	4 57	9 54	6 37	8 42	6 57	5 3	10 6	6 50
11	7 4	4 56	9 52	7 54	9 23	6 57	5 3	10 6	8 3
12	7 4	4 56	9 52	9 9	10 10	6 57	5 3	10 6	9 11
D	7 4	4 56	9 52	10 19	10 58	6 57	5 3	10 6	10 23
14	7 4	4 56	9 52	11 20	11 48	6 57	5 3	10 6	11 23
15	7 4	4 56	9 52	morn	morn	6 57	5 3	10 6	morn
16	7 5	4 55	9 50	0 21	0 43	6 58	5 2	10 4	0 21
17	7 5	4 55	9 50	1 17	1 47	6 58	5 2	10 4	1 15
18	7 5	4 55	9 50	2 18	2 53	6 58	5 2	10 4	2 12
19	7 5	4 55	9 50	3 20	3 59	6 58	5 2	10 4	3 12
D	7 5	4 55	9 50	4 17	4 52	6 58	5 2	10 4	4 8
21	7 5	4 55	9 50	5 15	5 43	6 58	5 2	10 4	5 4
22	7 5	4 55	9 50	6 7	6 22	6 58	5 2	10 4	5 56
23	7 5	4 55	9 50	sets.	6 59	6 58	5 2	10 4	sets.
24	7 5	4 55	9 50	5 37	7 36	6 58	5 2	10 4	5 48
25	7 5	4 55	9 50	6 34	8 13	6 58	5 2	10 4	6 40
26	7 5	4 55	9 50	7 32	8 46	6 58	5 2	10 4	7 40
D	7 5	4 55	9 50	8 30	9 21	6 58	5 2	10 4	8 36
28	7 5	4 55	9 50	9 29	10 28	6 58	5 2	10 4	9 33
29	7 4	4 56	9 52	10 23	11 33	6 57	5 3	10 6	10 26
30	7 4	4 56	9 52	11 23	aft 19	6 57	5 3	10 6	11 21
31	7 4	4 56	9 52	morn	0 55	6 57	5 3	10 6	morn

1840

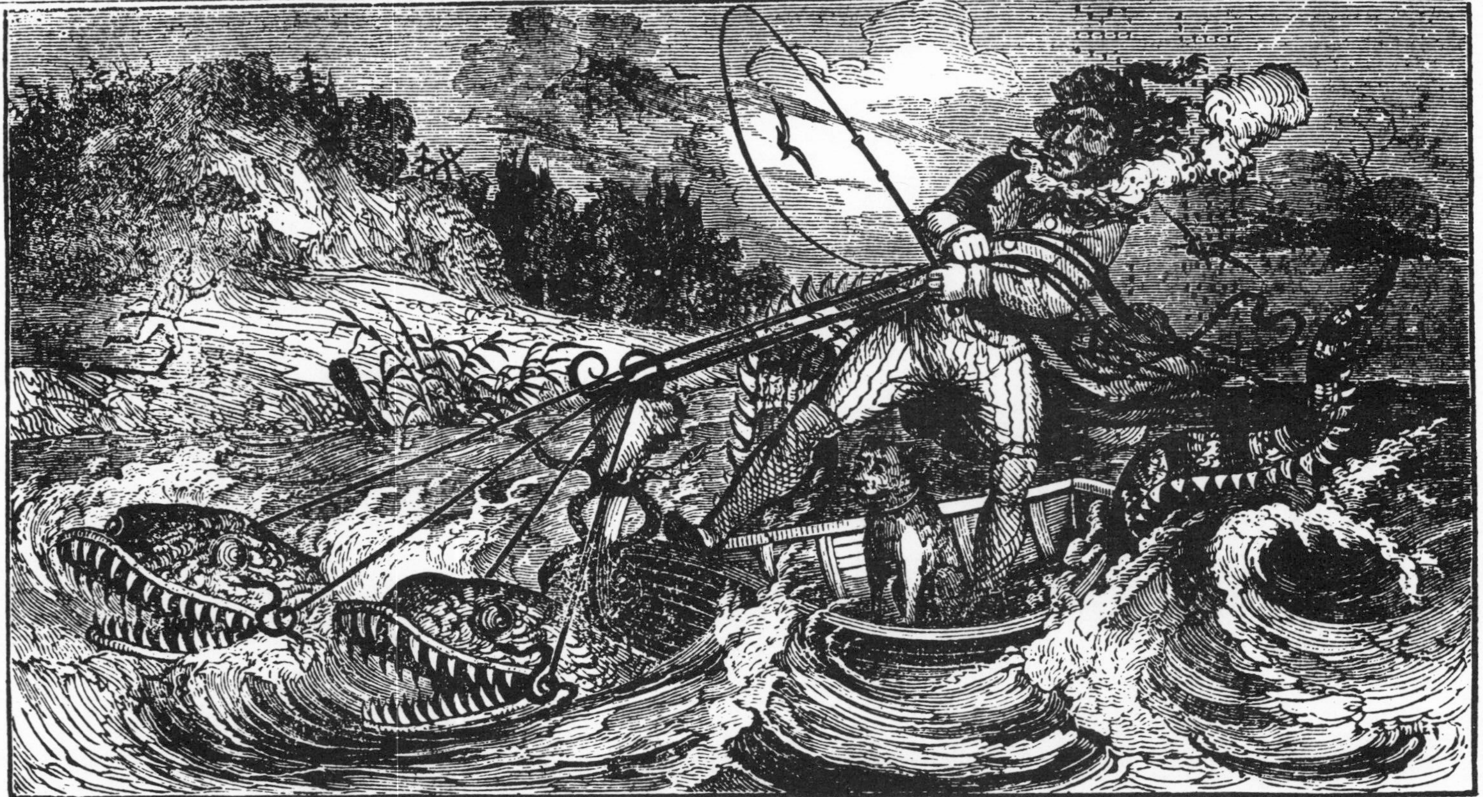

The Way they Travel in the West.....See page 28.

Vol. 2.] "GO AHEAD!!" [No. 3.

THE CROCKETT ALMANAC
1841.

Tussel with a Bear. See page 9.

Containing Adventures, Exploits, Sprees & Scrapes in the West, & Life and Manners in the Backwoods.

Nashville, Tennessee. Published by Ben Harding.

INTRODUCTION——by Ben Harding.

Having heered that my friend the Kurnill is alive, I hav sot up the Allmynack for another yeer, and thar is a plenty of rightings on hand, that haint been printed yet, and I intend to show a leg from yeer to yeer, and get out the allmyknack in onor of Kurnill Crockett. A depputashun of Kentucky chaps whose names is Oak Wing. Brush Grinner, Steven Horn, Price Beef, and Mortal Brown, all tickler friends of Crockett's, has cleared out for the mines, and expects to overhall the Kurnill, and restore him to his individdle rites in old Kaintuck, for they has been nobody fit to go to Kongress sot up for candy-dates cents he war grappled by the cussed heathens in Texias. When the Kurnill gets back, we will hav a plenty of his adventurs and scrapes among the Spaniards, and he will giv us the reeding of his log book cents he has been in the mines. Them as has seen Crocket, sez that he war very oneasy about how his allmyknack was gitting on in his absense; but when he heered that I had hoisted it aboard, he looks as pleezed as a sea-gull swallowing a little fish; and he whacked his spade into the ground, and sez he, "I hope I may be shot, if I aint glad to heer it, for I noes that my friend Harding will fishiate better as no other man except myself." So I was glad to hear that my friend, the Kurnill, had dun so much to author-eyes me to stand as cheef cook and bottle-washer in this bizziness, and I meen to crack on all I no, under a full press of canvass, till I giv the bografy of every wild cretur in these landings, and make the whole *world laugh and dance for joy.*

As to myself, I am getting to be along in years, tho I feel as spry as a young man, except that I am lade up with the ruemytiz and haz a wood leg and one hip outerjint. I spose according to the best kalkulashuns, I am drawing near to the eend of my voige, but if I only live to shake a fist with my old friend the Kurnill once more, I'll be content to run off the reel; but I'll keep up the allmyknack till I've drunk my *last bottle*, and then when death snuffs my *candle*, and puts my *pipe* out, I spose my job will be *awl* over at *last.*

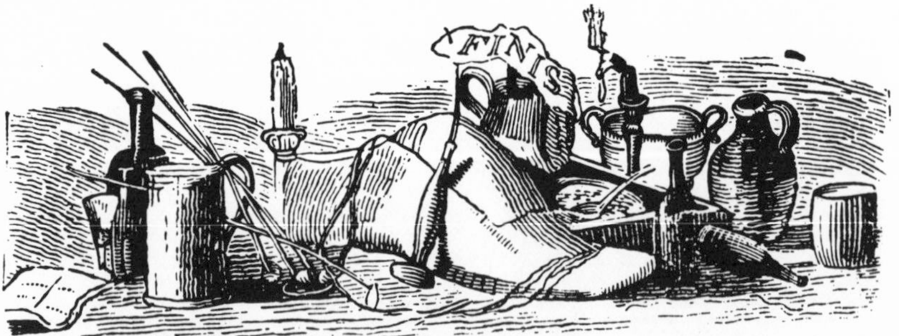

ECLIPSES.

There will be four Eclipses of the Sun, and two of the Moon. The first will be of the Sun—a small, partial eclipse, on January 22d, at the time of New Moon—visible only in the Southern extremity of the Southern Ocean. The second will be a total eclipse of the Moon, on February 5th—visible in the Western Continent and Pacific Ocean; commencing at 6 14 P. M., and ending at 11 39 P. M. The third will be a partial eclipse of the Sun, on February 21st, early in the morning—visible only in the North Atlantic Ocean, Iceland, and East Greenland. The fourth will be a partial eclipse of the Sun, in July, but invisible except in Baffin's Bay, Greenland, Iceland, Northern Ocean, Norway, Sweden, Lapland, Finland, Russia in Europe, Prussia, Italy, Germany, Scotland, and north of France. The fifth will be a total eclipse of the Moon, August 21—partially visible in this country. The sixth will be a small eclipse of the Sun, August 16th, P. M., invisible.

Morning and Evening Stars.

The Planet Venus will be Evening Star till May 14th, thence Morning Star through the year. Jupiter will be Morning Star till June 5th, thence Evening Star till December 22d, and then again Morning Star. Mars will also be Morning Star till April 17th, thence Evening Star to the end of the year. Saturn, likewise, will be Morning Star till June 21st, thence Evening Star till December 27th, when he will again be Morning Star.

Common Notes for 1841.

Solar Cycle, 2.—Epact, 7.—Lunar Cycle, 18.—Julian Period, 6554.—Dominical Letter, C.—No. of Direction, 21.—Roman Indiction, 14.—Dionysian Period, 170.

1841. **JANUARY.** **31 Days.**

These calculations are on a new plan, whereby much space is saved and all their usefulness retained. They will serve for all the United States, the Canadas, &c.

PHASES OF THE MOON.

○ Full 7th, 9 55 M.
☾ L. Q. 14th, 7 26 M.
● New 22d, 11 58 M.
☽ F. Q. 30th, 5 50 M.

D. M.	D. W.	Sun rises H. M.	Sun Sets H. M.	Sun's Dec. D. M.	Sun Slow. M. S.	Moon South H. M.	High Water. Boston.	High Water. New York.	Moon Rises and Sets. Maine.	Massachusetts.	New York.	Washington.	Charleston.	New Orleans.	ASPECTS, &c.
1	F	7 26	4 34	23 0	3 59	6 33	5 17	2 43	0 37	0 35	0 33	0 31	0 25	0 21	☉ Perigee. *About*
2	S	7 26	4 34	22 55	4 27	7 23	6 34	4 0	1 49	1 46	1 43	1 40	1 30	1 25	*this time, woollen mit-*
3	S	7 25	4 35	22 49	4 55	8 20	8 1	5 27	3 4	2 59	2 54	2 49	2 35	2 24	*tens in demand.*
4	M	7 25	4 35	22 43	5 22	9 22	9 14	6 40	4 25	4 19	4 13	4 7	3 46	3 37	*Loafers huddle around*
5	T	7 24	4 36	22 37	5 49	10 29	10 17	7 43	5 42	5 35	5 28	5 21	5 0	4 46	*the store. Hot*
6	W	7 24	4 36	22 29	6 15	11 36	11 10	8 36	6 51	6 44	6 37	6 30	6 9	5 55	Epiphany. *whiskey*
7	T	7 23	4 37	22 22	6 41	m	11 51	9 17	rises	rises	rises	rises	rises	ises	☽ Perigee. *punch*
8	F	7 22	4 38	22 14	7 7	0 39	a 38	10 4	6 0	6 5	6 10	6 15	6 30	6 40	Very high tides.
9	S	7 22	4 38	22 6	7 32	1 38	1 18	10 44	7 23	7 26	7 29	7 32	7 41	7 47	*drunk.*
10	S	7 21	4 39	21 57	7 56	2 31	1 56	11 22	8 41	8 43	8 45	8 47	8 53	8 57	*Attractive theatre bills.*
11	M	7 20	4 40	21 48	8 20	3 21	2 37	a 7	9 55	9 55	9 55	9 55	9 55	9 59	*White thin pants un-*
12	T	7 20	4 40	21 38	8 43	4 7	3 18	0 48	11 5	11 4	11 3	11 2	10 59	10 57	*comfortable in the eve-*
13	W	7 19	4 41	21 28	9 6	4 52	4 7	1 37	m	m	m	m	m	11 54	*ning. Icicles*
14	T	7 18	4 42	21 17	9 28	5 36	5 5	2 35	0 15	0 12	0 9	0 6	0 0	m	*on the eaves of houses.*
15	F	7 18	4 42	21 6	9 49	6 20	6 9	3 39	1 20	1 16	1 13	1 8	0 58	0 52	Low tides.
16	S	7 17	4 43	20 55	10 10	7 6	7 27	4 57	2 26	2 21	2 16	2 11	1 57	1 46	*Large fires, supposed*
17		7 16	4 44	20 43	10 30	7 55	8 38	6 8	3 32	3 26	3 20	3 14	2 56	2 43	*to be the work*
18	M	7 15	4 45	20 31	10 49	8 45	9 34	7 4	4 34	4 27	4 20	4 13	3 52	3 38	*of an*
19	T	7 14	4 46	20 19	11 8	9 36	10 21	7 51	5 29	5 21	5 14	5 7	4 46	4 32	☽ Apogee.
20	W	7 13	4 47	20 6	11 26	10 26	10 58	8 29	6 15	6 8	6 1	5 54	5 33	5 20	*incendiary*
21	T	7 13	4 47	19 52	11 43	11 16	11 32	9 2	6 53	6 47	6 41	6 35	6 17	6 5	*Vigorous skateing*
22	F	7 12	4 48	19 39	11 59	a 3	m	9 36	sets.	sets.	sets.	sets.	sets.	sets.	☉ Eclipsed, invis.
23	S	7 11	4 49	19 25	12 15	0 48	0 6	10 8	5 54	5 58	6 2	6 6	6 19	6 26	High Tides.
24	S	7 10	4 50	19 10	12 30	1 30	0 38	10 44	6 53	7 1	7 4	7 7	7 15	7 19	*near Boston.*
25	M	7 9	4 51	18 56	12 44	2 12	1 14	11 11	8 4	8 5	8 6	8 7	8 10	8 13	*Hot dinners.*
26	T	7 8	4 52	18 41	12 57	2 53	1 41	11 45	9 9	9 9	9 9	9 9	9 9	9 9	*Sundry Tailors*
27	W	7 7	4 53	18 25	13 9	3 35	2 15	m	10 16	10 14	10 12	10 10	10 6	10 4	*cheated.*
28	T	7 6	4 54	18 10	13 21	4 20	2 53	0 23	11 27	11 24	11 21	11 18	11 10	11 2	*about these times.*
29	F	7 4	4 56	17 54	13 31	5 9	3 37	1 7	m	m	m	m	m	m	
30	S	7 3	4 57	17 37	13 41	6 0	4 33	2 3	0 43	0 39	0 35	0 31	0 19	0 9	*Cold frosty weather.*
31	S	7 2	4 58	17 20	13 50	6 57	5 53	3 23	1 56	1 51	1 46	1 41	1 25	1 16	Low Tides.

"Sam, why did you bring that stupid ass, here? He knows nothing about his business, and has got me into two or three deuced scrapes by carrying billets to the wrong lady, and comporting himself without due circumspection on some very delicate occasions."

"Please yer honor, you told me to bring one here to act as a gentleman's gentleman."

"So I did, Sam, and I told you to bring somebody who had been *in the world.*"

"Exactly so, your honor, and my brother Phelim is exactly that same. For he was employed by Mr. Spadem, these sax years in claneing out wells, yer honor; and didn't he spend half his time down in the world yer honor, where neither you nor I has been?"

"That is *well*, Sam, but not at all to my purpose; I would have a man that has seen something of shifts, and turnings and revolutions, and knows how to accommodate his movements to the revolving scenes of life."

"Ah, yer honor, then Tom Screwhip would be just the boy, for he has been in the treadmill forty times, to my sartin knowledge."

Latest from the Mines.

The other day I war playin the soger in the door of my shantee, setting with my game leg in an old cheer, and smokin my pipe, when a long-sided feller reeched me the folleting letter, and I knowed the hand riting at wonst, so I riz rite up and gin 3 cheers, and then red it.

MEXIKAN MINES—THE FORTH DAY JULY 1840.

Bengimmin Harding, Escuire:

Deer Cir—This is the glorus day we fout and ganed our libberties, and hear I am amongst pesky Spanyards a diggin for the pretious mettles. I hope you keep up the Awlmyneck, and put in the peeces that you find in my old coonskin trunk in the garret. They ar awl true, and may be lyed on, and I think they will keep up my fame, for I ar very fond of posthumorous fame, but why don't you send sum won to git me out of these infarnal green-skinned varmints' hands, for it's very diffrunt from being in Kongress? Whar's Mike Greenin, Toby Wing, and Bill Salthead? Why don't they do sumthing to dig me out of this cussed burrow, for I don't like it at awl; and now they ar got a big chain around my leg, and it is wound around my middle, which makes it very onplesant, and I'll tell you the wreizon that they put this chane on to me.

You must no that arter bein hear so long I got dissatisfide and oneasy about my awlmyneck and wanted to see old Kaintuck wonst more, and heer the crack of my rifel and the bark of my dog, and if it war no more thon the yell of a painter, I thort it wood kynder sorter make a ludikkerous expression on my vitawls, and so sez I to myself, "what is the good for Davy Krockett to be treed in this pesky hole awl his days, when it war allowed all about our diggin that he could squat lower, skreem lowder, and run faster than any other feller there or in Kongress ither. Legs is legs awl over the kreeation, tho I most don't hardly bleeve this belongs to the Lord's kreeation, for it looks no more like Kaintuck than it looks like a dum klock." So I intermind I woodn't eet brown beens and bullock's heds no longer, and won day when we war goin to our dinner awl in droves like oxes and sheeps, I let my sugar-lofe hat fall off, bekase thar war a hi wind, and it blowed a a smart chanse from the plaice, and I run arter it, and the more I tried to ketch it the more I coodn't, bekase I happened to fall down when I got most to it, and so befur I coed git it I war behind a sorter hill, and the gards thort I war cummin back, but that wood be ridikulus, and so I giv my legs an almity strechin jist about that time. Pritty sune when I riz a hill, I seed the gards war arter me, and befour long sum war cumin on hosses with a slippen-noose kinder string that they calls a lassy. When sum on 'em cum neer me I squatted behint a stump an maid myself little. In this way I went till I cum to a sort of bay on the C shoar, and my hart jumpt for joy when I seed a big bote thar, about a quarter of a mild from the shoar. I jest dove into the drink, and never swum so lite in my life, for it seemed as if the water helped me. I got to this big bote and the men let me cum in, and when I telled 'em my name war Krockett, they gin 3 cheers and axed me down into a little suller in the hinder eend of the bote, whar war all sorts o' likker. Then I went up agin on the ruff. The bote had three pesky grate logs stuck up on it as hi as a pine tree, and all sorts of big black strings like a fish nett. So the saylors begun to tork to me, and I war tellin em about my kase, and how I war never kilt, when awl at wonst I seed a passel of them unsarcumsised Spanyards gatherin round the shore and pinting off to the bote. So I telled the Ginerawl what had kommand of the bote, and he telled me I had better go and hide. But I seed no bushes nor no where to go, only down into won of the sullers. I axed the Ginerawl if them logs war holler that stuck up perpendikkler, and he sed no; so I run down suller, and then the pesky sogers cum into the bote. I heered 'em jabbering like a passel of crows ovver a karkass, and pritty soon they cum jumpin down suller, and as soon as they seed me, they drawed their sords, and telled me to surrender. I lookt around for sum weppun but I seed none only a trumpet, and they seezed me rite off. I fit till I split my thum nale in the middle and tore my trowsis haff off; but it war no kinder use, and they snaked me up to the ruff of the bote, and the ginerawl didn't dast to say a word. They fotch me back and hear I ar with a chane on, and diggin for gold! Now I leeve it to you, Benjimmin, if this aint wusser than rassling with a nigger greeced, and as I place grate dependance on your judgment do you think it ar rite for a member of Kongress to stay in these diggins. Do say sumthing about it in the awlmyneck, for my sittyvation is getting to be onplesant.

Yourn to sarve. DAVY CROCKETT.

Rare Economy.

When I war a young feller thar war nothing I despised like I did a Yankee; speshally if he war a pedlar, and I sum think I'd never have got over it to this day if I hadn't gone among them in their own cleerings and seed wot sort of tracks they make. Cause Why? Didn't one on 'em sell me a famous match for my black switch tail horse at Vicksburg? and didn't I find out as soon as I got home that the pestiferous, nefarious, outdacious, egg-sucking, worse-than-a-methody-missioner had been in my pastur fust, and then travelled clear to Vicksburg to sell me my own "Streak o' Litening?"—and as if that war not aggravatious enuff, the sarpint had put off an old wooden clock that woodn't neither stand nor go, on my wife. Arter that it wood be superogatious to tell about the twenty pounds of sausages stuffed with salt pork and green baze—that war as much Judy's blame as hisn—she'd ought to hav knew better.

That's not all about it neither, nor haff nor quarter. I hated the Yankees for being sich a d——d stingy horsetentacious boat's crew as every body noes they be. Thar war won Adonijah Allsaint, wot made an improvement in Skunk's Cabbage Swamp, the same feller wot war caught picking his own pocket in his sleep. When he cum among us he war an emancipationer and tried to persuade all the nayberhood that niggers war human kritters and had soles like white men. By all the vartues of lead and gunpowder, he hadn't been a year among us afore he tied three of his sarvents naked in a swamp all night, and they war all stung to death by gallynippers, jist because he had too much yewmanitee, he said, to whip 'em. Then he was all for saving, saving: jist as if money war not made to spend and vittles to eat. He always used to have a wooden bacon ham on his dinner table, jist for a shew, and painted so nayteral it wood make your mouth water to look at it.—He said he did this to larn the vartue of self-denial.—All the Yankees what cum nigh us had jist the same smell of the woodpecker's nest they war hatched in. Adonijah died at last, and the Devil got his due—if he didn't I don't no what fire and brimstun are made for. The methodizers put these lines over him:

"Here lies a Christian, Parent, Friend—
A brother in the Lord;
A firm believer to the end,
In every *saving* word."

As true as my shooting machine at a hundred yards, I've seen worse lines on a tombstone than that. For all that, I'd seen so much of Adonijah's cajolery that I hated the very name of saving, and spent my money, when I had any, as fast as whiskey could melt it, or a fiddle cood go, or a race hoss cood run away with it. You may presume, then, stranger, how mad I war to be called a Yankee by an oncivilized Ingin savage, what noed no more of the world or of good manners than if he'd lived a thousand yeers in the hart of a limestone quarry, d——n his pickter.

You see, stranger, I war out on the trail of a Cherokee war party, what had been seducing away our hosses and cavorting among our wimmen with their tomahawks and skalpers, and sich like innocent amusements as cums nateral to 'em, and we cum up to 'em jist as they had crossed Red Warrior Creek whar it ar all of a quarter of a mile wide, and we coodn't get across at 'em no way we cood fix it. So they cum down to the edge of their convenient namesake and dared us to cum

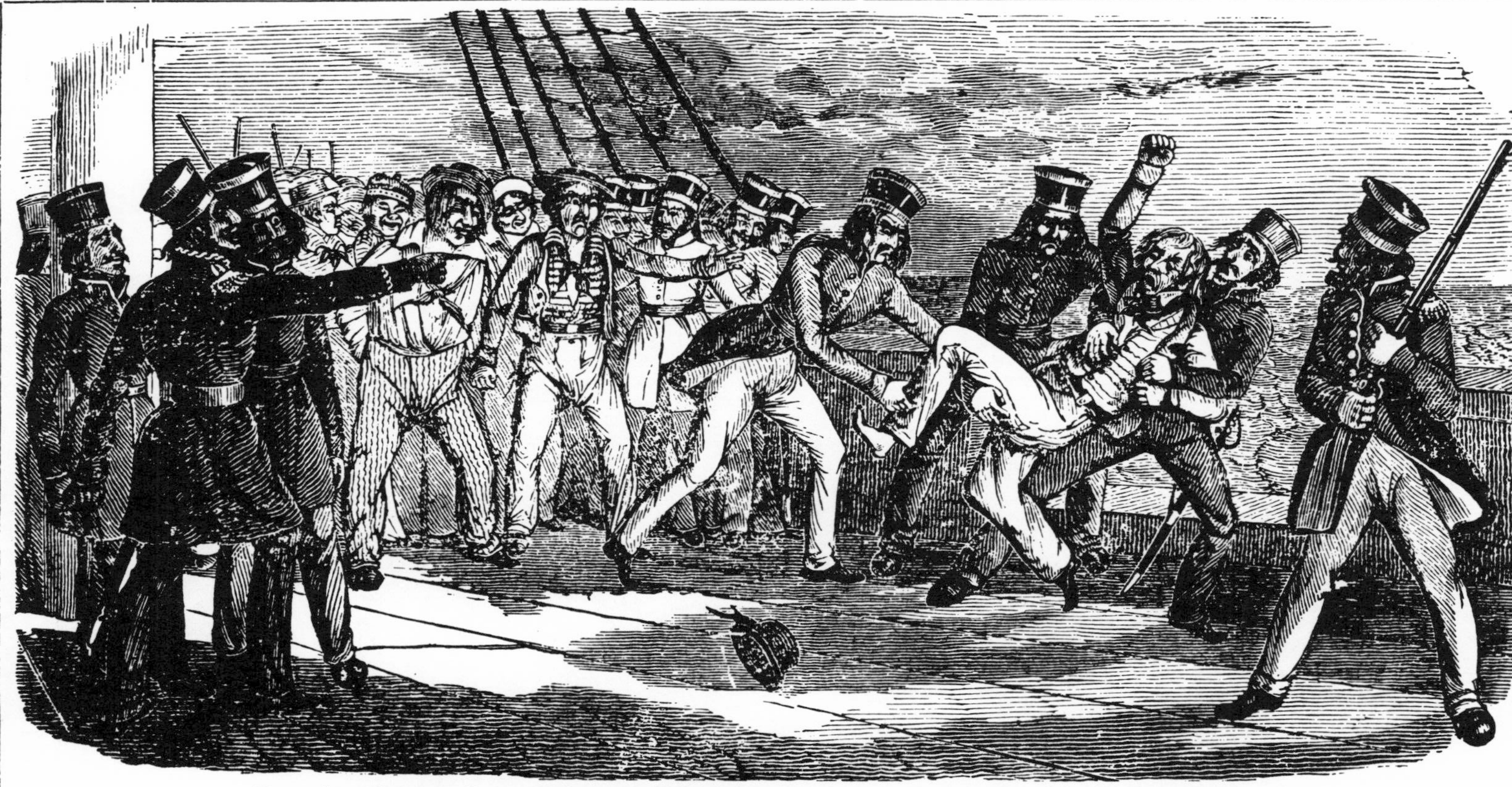

Crockett retaken after his Escape from the Mines.---See page 4.

Rare Economy---Continued from page 4,

over and hav our hair cut, which made us hugaceously mad, as who woodn't be, to heer himself abused when his hands war tied? Thar war won devil's kitchen tho', that made me more savagerous than all the rest, for he got into a peecan tree, and shewed us his posterum, if it ar not ondecent to say so, and very politely asked us to kiss it. Now I've known of many such invites being given, but I never knowed nobody accept none on 'em. Howsever I felt amazen wolfy at what he said and done, and took a blizzard at him. It war a long shot and all depended on luck, and I had my own share on it and another man's too. The screeching varmint tumbled out of the tree and never stirred agin, and his brother rogues ran away, arter they had a comfortable howl over him. When we crossed over we found that the Ingin's hide war not broke and not a drop of blood had cum from him.

Sum time arter, when peace war made with 'em, I war at the council, and one of the painted pagans talked the skimmage over. One of the beloved men, said that he had always heered the Yankees war a transcendental saving people; but he never knowed how stingy they war till he seen one on 'em shoot his brother Cockahoop Zigzacker across the Red Warrior without spiling his skin. He'd seen the ants and the bees lay up corn and honey for the winter, he sed, "but he a kind o' thort thar war no kritter but a Yankee that wood hav been so particklar about his leather." The brute thort I meant to tan his brother's skin or sell it, as he had seen the Yankees do by all other skins. Now, stranger, I'll leave it to you if sich ignorant wretches ort to be suffered to live.

Insult to Kentucky.

About eight year ago, thar war a feller from Down East, or sum other town in them parts, that cum into the cleering to religionize. He brot about 50 of his books with him, and set up his shanty for to convart the heethin. He giv the ingins an invite, and when they went to see him, he lent 'em books to reed jest as he wood to a sivilized cretur, but they took the leeves to lite their pipes with. So when he found he coudn't do nothin with the cussed red skins, he gin out that he would convart the natyves of Old Kentuck at haff a dollar a head. We war hugeously mad when we heered that, bekase he had gin the red skinned

Rare Economy---See page 4.

1841.	FEBRUARY.	28 Days.

These calculations are on a new plan, whereby much space is saved, and all their usefulness retained. They will serve for all the United States, the Canadas, &c.

PHASES OF THE MOON.

○ Full 5th, 8 55 E.
☾ L. Q. 13th, 1 27 M.
● New 21st, 6 11 M.
☽ F. Q. 28th, 2 54 E.

D. M.	D. W.	Sun rises H. M	Sun Sets. H. M	Sun' Dec. D. M.	Sun Slow. M. S.	Moon South. H. M.	High Water. Boston.	High Water. New York.	Moon Rises and Sets. Maine.	Massachusetts.	New York.	Washington.	Charleston.	New Orleans.	ASPECTS, &c
1	M	7 1	4 59	17 3	13 58	8 0	7 30	5 0	3 9	3 3	2 57	2 51	2 31	2 22	*Demand for clam soup.*
2	T	7 0	5 0	16 46	14 5	9 5	8 57	6 27	4 22	4 15	4 8	4 1	3 38	3 26	*Cold nights—several*
3	W	6 59	5 1	16 29	14 12	10 10	10 0	7 30	5 23	5 16	5 11	5 2	4 40	4 27	*conspicuous old maids*
4	T	6 53	5 2	16 11	14 17	11 12	10 53	8 23	6 11	6 5	5 59	5 53	5 35	5 24	☽ Perigee. *enter the*
5	F	6 57	5 3	15 53	14 22	m	11 35	9 5	rises	rises	rises	rises	rises	rises	☽ Ecli. vis. and total.
6	S	6 56	5 4	15 34	14 26	0 8	a 14	9 44	6 6	6 8	6 10	6 12	6 18	6 22	*state of double blessed-*
7	**S**	6 54	5 6	15 16	14 29	1 1	0 48	10 18	7 21	7 22	7 23	7 24	7 27	7 28	Very high Tides.
8	M	6 53	5 7	14 57	14 32	1 48	1 24	10 54	8 36	8 35	8 34	8 33	8 30	8 29	*ness.*
9	T	6 52	5 8	14 37	14 33	2 35	2 1	11 31	9 49	9 47	9 45	9 43	9 37	9 33	*Large noses look red.*
10	W	6 51	5 9	14 18	14 34	3 22	2 40	a 10	11 0	10 56	10 53	10 50	10 41	10 35	*Horses stamp in the*
11	T	6 50	5 10	13 58	14 34	4 8	3 25	0 55	m	m	m	11 54	11 40	11 32	*night. Musquitoes*
12	F	6 49	5 11	13 39	14 34	4 55	4 21	1 51	0 9	0 4	0 0	m	m	m	*very scarce.*
13	S	6 47	5 13	13 18	14 32	5 44	5 22	2 52	1 17	1 11	1 5	0 59	0 40	0 29	*Shiver-de-freeze.*
14	**S**	6 46	5 14	12 58	14 30	6 33	6 41	4 11	2 20	2 13	2 6	1 59	1 36	1 24	Low Tides.
15	M	6 45	5 15	12 38	14 27	7 26	7 57	5 27	3 18	3 11	3 4	2 57	2 34	2 22	*Great talk of spring.*
16	T	6 44	5 16	12 17	13 23	8 16	9 3	6 33	4 7	4 0	3 53	3 46	3 26	3 13	☽ Apogee.
17	W	6 43	5 17	11 56	14 19	9 7	9 53	7 23	4 49	4 43	4 37	4 31	4 12	4 1	*Ice creams very dull.*
18	T	6 41	5 19	11 35	14 14	9 55	10 32	8 2	5 23	5 18	5 13	5 8	4 53	4 44	*Shoemaker's wax freez-*
19	F	6 40	5 20	11 13	14 9	10 41	11 4	8 34	5 50	5 46	5 42	5 38	5 16	5 18	*es. A great deal of*
20	S	6 39	5 21	10 52	14 2	11 25	11 31	9 1	6 12	6 9	6 6	6 3	5 54	5 48	*cider drank.*
21	**S**	6 37	5 23	10 30	13 55	a 8	m	9 38	sets.	sets.	sets.	sets.	sets.	sets.	☉ Eclipsed, invis.
22	M	6 36	5 24	10 8	13 48	0 51	0 8	10 8	7 0	7 0	7 0	7 0	7 0	7 0	High Tides. ***Much***
23	T	6 34	5 26	9 46	13 39	1 33	0 38	10 41	8 7	8 6	8 5	8 4	8 1	8 0	Shrove Tuesday.
24	W	6 33	5 27	9 24	13 30	2 18	1 11	11 18	9 18	9 15	9 12	9 9	9 0	8 57	Ash Wednesday.
25	T	6 32	5 28	9 2	13 21	3 6	1 48	11 57	10 31	10 27	10 23	10 19	10 7	9 58	*talk about finishing*
26	F	6 30	5 30	8 40	13 11	3 57	2 27	m	11 45	11 40	11 35	11 30	11 15	11 4	*B. H. Monument.*
27	S	6 29	5 31	8 17	13 0	4 53	3 27	0 57	m	m	[illegible]	m	m	m	*Cold weather.*
28	**S**	6 28	5 32	7 54	12 49	5 52	4 29	1 59	1 2	0 56	0 50	0 44	0 24	0 13	1st Sund. in Lent.

Perhaps the reader may not be aware of the source from whence arose metal heels to fashionable boots and shoes. The following veritable history will illustrate the matter: One Thomas Overdone, had been much pestered with boot-jacks, none of which appeared calculated to suit his purpose. Having been much vexed with one of these useful articles, one evening, he threw it into the fire, and swore that he would abandon the use of the instrument, henceforth and forever.

When the next evening came, he was driven to his wits end; for the thought of sleeping in his boots, however endurable to himself was violently opposed by his better half, who had the horror of barked shins before her eyes. Accordingly he had recourse to a man of science. The latter advised him to nail to his boots a piece of steel, and procure a powerful magnet, which last was firmly attached to a post. Placing his heels near this magnet, the boots were drawn off in a trice. Since that time metal heels have been worn, and although they have made much noise, yet few knew their origin.

"I think I have heard of you before, sir." "Very probable, sir. My name is *Brown.*"
"Oh bless your soul, yes. I've heard of fifty of you."

varmints the fust chance to git to heaven; wich war a thing never heered on in our diggins befour, as them and the niggers always had to wate till thar betters war sarved. Besides, he war sent out to convart the heethin, and it war kinder oncivil to call white fokes by that name. Only think of it, deer reeder, to call a member of kongress a heethin! Thar war sum tork of lynching him; but we thort it war best to katekise him fust, to see if he wood poligize, and if he was found out to be true game, and willin to do what war write, we would accept of his tarms, only he must convart the children for half price. I bleve this war rite, for seein as religun is a verry good thing in its place, we wanted to be sivil with the cretur, and not go for to play possum with the word of God, wich would be ridiculous. So we chose a committe of won to call and see him, and that war Mike Cunningham the teemster, who had been clark to a lawyer in his young days, and so he war the only won in the cleering who knowd how to expostalize on the scriptur.

Mike went rite off, and took his little boy with him so as the feller mite try his hand on him fust, and se how he made out, for he knowd if he didn't circumbobolate the boy, he couldn't do nothin with groan fokes. As soon as Mike went in, the religionizer axed him his bizness, and Mike telled him he had cum to see if he wood do rite, or else he must be lynched. Then the feller war verry perlite, and axed Mike to take a cheer, but he wouldn't. Then the feller sed he didn't meen no insult to the white fokes, but he only offured to convart the ingins fust, bekase he thort they needed it most, as they worshipt idles and jiggerknots, and the widders burnt themselves up with thar husbands. Then Mike noed he lyed, bekase thar are no sich doins, and it war skandeliferous to lye about the red skins that are bad enouff when the truth is told. So Mike telled him rite off that he war a skunk and no gentleman. The feller got mad then as a hot gridiron, and he sed he wood hav Mike parsecuted for refformation of karaktur. Then Mike crooked his thum, and begun to squint most awfully at the feller's rite eye. So he cooled down in a minnit, and cum to tarms, and sed he would do whatever Mike sed war rite.

"Very well"—sez Mike—"then you must convart the children for haff price."

"May I be crucified if I do!" sez he—"for I made up my mind 3 year ago not to tantrivate with sucklings at awl; bekase sum of them are the very devil. They ar like a young tode that is full of venom. I took a young won to do for about 5 year ago, and licked him with a bunch of birches till the skin was all off his back, but I couldn't git the grace o' God into his natur anny more than you can nokulate a feller that's had the small pocks. No, railly sir, I can't make a livin at it, I assure ye."

Mike felt as cross as 2 crooked gate posts, and he shook his head like a bull when you fling a rope round his neck. Then the religionizer sed he would split the diff'runce and convart the groan fokes by the pound. He sed he knowed thar war a plenty of unsarcumsized sinners in our diggins, but he bleeved thar war a good menny that hadn't bowed the nees to a varmint he called Bale. Mike telled him thar war no sich cretur as that in our diggins, that he had seen painters, and wolves, and bares, and wild cats, and had got a jint of a mammouth at home; and so when he seed the feller war green in the forrest, and didn't no nothin, he telled him he wood let him off with a bit of a prayer, and wood give him a levenpenny bit for it. So when he seed Mike put his hand in his pockit for the munny, he got down on his nees, and begun to put on the steem. When he got warm in his prayer, he said sumthing about the wicked Kentuckians, and Mike took hold of his eer and pinched it till he made him take it back, and sware that they were all fine fellers. Finally, Mike reported that the religionizer want fit for his bizziness, and we held a meetin, and I war put in the cheer, wich war a pine stump, and we decided that thar war no need of any more religion in Old Kaintuck, and that it war too expensive to think of byin any more; and that this new man shood hav the privilege to tar and fether himself. On the next day, we sent Mike with a bag of fethers and a kittle of tar, and he took 'em into the religionizer's room, and set 'em down, and sez he, "we ar concluded that you ort to be lynched, but we give you the privilege to do it awl yourself. So I will cum back tomorro about this time, to see that you hav dun it according to order."

When Mike went back, the nixt day, he found the feller war gone with awl his plunder and hadn't used the tar and fethers at awl.

Tussle with a Bear.

I salled out from hum, one rainy arternoon, to go down to Rattle-snake Swamp to git a squint at a turkey-buzzard, for thar war a smart chance of them down that way, and I had hered how thar war to be a Methodist parson at my house on the next day, and my wife wanted me to git sumthing nice for his tooth. She said it would help out his sarment almighty much. So I took my dog and rifle and sallied out rite away. I had got down about as fur as where the wood opens at the Big Gap, when I seed it war so dark and mucilaginous that I coodn't hardly see at all. I went on, howsever, and intarmined in my own mind, to keep on, tho I shood run afoul of an earthquake, for thar is no more give back to me than thar is to a flying bullet when a painter stares it rite in the face. I war going ahead like the devil on a gambler's trail, when, all at once, or I might say, all at twice, for it war done in double quick time, I felt sumthing ketch me around the middle, and it squeezed me like it war an old acquaintance. So I looked up and seed pretty quick it war no relation of mine. It was a great bear that war hugging me like a brother, and sticking as close to me as a turcle to his shell. So he squeezed an idee into my hed that if I got him as ded as common, and his hide off of his pesky body, he would do as well for the parson as any thing else. So I felt pretty well satisfied when I cum to think I had my Sunday's dinner so close to me. But when he railly seemed to be cuming closer and closer, I telled him to be patient for he wood git into me arter he war cooked; but he didn't seem to take a hint, and to tell the truth, I begun to think that although there war to be won dinner made out between us, it war amazing uncertain which of us would be the dinner and which would be the eater. So I seed I ought to hav ben thinking about other matters. I coodn't get my knife out, and my rifle had dropped down. He put up won of his hind claws agin my side, and I seed it war cuming to the *scratch* amazing sudden. So I called to my dog, and he cum up pretty slow till he seed what war the matter, and then he jumped a rod rite towards the bear. The bear got a notion that the dog was unfriendly to him, before he felt his teeth in his throat, and when Rough begun to gnaw his windpipe, the varmint ment there should be no love lost. But the bear had no notion of loosening his grip on me. He shoved his teeth so near my nose that I tried to cock it up out of his way, and then he drew his tongue across my throat to mark out the place where he should put in his teeth. All this showed that he had no regard for my feelings. He shook off the dog three or four times, like nothing at al!, and once he trod on his head; but Rough stood up to his lick log and bit at him, but the varmint's hairs set his teeth on edge. All this passed in quicker time than a blind hoss can run agin a post, when he can't see whar to find it. The varmint made a lounge and caught hold of my rite ear, and so I made a grab at his ear too, and caught it between my teeth. So we held on to each others' ears, till my teeth met through his ear. Then I tripped him down with one leg, and the cretur's back fell acrost a log, and I war on top of him. He lay so oncomfortable that he rolled off the log, and loosened his grip so much that I had a chance to get hold of my nife, and Rough dove into him at the same time. Seeing thar war two of us, he thought he would use one paw for each one The varmint cocked one eye at me as much as to ax me stay whar I war till he could let go of me with one paw, and finish the dog. No man can say I am of a contrary disposition, though it come so handy for me to feel the haft of my big butcher, as soon as my rite hand war at liberty, that I pulled it out. The way it went into the bowels of the varmint war nothing to nobody. It astonished him most mightily. He looked as if he thought it war a mean caper, and he turned pale. If he didn't die in short time arterwards, then the Methodist parson eat him alive, that's all. When I cum to strip, arter the affair war over. the marks of the bear's claws war up and down on my hide to such a rate that I might have been hung out for an American flag. The stripes showed most beautiful.

A Sailor's Yarn.

I always put grate dependence in my frend Ben Harding, and he never telled me any tuff yarn that warn't true; for I have seen as big wunders in the forrest, as he ever seed on the water. So put that to that, as the cat said when she stuck her tung into the kreem pot, and it proves 'em both true. Ben's last yarn war sumthing like this:—

I had a shipmate by the name of Bill Bunker. Bill was a queer chap, and was up to as many moves as a minnit watch that strikes every second. He want content to get threw the world with a reg'lar breeze and a moderate sea; but war always for having sum shine or another. He wood sooner clime over a coach than turn out for it; and whenever he fell down, he wood make bleeve he war drunk jist to raze a row with the watchmen.

Bill went won seeling voige in a little skooner called the Blackbird. I never telled you, Kurnill, how they knock them fellers over the nose; but that's neither here nor thar—Bill's scrape war on an ileand. Arter they had got pretty neer full of skins and sea-mammouth ile—sum calls 'em sea-illifants, but I spose when I tork to a Kongressman I must use high-floun lingo—they then steered away for home. They expected to make the land the nixt morning; but they seed nothing but an ileand. It war an outlandish place enuff, so full of scraggy trees and rocks that it looked as if you cood not find room to set down without scratching your fundaments to pieces. The Cappen concluded to lay under the ileand a few days, and so they cum to ankur. While they layed there they tarred down the rigging, painted the black streek on the vessel's side, korked the decks, and mended sales. But they didn't go ashore, as the Cappen had seen sum awful looking Ingens that war so ondecent as to ware very few close. Bill sed he wood be sworn thar warn't a tailor in the ileand that knowed how to make a pare of christian breeches.

So it war won fine sunny day when they war intending to be off the nixt morning. and they had the sales loosed to dry, when Bill, all at once, axed the Cappen to let him go ashore and have a kruice. This war a poser for the Cappen, as Bill was the only able seeman he had aboard, and he felt sartin that if he went ashore, he wood lose the number of his mess; for he wood hav his frolic out, and wood dance a jig if he war hanging on a gallus. He cood dance on a coffin or play kards on a tomb-stone. Bill woodn't take no for an ansur, and so the Cappen let him hav the boat. He skulled her ashore, and then walked into the intereur of the ileand. He found it looked better, as he went on. Thar war a plenty of green grass, and good water, and the birds war so thick, he wood hav thort he had been in the woods, if their wings had only been branches, instead of feathers. But he coodn't find no grog-shop, and so the water war almost as good as none, for every body knows that water without sumthing strong in it, is like a hansum bird that don't no how to sing.

Howsumever, when he got tired of walking about and seeing noboddy, he worked down towards the shore; and now he detarmined to leeve his canishaw's on a big rok, befour he went aboard. So he got an old korking iron out of the bote, and begun to kut the fust letters of his name. Whilst he war at work, he seed out of won korner of his i, that thar war a little critter behind a tree—and then he watched slyly till he got a glimpse of its eyes. So he flung down his things and run thar. It war a Ingin gal, and Bill swears she war hansum. She tried to run, but Bill got up to her so quick she coodn't. Then she sunk back agin a tree, with her eyes on the ground, and looked as bashful as a monkey with his back broke. That struck Bill all aback, and he coodn't make up his mind rightly how he shood hail her, but he ranged up along side, and war going to mince up his mouth to speak her fair, when he sum how stuck the end of his queu into her eye. He didn't do it a proppus, but she jumped back, and thort he war going to board her in the smoke. He begun to make his polly-gees, and axed her pardun, and all that, but she woodn't trust him for a good while She chattered away in her own lingo, and every once in a while she wood ketch hold of his queu and give it a twitch, and I spose she war sneering about it in her own language.

At last she got kinder kooled down, and then she let him take hold of her hand, while she led him to the place whar she lived—though she kept a lookout for the queu all the time, as she war afrade it wood be playing its tricks with her agin She took him to a hut whar war about twenty savagers, and they all got up and run towards them making as big a noise as if the imps of the infarnul reguns had jist got a half holiday on a Saturday arternoon. Bill soon found out that this war the king's dawter, and while she telled 'em about the queu, they listened with their eyes and mouth wide open. As soon as she had done, they seized on Bill and tied him, hand and foot. Then they bro't out a log of wood, and a ax that war made of flint, and sharp as need be. Bill begun to be skared; and then they took and laid him down with his hed on the log, and won grum looking feller caut up the ax. Bill thort his time war cum. His neck felt queer enuff. So he hurried and sed a short prayer and whistled won or two sam tunes for the good of his sole. Then the big savager lifted the ax over his hed, and down it cum—not on Bill's neck but on the queu, which it took off smack smooth close to his hed. The gal caught it up, and as soon as Bill war loosed, he didn't stop to see what she did with it, but cut dirt for the bote and got safe aboard the skooner.

A Sailor's Yarn---See opposite page.

1841. MARCH. 31 Days.

These calculations are on a new plan, whereby much space is saved and all their usefulness retained. They will serve for all the United States, the Canadas, &c.

PHASES OF THE MOON.

○ Full 7th, 8 29 M.
☽ L. Q. 14th, 9 14 E.
● New 22d, 9 33 E.
☽ F. Q. 29th, 9 57 E.

D. M.	D. W.	Sun rises H. M	Sun Sets. H. M	Sun's Dec. D. M.	Sun Slow. M. S.	Moon South H. M.	High Water. Boston.	High Water. New York.	Moon Rises and Sets. Maine.	Massachusetts.	New York.	Washington.	Charleston.	New Orleans.	ASPECTS, &c.
1	M	6 26	5 34	7 32	12 37	6 53	5 46	3 16	2 12	2 5	1 58	1 51	1 28	1 16	*Windy weather. Cool*
2	T	6 25	5 35	7 9	12 25	7 57	7 24	4 54	3 12	3 5	2 58	2 51	2 28	2 16	*nights and mornings.*
3	W	6 23	5 37	6 46	12 12	8 58	8 49	6 19	4 4	3 58	3 52	3 46	3 27	3 14	*Money scarce.*
4	T	6 22	5 38	6 23	11 59	9 55	9 47	7 17	4 44	4 39	4 34	4 29	4 14	4 5	☽ Perigee. *Oyster*
5	F	6 21	5 39	6 0	11 45	10 49	10 35	8 5	5 16	5 12	5 8	5 4	4 52	5 45	*suppers. Weather*
6	S	6 19	5 41	5 37	11 31	11 40	11 13	8 43	5 43	5 40	5 37	5 34	5 25	6 19	*beginning to grow*
7	S	6 18	5 42	5 13	11 16	m	11 49	9 19	rises	rises	rises	rises	rises	rises	2d Sunday in Lent.
8	M	6 17	5 43	4 50	11 1	0 27	a 28	9 58	7 28	7 27	7 26	7 25	7 22	7 18	High Tides. *warmer.*
9	T	6 15	5 45	4 26	10 46	1 14	0 59	10 29	8 41	8 33	8 35	8 32	8 24	8 19	*Dry Good dealers very*
10	W	6 14	5 46	4 3	10 30	2 1	1 37	11 7	9 53	9 49	9 45	9 41	9 28	9 21	*polite. No news in*
11	T	6 12	5 48	3 39	10 14	2 50	2 16	11 46	11 3	10 58	10 55	10 48	10 32	10 23	*the papers. Fiddlers*
12	F	6 11	5 49	3 16	9 58	2 39	3 5	a 35	m	m	11 59	11 53	11 35	11 23	*in demand. Grocers*
13	S	6 10	5 50	2 52	9 41	4 30	3 53	1 26	0 11	0 5	m	m	m	m	*refuse to trust stran-*
14	S	6 8	5 52	2 29	9 24	5 22	4 59	2 29	1 12	1 5	0 58	0 51	0 29	0 20	3d Sunday in Lent.
15	M	6 7	5 53	2 5	9 7	6 14	6 7	3 37	2 6	1 59	1 52	1 45	1 22	1 11	*gers. Several persons*
16	T	6 6	5 54	1 41	8 50	7 5	7 27	4 57	2 50	2 44	2 38	2 32	2 13	2 0	☽ Apo. Low Tides.
17	W	6 4	5 55	1 18	8 32	7 55	8 34	6 4	3 29	3 23	3 17	3 11	2 52	2 43	St. Patrick. *take cold.*
18	T	6 3	5 57	0 54	8 14	8 42	9 24	6 54	4 0	3 55	3 50	3 45	3 29	3 20	*During this month or*
19	F	6 2	5 58	0 30	7 57	9 27	10 7	7 37	4 24	4 20	4 16	4 12	4 0	3 53	*the succeeding one, a*
20	S	6 0	6 0	S. 6	7 38	10 11	10 39	8 9	4 47	4 44	4 41	4 38	4 29	4 23	Vernal Equinox.
21	S	5 59	6 1	N. 17	7 20	10 53	11 12	8 42	5 6	5 5	5 4	5 3	4 58	4 56	4th Sunday in Lent
22	M	5 58	6 2	0 41	7 2	11 36	11 45	9 15	sets.	sets.	sets.	sets.	sets.	sets.	*thaw may be expected.*
23	T	5 56	6 4	1 5	6 44	a 21	m	9 50	7 8	7 6	7 4	7 2	6 56	6 52	*Measles prevalent.*
24	W	5 55	6 5	1 28	6 25	1 8	0 20	10 27	8 23	8 20	8 17	8 14	8 5	7 57	High Tides. *Consid-*
25	T	5 53	6 7	1 52	6 7	1 59	0 57	11 7	9 39	9 34	9 29	9 24	9 9	9 0	Annuncia. or holyday.
26	F	5 52	6 8	2 15	5 48	2 54	1 37	11 51	10 55	10 49	10 43	10 37	10 18	10 6	*erable talk of finishing*
27	S	5 51	6 9	2 39	5 30	3 52	2 21	m	m	m	11 55	11 43	11 25	11 12	*Bunker Hill Monu-*
28	S	5 49	6 11	3 2	5 11	4 54	3 17	0 47	0 9	0 2	m	m	m	m	5th Sunday in Lent.
29	M	5 48	6 12	3 26	4 53	5 57	4 28	1 58	1 14	1 7	1 0	0 53	0 30	0 18	*ment.*
30	T	5 47	6 13	3 49	4 34	6 58	5 55	3 25	2 8	2 2	1 56	1 50	1 31	1 19	Rather low Tides.
31	W	5 45	6 15	4 12	4 16	7 56	7 26	4 56	2 51	2 46	2 41	2 36	2 22	2 11	☽ Perigee.

A Jonny Raw, from Squantum, applied to a noted Surgeon, and announced his intention of learning the art and mystery of dissection. He boasted much of his steady hand, having signed the temperance pledge early in life: and thought he could practice upon the defunct human body with great tact and precision. The surgeon was surprised at the singular taste of the youth; but told him that he must not expect to arrive at the top of the profession in one leap. "Go first, my lad," said he, "and begin at the bottom of the ladder. Try the rudiments of the art first."

The young man departed; and sometime afterward the surgeon met him in the street, but in a guise not well adapted to a professional character.

"Ah! my lad," cried he—"you have given up the idea of dissecting human bodies, I presume."

"Not at all, sir," answered the enthusiast—"I have commenced as you advised me, at the bottom of the ladder, and am now employed in *opening oysters*, in Mr. Brown's victualing cellar."

Letter from Ben Harding to Col. Crockett.

GALLIANT KURNILL.—I haint had no ansur to my last letter, and so I taik my penn in hand to inform you that I am well, eccepting that I hav got a hard tutch of the rumatiz, and hope these few lions will find you engoying the same blessing. As you wanted me to cum up hear to the hed of Squaw River to drumm up voturs for you at the nixt eleckshun I have dun the best I cood, and hope to grapple a good menny more. I hav ben to Little Pucker Pond, Gr'n Island, Bear's Tail Inlet, Squaw's Foot village, and Salt River Pint. When I fust wayed ankur from your house, I kruced rite thro the hart of Gum-tree woods and didn't heave in site of a human craft for haff the day, tho I raised five or sicks foxen, and one wolf, and about fifty skool of Burds, and then I sot down to black Betty and whet up with sumthing like a pint. It never tasted better, and I only wisht you was thar to take a horn with me, for as the wise man sez in scripter, a friend's face sharpens iron. Wile I wos doing my duty over the white face, there hove in site 2 fellers and I bleeve they were duchmun, by their lingo. I offured them a drop and then I axed em to vote for Kurnill Krockett. They sed they had ben in this cuntry ony 2 yeer and want sivilized yet, so they couldn't vote, but they give me their hands upon it that they wood vote for you as soon they got their tickets where they belong, up in the state of New York. I made sale from there, and the nixt place that brot me up war Red Hill Swamp, close aboard of Great Swallow Muddy. I twigged a villidge close by, and so I hauled my wind, and went up to it, and axed for the tavern. As soon as I had put sumthing warm under my skin, I telled the men there, sez I, "Shipmates, good even,—I'm cum from Krockett with a roring commisshun to git votes, and I spose there's none here that will say black is the white of his eye. Any man that sez a word agin Davy Crockett, is a swab and a soger, and a big eater, and his messmates don't like him."— With that a long slab-sided feller told me to stand out for a bend, that he was Krockett's rifle, and had been put up for Kongress agin him. Sez he, "I've got more votes in won town than he's got all over the cuntry," and he wanted to fite it out, and telled 'em to hold him bekase he was afeared he should kill me. He telled 'em to jist sprinkle a handful of salt on my hed, and he would take me down his infarnul long throte jest as I stood. Sez I, "Look hear, mister, do you think I am a green hand or a fresh water lobster? I've ben on the levvy at New Leens when there war a dozen sich fellers as you gutted out clear from stem to starn. Pull off your breeches before you begin upon me, so that your hares may have sumthing left 'em, for I wont leeve a peace of you big enuff to bild a grave stone over it." With that the long-gutted soger got his grapplings on my Q, and sed he'd larn me to try to keep him out of Kongress. I fetched him a wipe with my left hand acrost the nose and stunted him, so that he fell down. Then the crowd all hollered "hurra for Krockett!" and they give me their hands on it that they would vote for the Kurnill.

Next morning I maid a raft to kross over to tother side of Salt River. I got to about the middle of the river, and was going under a bridge when I seed a man and a boy on the bridge ketching fish. I haled the man and hollered out to him to vote for Krockett, and he and the boy war so skeered when they see me—the fresh water lubbers—that the boy let his basket of fish fall overboard, and the man giv his line sich a jirk that he broke it off and his fish fell back into the water. Then they run off to the clecring on tother side, and told such a yarn about me that an infarnul big mob cum runnin down to the landing to see if I war a maremade or a shark. Sez I to 'em, "I spose you don't know me, but I'm arter votes, and if any of you wants to no my name, it is Ben Harding, the messmate of Davy Krockett, and my name's in the allmy knack!" When I sed that, the Justass of the peace cum rite up to me, and took off his hat and axed me to his house, and he intraduced me to awl his family, and telled 'em I wos a extinguished orthur. I axed for sumthing to do onor to my frend with, and I took the biggest horn of whiskey that has gone into my cataplasm for a week.

I expect to get awl the votes up this way, and I'm pickin 'em up all round the cumpass, for I meen to git you into Kngress, if I lose my jacket. Between you and me, Kurnill, I've been thinking whether I couldn't do sumthing for myself too. Sum on 'em thinks I ort to be up for a offiss of that kind, and I'm sure I deserves sumthing of my country seein as I hav sarved as bosun's mate, captin of the foretop and quarter master aboard the friggit. They has sum fellers in Kongress that can't hand, reef, and stear, and sum that don't know a juel block from the cook's coppers. I expeck you will try your hand for me one of these days, for I'm gitting old and lame, and I must git a burth in Kongress or the alms house pretty quick. Yourn till death.

B. H.

Love in a Chest.

"They tell me, Mr. Harding, that a saylor has a wife in every place whar he goes. Now I don't mean to insinnivate enny thing, but as you noes, Ben, praps you could tell how that is."

"Blow my timbers, Kurnill! but that is a hard word, to say it to a seaman too. But never mind, I don't get mad at trifles. You landsmen who has so many women to expose of—why you don't vally a petticoat; you don't know how to feel for 'em. But a saylor always twigs one of 'em when he can. My mother was a woman, Kurnill."

"So you told me before, Ben—but I would'nt hav beleeved it the fust time I seed you floating down the Massissippi, for you hadn't the apperunce of ennything that war ever born of woman."

Ben rolled up his eyes and turned over his cud with his tung, and after he had settled it to please his mind, he sez, "Then Kern ll, praps you wont bleeve that I've ever been in love, sense you think so hard of my looks."

"I've nothin to say agin that," sez I—"for every critter has his mate. Every thing cums to sum useful purposs, and your face wich is so ruff mite sarve for a gall to scratch her back aginst when it itched. I've no doubt that if you ever war in love, Ben, you loved very hard, bekase you ar a very hard favored man."

"That I did Kurnill!" sez Ben—"I loved so hard that my hart seemed to be skinned and my throte and bowels war all raw. My eyes! I thort I war going to shake to peaces from stem to starn, bekase my insides kept up such a combobolation. You see the way of it was this, that Goverment wanted a draft of men to go to the lakes, when we had the last kick up with John Bull, I got captured among the rest, and was ordered to march into the inferior, and go on the lakes, and you see I'm no fresh water fish, and I felt as savage as a struck porpuss, when arter sarvin a reg'lar prenticeship on salt water, I was transmografied into a fresh water lubber. So when we formed into a company and war put into marching shape, we lookt like a pack of sogers going thro the country, and I got a conceit into my head that I woodn't go fur. So won day when we was turned into a barn to sleep, I jest squeezed off won of the bordes, and my name war o-p-h off. I warked about five mile that nite, and didn't noe whar I war enny more than a codfish off soundins. Towards morning I lade down to sleep, and I hadn't slept long before I war waked up by the sun shining on my eyes: and then I heered the voice of our lefftennent, and I thort my name war Dennis, for they war close aboard of the place where I had cum to an ankur. But I war down in the long grass, and there war sum rocks thereaway, and their peepers warnt sharp enuff to twig dungarven. As soon as all war still, I got up and lookt around me; but jest at the minnit an infernal little reefer, who happened to be astarn of the rest, fixt his eyes on me, and he cum runnin towards me and yelping for help. I knowed it was time to drop my courses and set my skysails, and I put one foot before the other as if I was measuring land by the job. I didn't see which way I went, but they war all arter me, like a whole fleet of frigates in chase of a 74. I run about a mile, and as I hadn't got my land legs on I was tired a little, and then I seed a small house and a fence. "Any port in a storm," sez I,

1841.	APRIL.	30 Days.

These calculations are on a new plan, whereby much space is saved, and all their usefulness retained. They will serve for all the United States, the Canadas, &c.

PHASES OF THE MOON.

- ○ Full 5th, 8 32 E.
- ☾ L. Q. 13th, 5 8 E.
- ● New 21st, 9 37 M.
- ☽ F. Q. 28th, 4 4 M.

D. M.	D. W.	Sun rises H. M.	Sun Sets H. M.	Sun's Dec. D. M.	Sun Slow. M. S.	Moon South. H. M.	High Water. Boston.	High Water. New York.	Moon Rises and Sets. Maine.	Massachusetts.	New York.	Washington.	Charleston.	New Orleans.	ASPECTS, &c.
1	T	5 44	6 16	4 35	3 58	8 48	8 38	6 8	3 26	3 22	3 18	3 14	3 3	2 54	*April Fool Day.*
2	F	5 43	6 17	4 59	3 39	9 38	9 31	7 1	3 53	3 50	3 47	3 44	3 36	3 32	*Weather continues to*
3	S	5 41	6 19	5 22	3 21	10 26	10 16	7 46	4 15	4 14	4 13	4 12	4 9	4 5	*grow warmer. Muddy*
4	**S**	5 40	6 20	5 44	3 3	11 13	10 53	8 23	4 37	4 37	4 37	4 37	4 37	4 37	Palm Sunday. *streets*
5	M	5 39	6 21	6 7	2 46	11 59	11 29	8 59	rises	rises	rises	rises	rises	rises	*—several ladies lose*
6	T	5 37	6 23	6 30	2 28	m	a 5	9 35	7 41	7 37	7 33	7 29	7 16	7 9	*their slippers in the*
7	W	5 36	6 24	6 52	2 10	0 42	0 40	10 10	8 52	8 47	8 42	8 37	8 21	8 12	High Tides. *mud—*
8	T	5 35	6 25	7 15	1 53	1 37	1 19	10 49	10 1	9 55	9 49	9 44	9 24	9 13	Maundy-Thursday.
9	F	5 33	6 27	7 37	1 36	2 27	2 2	11 32	11 5	10 59	10 53	10 47	10 28	10 14	Good Friday. *Boot-*
10	S	5 32	6 28	8 0	1 20	3 20	2 47	a 17	m	11 56	11 49	11 42	11 20	11 8	*blacks curse and swear*
11	**S**	5 30	6 30	8 22	1 3	4 12	3 39	1 9	0 3	m	m	m	m	11 56	Easter. *terribly. The*
12	M	5 29	6 31	8 44	0 47	5 4	4 34	2 4	0 52	0 45	0 38	0 31	0 8	m	☽ Apogee. *Legisla-*
13	T	5 28	6 32	9 5	0 31	5 54	5 36	3 6	1 32	1 26	1 20	1 14	0 55	0 44	*ture make long speeches*
14	W	5 27	6 33	9 27	0 16	6 43	6 45	4 15	2 5	2 0	1 55	1 50	1 34	1 25	*—Molasses candy scarce*
15	T	5 25	6 35	9 49	S. 1	7 28	7 49	5 19	2 32	2 28	2 24	2 20	2 8	2 0	Low Tides. *and in*
16	F	5 24	6 36	10 10	F. 14	8 11	8 48	6 18	2 55	2 52	2 49	2 46	2 37	2 31	*great demand. Fresh*
17	S	5 23	6 37	10 31	0 28	8 54	9 34	7 4	3 16	3 14	3 12	3 10	3 4	3 0	*Hal but. Umbrellas in*
18	**S**	5 22	6 38	10 52	0 42	9 37	10 17	7 47	3 37	3 36	3 35	3 34	3 31	3 29	Low Sunday. *demand.*
19	M	5 21	6 39	11 13	0 56	10 21	10 52	8 22	3 56	3 57	3 58	3 59	4 2	4 2	*Potatoes very poor—*
20	T	5 19	6 41	11 33	1 9	11 8	11 27	8 57	4 18	4 20	4 22	4 24	4 30	4 34	*many of them rotten.*
21	W	5 18	6 42	11 54	1 22	11 57	m	9 38	sets.	sets.	sets.	sets.	sets.	sets.	*Violent hail storm.*
22	T	5 17	6 43	12 14	1 34	a 51	0 8	10 20	8 43	8 38	8 33	8 28	8 12	8 3	High Tides. *Talk of*
23	F	5 16	6 44	12 34	1 46	1 50	0 50	11 4	10 1	9 55	9 49	9 43	9 24	9 12	*finishing Bunker Hill*
24	S	5 14	6 46	12 54	1 57	2 53	1 34	11 59	11 11	11 4	10 57	10 50	10 27	10 17	*Monument.*
25		5 13	6 47	13 14	2 8	3 57	2 30	m	m	m	11 58	11 52	11 32	11 22	2d Sund. af. E. ☽ Per.
26	M	5 12	6 48	13 33	2 18	5 0	3 22	0 52	0 10	0 4	m	m	m	m	*An Editor gets his nose*
27	T	5 11	6 49	13 52	2 28	5 58	4 30	2 0	0 58	0 53	0 48	0 44	0 27	0 20	*pulled. A ghost seen*
28	W	5 10	6 50	14 11	2 38	6 52	5 55	3 25	1 33	1 29	1 25	1 21	1 11	1 3	*in School street.*
29	T	5 8	6 52	14 30	2 47	7 41	7 3	4 33	2 3	2 0	1 57	1 54	1 46	1 40	Low Tides.
30	F	5 7	6 53	14 43	2 55	8 29	8 14	5 44	2 27	2 25	2 23	2 21	2 15	2 11	*Weather grows warm.*

YOUNG LADY'S DIARY.—Arose at 11 A. M. Was dressed at twelve. Dropped in at Miss William's and learned the name of Margaret Flury's beau. At 2 stopped in at Jones's, and looked at several pieces of goods, together with ribbons without number. Threatened to call again. Shopkeeper very polite. Saw a handsome young man behind the counter. He looked like Sandy Jenkins. At 4 o'clock had a call from Mr. Fitz; he was very agreeable, and gave a full account of the ball at M———'s. Thought he should come again. At 6 prepared to go to the theatre. Went with our party, and was first bored with a tedious play written by that dull fellow, Shakspeare. After that came a new farce—I forget the name, but it was delightful, especially when one of the characters fell into a basket of crockery. Got my feet wet on the way home; but Mr. Brown, our beau, was very kind. He lent me his India-rubbers. They were too large for me, but as it was dark, no one could see the size of my feet. Got safe home, and went to bed. Lay awake till two o'clock, engaged in reading a sweet novel, by the dear, delightful Bulwer. Went to sleep at last, and dreamed Mr. Fitz wanted to propose, and just as he was on the point, I was called to breakfast by Kitty. I will get ma' to turn off the impudent creature.

and I bounced rite thro the gate into a kind of a garden, and thar war a fine plump looking gal there all alone. She was jest pickin a pare off a young tree; and she turned her head the minnit she heered me cum thro the gate. I telled her not to be fritened, and she stood still. Then I took off my hat, and made about a dozen low bows to her, and telled that I am chased by sum rascals who wanted to make a soger of me, and I put on the soft soap so thick, that she telled me to cum into the house, and it's well she did, for I seed the bosun's head pop up over the fence jest as she shut the door. She took me up garret and put me into a big chist. There I laid as snug as a ground beet butt, and the offissers was soon afoul of the gal, for they swore they seed me dodge into that gate. She told 'em it war a foolish story of theirn, for she hadn't seen no man till they cum, and she wished they would cleer out all of 'em, as it would be agin her karaktur to have 'em there when her father and brothers war away from home. At last, they hauled off grumbling, and then the gal let me out of the chist. So I thanked her kindly, and she smiled and she tauked, and used such dictionary words that I perseeved she was high larnt. I begun to feel strange when I seed her hansum shape, and her plump catheads, and all that sort-o-thing, and at last I got in love. In two hours her fokes got home, and I telled 'em how she had slipt off the sharks, and they said she was true blue. I staid there four or five days, and all that time I was in love, and I thort they all liked for the gal to be a sailor's wife; but all of a sudden, they got to drinkin with me, and got me drunk one day, and when I cum to myself, I was about two hundred miles from the place, and never could get the latitude and longitude of it sense I spose they carred me off so that I needn't marry the gal, and they didn't want to hurt my felins by refusing: so they transferred me. So seein I couldn't ever find the gal agin, I took a good cruse on the strength of it, and had a fortnite's drunk, and that cured my love—but it was tremendous while it lasted.

Cobbing the Cook.

You axed me to tell you what I meant by cobbing the cook. Now, Kurnill, you don't have any sich doins up in this latitude, but aboard of a ship, the feller what cooks the vittles has all the slush for his parquisit; and so to make up for that, he must be cobbed when he don't do his duty. When a ship's company hangs together, and carrys on every thing reg'lar, the cobbing of the cook is always done hansumly and without any trubble, but sumtimes there is ruff ally fellers aboard, who will stick up for the cook in hopes of gitting the windurd side of him. He will give them a peace of soft tack, or let them have a gob of slush to eat on their bread; and then when the cook is brought to the windlass and the handsaw laid agin his starn, they will grumble, the lubbers, and try to stand up for him.

We war wonst saling in the gulf streem in the old ship Susannah—a very good craft, but rather wet on the fourcastle—when we found the cook was growing keerless about our vittles. We stood it as well as we cood, till won day we hauled a biled rat out of the been soop, and then we swore the cook should be cobbed if it cost us six months' wages. I went up to the cabuse, and sez I, "Cum out here, you black scorpion, and stand by to be cobbed!" He rolled up the whites of his eyes like a duck in a thunder storm, and he ketched up the tormentors, which, you must noe, is a grate iron fork, and he sed he wouldn't stur tack nor sheet. Then I put my grapplings rite into blackey's wool, and bowsed away. He made a jab at me with his tormentors, and Bill Davis pulled 'em out of his hand. He fout and bit and stunk, all under won. "Cum along, you d——d soger!" sez I, "and take your pilotage for steerin a dead rat into our kid." I got him as fur as the windlass, while Bill Davis bored holes in a barrel stave, for to spank his backside with; but jist as I was hollering for spunyarn to seize him down to the windlass, I felt a wipe on the side of my head that almost knocked me on my beem eends. I turned round and seed a lubber of a marine that we had shipped in Cuba, and noed rite off what it ment; for he war always laying off and on the cook's galley, to git sumthing good to put into his bred basket. I kicked up behind and planted my heel in the marine's bowels, and he grunted like a struck porpuss. By this time, every won war up for a row. Sum on 'em stuck up for the cook, and sum on 'em war for lending me a hand to bring the cussed nigger to justice. Now it war the devil to pay and no pitch hot. In a minnit, two or three war down in the lee skuppers. Some on 'em had black eyes, and the claret war running like a reg'lar naval action.—Hugh Jones found a bottle of rum in the cook's galley, and he swigged upon that in the midst of the fite. As for me, Kurnill Crockett, I don't strike my flag to any craft that wears purser's shirts; but I war raked by a pare on 'em; for the cook took me in front, and the infarnal marine cum up agin in my wake. The d——d nigger got me by won leg and was going to throw me overboard, and then the marine got hold of my cue with his teeth. But I shet up my corn grinders and got blackey's hand between my teeth, when he let go of me, and I follered him with a handspike till he run clear over the ship's side. I never seed him agin, and its no hard work to giss what becum of him, for the sharks has a nat'ral puncheon for nig's meat The fite was kept up till it got to be a rai'l mutiny; for they broke open the Cappin's liquor case, and the way the square bottles flew about the decks war nixt to a white squall. The Cappin seed every thing going to rack, and he didn't no now to carry sale in sich a sqall. He begged the men to be easy, but it was no use, for he got a dab in his own chops. But the second mate was as cunning a young devil as ever pulled out a weather eering, and when he saw how 'twas, he went aloft, and pretty soon he bellowed out from the cross-trees, "Call the Cappin quick, for I see a British man-o-war in the horizon." The hands on deck soon understood his lingo, and there was a scampering and clawing off, like a harpoon thrown into a pod of fish. Every won run down below and kept as quiet as a louse in a clean shirt, for they war so a-feared of getting pressed that they wood have let a rum cask leak out without ketching a drop sooner than to show their profiles on deck.

[See page 19.]

Portrait of the Girl

Who secreted Ben Harding in a Chest, while the crew were in pursuit of him. See the story of Love in a Chest, page 14.

1841. MAY. 31 Days.

These calculations are on a new plan, whereby much space is saved and all their usefulness retained. They will serve for all the United States, the Canadas, &c.

PHASES OF THE MOON.

○ Full 5th, 9 13 M.
☾ L. Q. 13th, 11 29 M.
● New 20th, 6 52 E.
☽ F. Q. 27th, 10 16 M.

D. M.	D. W.	Sun rises H. M.	Sun Sets H. M.	Sun's Dec. D. M.	Sun Fast. M. S.	Moon South H. M.	High Water. Boston.	High Water. New York.	Moon Rises and Sets. Maine.	Massachusetts.	New York.	Washington.	Charleston.	New Orleans.	ASPECTS, &c.
1	S	5 6	6 54	15 7	3 3	9 15	9 8	6 38	2 49	2 48	2 47	2 46	2 42	2 41	*Lads and lasses riding*
2	S	5 5	6 55	15 25	3 11	10 0	9 55	7 25	3 10	3 11	3 12	3 13	3 17	3 13	3d Sunday after E.
3	M	5 4	6 56	15 42	3 18	10 47	10 35	8 5	3 31	3 33	3 35	3 37	3 43	3 47	*out; girls talk and*
4	T	5 3	6 57	16 0	3 24	11 35	11 11	8 41	3 55	3 58	4 1	4 4	4 13	4 19	*laugh very loud.*
5	W	5 2	6 58	16 17	3 30	m	11 49	9 19	rises	rises	ises	rises	rises	rises	*Chaise will overset*
6	T	5 1	6 59	16 34	3 35	0 25	a 27	9 57	8 57	8 51	8 45	8 39	8 19	8 9	High Tides. *about*
7	F	4 59	7 1	16 51	3 39	1 16	1 7	10 37	9 58	9 51	9 44	9 37	9 14	9 1	*this time, corner of Ann*
8	S	4 58	7 2	17 7	3 44	2 9	1 48	11 18	10 50	10 43	10 36	10 29	10 6	9 53	*and Blackstone streets.*
9	S	4 57	7 3	17 23	3 43	3 1	2 30	noon	11 32	11 26	11 20	11 14	10 54	10 44	4th Sund. aft. Easter.
10	M	4 56	7 4	17 39	3 50	3 51	3 16	0 46	m	m	11 57	11 52	11 36	11 27	☽ Apogee. *Snow*
11	T	4 55	7 5	17 55	3 52	4 40	4 3	1 33	0 7	0 2	m	m	m	m	*melts fast. Weather*
12	W	4 54	7 6	18 10	3 54	5 26	4 51	2 21	0 36	0 32	0 28	0 24	0 11	0 4	*grows warmer.*
13	T	4 53	7 7	18 25	3 55	6 9	5 47	3 17	1 1	0 58	0 55	0 52	0 42	0 37	*Fine weather for dig-*
14	F	4 52	7 8	18 39	3 56	6 51	6 51	4 21	1 21	1 19	1 17	1 15	1 8	1 5	Low Tides. *ging*
15	S	4 51	7 9	18 54	3 56	7 33	7 53	5 23	1 41	1 40	1 39	1 38	1 35	1 33	*Clams. Long days.*
16	S	4 50	7 10	19 8	3 55	8 16	8 54	6 24	2 1	2 1	2 1	2 1	2 2	2 2	Rogation Sunday.
17	M	4 50	7 10	19 21	3 54	9 0	9 42	7 12	2 21	2 23	2 25	2 27	2 33	2 36	*Girls meet at the cor-*
18	T	4 49	7 11	19 35	3 52	9 48	10 23	7 58	2 44	2 47	2 50	2 53	3 3	3 8	*ners of the streets and*
19	W	4 48	7 12	19 48	3 50	10 40	11 11	8 41	3 11	3 15	3 19	3 23	3 36	3 43	*giggle much.*
20	T	4 47	8 13	20 0	3 47	11 38	11 59	9 29	sets.	sets.	sets.	sets.	sets.	sets.	Ascen. D. Holy Th.
21	F	4 46	7 14	20 13	3 43	a 41	m	10 15	8 58	8 51	8 44	8 37	8 14	8 1	*Loafers begin to thaw*
22	S	4 45	7 15	20 25	3 39	1 45	0 45	10 59	10 3	9 56	9 49	9 42	9 19	9 6	☽ Per. Very H. Tides.
23	S	4 44	7 16	20 36	3 35	2 50	1 29	11 47	10 56	10 50	10 44	10 38	10 18	10 8	Sunday after Ascen.
24	M	4 44	7 16	20 48	3 30	3 51	2 17	m	11 34	11 29	11 24	11 19	11 2	10 54	*out, and sun themselves*
25	T	4 43	7 17	20 59	3 24	4 49	3 9	0 39	m	m	11 58	11 54	11 41	11 34	*on the Common. About*
26	W	4 42	7 18	21 9	3 18	5 39	4 7	1 37	0 6	0 2	m	m	m	m	*this time a great robbery*
27	T	4 41	7 19	21 19	3 11	6 27	5 9	2 39	0 31	0 29	0 27	0 25	0 18	0 14	*will be perpetrated in*
28	F	4 41	7 19	21 29	3 5	7 14	6 19	3 49	0 52	0 51	0 50	0 49	0 46	0 44	Low Tides. *the upper*
29	S	4 40	7 20	21 39	2 57	7 58	7 28	4 53	1 13	1 14	1 15	1 16	1 19	1 21	*part of Washington*
30	S	4 39	7 21	21 48	2 49	8 43	8 34	6 4	1 34	1 36	1 38	1 40	1 47	1 50	Pentecost. Whit S.
31	M	4 39	7 21	21 56	2 41	9 29	9 24	6 54	1 57	2 0	2 3	2 6	2 16	2 21	Whit Mond. *street.*

All the world has heard of Mr. Nobody. Every one knows he is more mischievous than any other wight on earth. He is every young lady's beau, every thief's accomplice, every loafer's scape goat. Dr. Young says, "The things unseen do not deceive us;" and thus it is with Mr. Nobody, who although never seen is sure to do all the mischief there is done. If you see a broken window, a molasses stopple left out, or a demijohn overset, you run no risk of being deceived with regard to the author of the calamity. It was Mr. Nobody, without doubt. There are occasions, however, when you may be certain Mr. Nobody will be absent, and his place will be supplied by solid flesh and blood. These are such cases as the following: When the bell rings for dinner, when pay day arrives, when your taxes are due, when a lecture is to be delivered gratis, when money has been found and advertised, and when a vacant sinecure requires filling. In short Mr. Nobody is a very modest gentleman, and never occupies a station which any other person is desirous of filling. Having committed crimes innumerable, he ever escapes punishment: his infamous character destroys not his influence; every prude affects his company, and the chastest maiden thinks it no disparagement to seek him constantly.

Cobbing the Cook---See page 16.

19

1841.	JUNE.	30 Days.

These calculations are on a new plan, whereby much space is saved, and all their usefulness retained. They will serve for all the United States, the Canadas, &c.

PHASES OF THE MOON.

○ Full 3d, 10 48 E.
☾ L. Q. 12th, 1 3 M.
● New 19th, 2 18 M.
☽ F. Q. 25th, 5 39 E.

D. M.	D. W.	Sun rises H. M.	Sun Sets H. M.	Sun Dec. D. M.	Sun Fast M. S.	Moon South H. M.	High Water: Boston.	High Water: New York.	Moon Rises and Sets: Maine.	Massachusetts.	New York.	Washington.	Charleston.	New Orleans.	ASPECTS, &c.
1	T	4 33	7 22	22 5	2 32	10 18	10 12	7 42	2 21	2 26	2 31	2 35	2 53	3 0	Whit Tuesday.
2	W	4 38	7 22	22 13	2 23	11 8	10 51	8 21	2 52	2 58	3 4	3 10	3 30	3 40	*Great talk about the*
3	T	4 37	7 23	22 20	2 14	m	11 30	9 8	rises	rises	rises	rises	rises	rises	*next President.*
4	F	4 37	7 23	22 27	2 4	0 0	a 8	9 38	8 42	8 35	8 28	8 21	7 58	7 46	Rather High Tides.
5	S	4 36	7 24	22 34	1 54	0 52	0 48	10 18	9 28	9 21	9 14	9 7	8 44	8 31	*Politics run high, and*
6	**S**	4 36	7 24	22 41	1 44	1 44	1 25	10 55	10 5	9 59	9 53	9 47	9 27	9 17	Trinity Sunday.
7	M	4 36	7 24	22 47	1 33	2 32	2 [illegible]	11 32	10 35	10 [illegible]	10 25	10 20	10 3	9 55	☽ Apogee. *many*
8	T	4 35	7 25	22 52	1 22	3 18	2 [illegible]	a 9	10 59	10 55	10 51	10 47	10 34	10 27	*triumphs of principle,*
9	W	4 35	7 25	22 57	1 10	4 1	3 18	0 48	11 23	11 20	11 17	11 14	11 4	10 59	*both on the whig and*
10	T	4 35	7 25	23 2	0 59	4 44	3 59	1 29	11 42	11 40	11 38	11 36	11 29	11 26	*democratic sides.*
11	F	4 34	7 26	23 6	0 47	5 25	4 44	2 14	m	m	m	m	m	m	*A pair of white pants*
12	S	4 34	7 26	23 10	0 35	6 6	5 42	3 12	0 0	0 0	0 0	0 0	0 0	0 0	*seen in Tremont street.*
13	**S**	4 34	7 26	23 14	0 22	6 48	6 49	4 19	0 20	0 21	0 22	0 23	0 26	0 28	1st Sun. aft. Trinity.
14	M	4 33	7 27	23 17	F. 10	7 32	8 13	5 43	0 38	0 41	0 44	0 47	0 56	1 2	Low Tides. *the first*
15	T	4 33	7 27	23 20	S. 3	8 22	9 8	6 38	1 5	1 9	1 13	1 17	1 30	1 37	*this season.*
16	W	4 33	7 27	23 22	0 16	9 16	10 7	7 37	1 35	1 40	1 45	1 50	2 7	2 15	*Foreign news very in-*
17	T	4 33	7 27	23 24	0 28	10 16	10 57	8 27	2 14	2 20	2 26	2 32	2 52	3 2	*teresting. Fight*
18	F	4 33	7 27	23 26	0 41	11 19	11 48	9 18	3 2	3 9	3 16	3 23	3 46	3 58	*in Cornhill between two*
19	S	4 32	7 28	23 27	0 55	a 26	m	10 5	sets.	sets.	sets.	sets.	sets.	sets.	*loafers Jug of Molas-*
20	**S**	4 32	7 28	23 27	1 3	1 32	0 35	10 48	9 26	9 21	9 16	9 11	8 54	8 46	☽ Perigee. *ses broken*
21	M	4 32	7 28	23 28	1 21	2 33	1 18	11 29	10 2	9 58	9 54	9 50	9 37	9 30	Very High Tides.
22	T	4 32	7 28	23 28	1 34	3 28	1 59	m	10 33	10 [illegible]	10 27	10 24	10 14	10 9	*at the corner of Con-*
23	W	4 32	7 23	23 27	1 17	4 18	2 42	0 12	10 53	10 52	10 51	10 50	10 46	10 45	*gress street—molasses*
24	T	4 33	7 27	23 26	2 0	5 5	3 27	0 57	11 14	11 14	11 14	11 15	11 14	11 15	St. John Baptist.
25	F	4 33	7 27	23 25	2 12	5 52	4 24	1 54	11 35	11 37	11 39	11 41	11 46	11 51	*totally lost. Talk*
26	S	4 33	7 27	23 23	2 25	6 37	5 25	2 55	11 57	m	m	m	m	m	Low Tides. *of finish-*
27	**S**	4 33	7 27	23 21	2 38	7 22	6 33	4 3	m	0 0	0 3	0 6	0 16	0 21	3d Sun. after Trinity.
28	M	4 33	7 27	23 18	2 50	8 10	7 48	5 18	0 20	0 24	0 28	0 32	0 45	0 52	*ing Bunker Hill Mon-*
29	T	4 33	7 27	23 15	3 2	8 59	8 51	6 24	0 49	0 54	1 1	1 4	1 21	1 29	*ument.*
30	W	4 34	7 26	23 12	3 14	9 50	9 17	7 17	1 23	1 29	4 35	1 41	2 1	2 11	*Fishing party.*

HOW TO FIND OUT A MAN OF SENSE.—If you would find out whether a man is possessed of a first rate intellect or not, you have but to inquire whether he agrees with you in opinion or not. If he does, he is, of course, a man of sense: but if he has not come to the same conclusions with yourself, it is very plain that he is an ignorant fellow, who is wholly unfit to manage his own business. You would risk little in pronouncing him an idiot. But it is not only in matters of religion, taste, and philosophy that this rule applies. If you are fond of mutton-chop, and your neighbor prefers a roasted duck; if you drink wine and he drinks beer; or if you prefer land travel and he takes the steamboat, you have a right to set him down an ass. But if you change your opinions, or your taste, and subsequently come over to his ground, then, of course, he becomes a wise man. Your change of sentiment must be imputed to him for wisdom, for although he does not think as you once did, yet he thinks as you do now. There are some exceptions to this rule. If he takes a fancy to the same maiden that you love, or is a candidate for the office to which you aspire. He is then, of course, a most worthless fellow; and any opprobrious name that you think fit to apply to him, will be, to the last degree, apropos.

A Ride.

Thar war a little ditty that happent the fust time I war sot up for Kongress, that I never telled nobody nothing about; partly bekase every boddy knowed it, and partly bekase I war intermined to keep it a secret. Davy Crocket never duz any thing he is ashamed on, this I did not do myself, for I tried not to do it. I war going to election and had my rifle with me, with my dog Tiger, with two bottles of white face in my pockets. When I got about ½ way thar, and war in the forrest, I seed a cattymount up in a tree, and I clum up to git a fare shot at the cretur, and told tiger to be on hand if he war wanted. I war got on to the nixt branch to the won that the varmint war on, when he jumped down on to the limb and lit close to my elbow with his mouth to my ear, as if he war going to whisper sumthin mity private. I thort I war a gone sucker, but jist at that minnit the limb cracked and snapped off. I didn't stop to see what becum of the cattymount, but I went down, and wood ha' gone into the mud, only thar war a big elk under the tree, and I lit upon his hind parts, and he giv a rankantankerous jump which slid me down betwixt his horns like a gal in a sighed saddle, and then he put in all he knew. I like to ha' got my branes nocked out by the branches, and the way he went thro the forrest war like a driving snow storm.—All the trees and rocks seemed to be running the tother way; and Tiger couldn't keep up with us, and his pesky noise only maid the cretur run faster. I held on upon my rifle, and I couldn't help thinking of Kurnill Tonson's mounted riflemen only I shood ha' found it hard work to taik aim, bekase the cretur woodn't give me a chance. Howsever he soon begun to git out of the forrest, and then I war terribly ashamed for feer sum human wood see me, but I coodn't see them as every thing looked streeked as if the American flag war spred over all natur. We went ahed this way till all at wonst I seed thar war sumthing befour us, but I didn't have time to xamine it as we war jumping on like chain litening when it skips down the Mississippy. I soon found what it war, for we dove thro the door of a house, and when the door flew off its hinges, it went agin the wall so hard it stuck thar.—Then the elk pitched agin the door opposite, and tho it war locked, yet that flew into the middle of the flore, and upset a cat, and a table, and a candle that had been used to melt seeling wax. A young feller and a gal that war korting thar jumped up haff skeered to deth.

I railly thort this war the eend of my travels, but the pesky varmint wheeled about, and went hed fourmost out the door agin, and shot ahead on the jump, four mile farther, till he cum to the little eend of the Little Fork of Great Skunk's Liver River. We went rite thro the mob for the poles war held ther, and every boddy pulled off their hats and gin 3 cheers for Krockett, and that made me wrathy, and graniverous as a parched corn; bekase they didn't try to stop the varmint at all. But they all hurried out of the way, and bauled—Hurrah for Crockett! Won feller from down East sed he sposed that war the way that our candydates war *run for Kongress*. I spose the elk war so skeered that he didn't no what he war about. But it helped my lection, for they all thort it war an invention of my own, for to gratify the public. The elk had only gone a small peace further when we past by a store whar I war in dett a few dollars, and it war kepp by a Yankee, and he thort I war running away from my creditors. So he razed a hue and cry arter me, and in a munnit the hole village of Apple Toddy Creek war razed. They skeered the elk fust won way and then the tother, and he swung about and jostled me so that it skraped all the skin off my hinder eend, and I begun to feer if I got a seet in Kongress it wouldn't be of no use to me. Howsever the court war settin at the time, and the peeple skeered the cretur so that it run that way, and as the court house door was open, it run rite in. As soon as the judge seed me, sez he, "Thar's Crockett now! We war jist wanting yer for a witniss in this ere kase of the Widder Strapup. You've cum in the nick of time."

The lawyer that war pleeding agin the widder stared open his eyes, and sez he, "I bleeve it is the Nick o'time, for the devil must ha' brot him to spile my kase."

I jumped rite off the elk, and gin my evidence, and that saved the widder's property; so she took the elk under her protexion, and arter he war broke, she used to ride him to meetin.

Colonel Crockett and the Honey Bees.

It must be allowed that bees are curous creturs, speshaliy for making honey. Thar's but two things more curouser, and that ar a Yankee and an Irisher. The Yankee may be all his life making honey, or money, and that's all the same thing in Dutch, but you never ketch him eating any on it himself, which shews he haint got so much sense as a bee, with all his industriousness and ingenuity. Not he—none of his honey is of no use to nobody till grim death has smoked him out of his hive.

Thar's this difference between a Yankee and an Irisher—a Yankee always thinks before he speaks, and an Irisher always speaks before he thinks. You have to hammer a Yankee to a red heat before he strikes, and you must hammer an Irisher dead before he is cool. A Paddy is suspicious his own country is better than enny other, and a Yankee calkilates enny country is better than his own—but I expect I'm getting to philosopherising and that's a waste of time, and so stranger, if you pleasê, we'll jist take a dust of grog.

Onst I hired an Irisher to help me logrolling and house-raising, and a fine fellow he war when he war sober, which happened as often as twice a week; but when he war a little exflunctified, the Lord forgive me for a liar if he war not the most consumminated braggadocious I ever seen or heern tell on. His name war Teddy O'Rourke, and he used to swear that in his country the moon war as big as four of owrn, and the thunder four times as loud. He stumped all Kaintuck, and Tennessee, too, and said he could ride rusty on enny man born this side of the big water, xcepting Colonel Crockett. He had more sense than not to leave me out, tho he war a blundering bull of the bogs. But he licked Jimmy Twiggs and Bill Broadhern, and cum off first best from Sam Scrowger with very little damage, for he only lost one eye and a small bit of his nose, and thar ar few chaps that can git away from Sam so easy. But what made him prouder than a dog with two tails was, killing a bare by cutting him on the nozzle with a hoe, and arter that he eenamost grew out of his breeches, and swore he could lick any wild beast of American growth.

I didn't more than haff like this, and as I had a sort of kinder kyindness for Teddy, I rewmynated like a cow on a stale cud, about the best way to take the vanity and consate out on him. I did think of rowing him a mile or two up Salt River myself; but I didn't very well like to hurt his feelings, and besides I never skulp a man that's not my match. I shood have been obleeged to excoriate him for all that, if I hadn't had a piece of good luck won day—perhaps I mought say two pieces.

I war sneaking along the edge of Big Bear's Grass Bluff arter a buck, when I cum spontanatiously on a bee's neest in the grass, and at fust I war going to kill the varmints and take the honey—I a kinder thought I wood, and then I kinder thought I woodn't, and finally I felt a kinder woodn'ter. "No, no," says I, "these ere wild bastes of American growth, as Teddy calls 'em, will jist sarve his turn for a fite." And presently, in less than no time, the Lord war uncommon good to me agin, for I lit on a hornet's neest hanging to the branch of a persimmon bush before I noed it. I blazed a tree close by to no the place agin, and at nite I cum back and stopped up the hole with a plug, and took the neest down. I met a wolf and two catamounts on my way back hum; but I war in too good a humor at what I had done to hav the hart to hurt 'em—so I jist kicked 'em out of the track, and told 'em I war Col. Davy Crockett. When they heered that they powdered away with their tails between their legs, thanking me for their lives.

We had a corn husking at my clearing that nite and sum of the most savagerous fellers, and the prettiest, rosiest, holesomest corn-fed gals war thar that ever gouged out an eye, or war brushed by a beard. Arter work war done, the water of life jug went round and Teddy war in his glory. He swore he cood drive any man thar up to his neck into the floor like a nail, with one stroke of his five blessed bones, and that he cood pull the rainbow out of the sky and tie both eends in a bow knot. Now sum of the company were skeered at Teddy, and others didn't want to hurt him, and so nobody offered to stop his moderate headway till he most impudaciously boasted that he could whip twice his weight of any wild meat west of the mountains, and then I took it up. I offered to bet him the liquor all round, that I wood find him fifty little Kaintuckians the next day, that could make him say enuff, and the way he took me up war beautiful to hear.

Next morning I started Jem Flatfoot into the bush to git the neest, all drest and painted up like a Pottowottomy Ingin, and then follered arter with the boys and Teddy, all itching for a fite. On the way I led Teddy slam bang into the bees' neest, and I suspect you never seen a man shew so much rale grit. The bees out and at him like small shot on a blue winged teal, and at fust he war as much astonified as if he'd tumbled into a mare's neest. He didn't offer to cut dirt, tho'; but stood and danced on the neest like a feller named Potter, what I seen cut a pigeon wing among eggs in New York, singing out—och, I'm kilt, and murdhered and spilt intirely! Ceade millia diaoul! He made more noise than a hundred saw mills. May be he didn't stamp the sweeteners all to death, and when he'd got through and his physog looked more like a punkin than a gentleman's mug, I war obliged to give in that he'd fairly whipped the varmints. But he had a little smarter chance of work afore him.

When we cum to the persimmon bush there stood Jimmy Flatfoot with the yaller jackets' neest in his hand. "Hallo, Sackarup!" says I, "here's the animaul what will show you the bear hug." "Humble bumble kixawix tomensodle foodle foo!" says Jimmy.—"What's that the spalpeen is being arter saying?" sez Teddy. "He's axin me," sez I, "if you ar the little boy that ar to tite him, and he wants to no how many more you've bro't to begin to help you." "Mr. Lugin," sez Teddy, "you and I will soon be better acquainted, plase God, as the thief said to the halter." And then he made a dip rite at Jimmy, looking not at all like a quaker, but jist as if he ment to use him up from the eend of his snout to the tip of his tale; but Jim didn't stop for him. He pulled the plug out of the neest and give it a shake, and pulled foot like a whitehead, abusing Teddy in a most onchristian fashun all the way. That made Pat streak it harder arter him; but he might as well have chased a streak of forked lightning, for Jim could run down a buck. Now you must no, if you didn't no it afore, that neither a bee nor a yaller jacket can fly so fast as a man can run, and as Jim gallivanted thro' the bush he shook the beasts out of the neest and as they coodn't catch him, they naterally flew rite into Teddy's face, for he war close behind, so mad that he didn't feel the stings no more than if they war drops of Cologne water. So that they had it hip and thigh more then two miles, screeching and hollering like Henry A. Wise on the floor of Kongress, when he's mad; till poor Teddy dropt down and fainted away; for it was not in natur to stand it. Then I carried him hum and give him half a gallon of Tally Valley Cord to cumfort his stummuck, and he made nothing of it in less than an hour. I've heern tell that Irishers haint got no souls, and if that ar true the devil war very nigh gitting another apple to roast that time, for the ignorant cretur cum so near dying, thar war no fun in it; but it war the best taste of sport I ever had in my life.

Teddy never bragged arter that of what he coold do, but always affirmated that if the thing had happened in Ireland he wood have been crusified without benefit of clargy, for he said that the yaller jackets thar war as large as a turkey gobbler, and carried grindstones under their wings, to sharpen their bills on; but whether that ar true or no I leave to them what hav travelled in forrin parts. [See last page.]

A Scienterifical Courtship.

No doubt the reeder has heern of Wicket Finney; and if he hasn't heern of him, of Meg Wadlow. At any rate, between 'em both, he must hav heern of one or tother of 'em. Wicket considered himself inticingly wonderful whar thar war a gal to be treed, and all the female kyind of our diggins war voracious to git him and his plunder. Whenever Wicket axed a gal to set up with him she war rite off as tender as a oak tree with the bark off, and played possum to every feller, for six months arterward. But Wicket didn't take any of 'em for life, bekase why? It war so easy to git 'em, jist as when I war in a whole herd of buffaloes, I didn't draw trigger bekase I war in no hurry. Now Meg Wadlow hadn't cum to them parts then, for she war gone to live with her ant up in Queen's Creek Village, close to the Blue Notch, and her ant had sent her to bording skool for to finish her eddication. So the tork war all about our parts that she war coming home, and her fokes war in a dreadful fixin about it. Her mother was skeered ½ out of her wits, bekase she new that Meg wood xpect to see every thing in the perliterest fashion. She maid her husband wrence out his cap in cold water, and scour up his rifle as bright as two niggers' eyes; and she died her bare-skin pettycoat yaller, and bort two new woodden boles of a peddler for to put into the best room. At last Meg cum in good arnest, and when she got down upon the ground from the karridge, she held up her gound with won hand, jist as if Kaintucky ground war too mean for her to tred upon. Her father stood in the door, and held his breth, for he war so terrificaciously frightened when he seed her skooleriferous perliteness and all her other vississitudes, that he had rather a' faced a painter on the cleerins without his rifle. Her mother run and got behind a fence till the danger war over and peaked at Meg thro a not-hole. I don't no what past arter she got into the house: but in a few days, her father sent to town for a piane, bekase Meg wood hav won; and he went about the diggins torking about northing but the wonderful accomplifications and corruptions of his darter.

Wick Finny heered of all this and it sot his dander rite up. All the other fellers fout shy, and never dast to speek to Meg arter she got home any more than they wood look into Davy Crockett's rifle when his finger war on the trigger. But Wick war not the man to hang fire whar thar war anything of the she kind. He went up into Wolfhead Clearings and got him a soot-o-close that war bran new, and he made the shop keeper show him how to put 'em on. He went home with 'em, and felt so mity odd in his new close that he couldn't hardly turn his hed and lift up his legs, but he noed he war all in the hiter-fashion, and Meg wood have to own it, when she seed him. He war afeered to take his close off for fear he couldn't git 'em on agin, as he had forgot how it war done, and so he slept in 'em all that night.

On the nixt day jist as the sun had begun to squat, he blacked up his boots with a gob of bare's greece, filed sum of the rust off his teeth, and courled his hare with a peace of a broken rake. Then he sot out for Meg's house. He went rite in, and axed for Meg. Her mother didn't no him in his new close, and she curched so hard that she spraint her ankle. She showed him into the room war Meg was, and true enuff she war playing on her piane. He sot down on a kynd of a bench they coll a sophy, and then Meg lookt rite at him. He felt queer enuff when he seed her perlitenes and all that are kynd of personification. But he sez, sez he, "I spose it is a good while sense you hav ben up in these diggins be 4."

"I beg your pardon, sir," sez she, "I war jist sittin down to my piny forty."

"You needn't beg my pardon, I'm not a going to lick ye," sez he. "But should kindly thank ye jist to play upon that mashine a little; what do ye call it?"

She telled him it war a piny forty, and then she begun to make it tork whilst she sung a song that she called *Scots wee hay*.

He sed it war the prettiest thing he had ever heered since his sister broke the conch shell by blowing so hard that she split it in two. When Wick sed that, she held up both of her little white hands, and declared she didn't no what a conch shell war. When Wick heered that, he pulled won out of his pocket, and put it to his mouth and blew sich a winder that she put both her hands on her ears, and jumped up, and hollered rite out; for Wick had as much wind as a race-hoss, and when he blowed on the shell, it shook the hole house and made the wooden dishes rattle. When she sot down agin on the sophy, Wick sez, "Miss Mag'ret I spose you knows that I've cum to to try to—you know what," and then he winked so affectificaciously that she seed trap in a minnit.

"Oh, sir!" sez she, "my trough is invocably plagued to another," and then she laied her hand right on her stumark, and sed "Oh sir, my hart is deceptible to your honors in axing for my hand, but thar is another won as I is defianced to."

When Wick heered that, he jumpt right up and crowed 3 times, and he sez, "Tell me who the varmint is, right off, and I'll bring ye his two eyes in my pocket before you can wink agin. I'll let him no that when I'm on trail and their's a gal to be fout for, I'm all brimstone from my toes upwards."

When the gal seed that Wick war in arnest, and war going to fite for her, she looked down and blushed up like a red cabbidge. Then Wick sidled up to her, and giv her a smack that might be heered as far as a painter's squall. Then she noed Wick war true pluck, and she begun to feel worser and worser, and she sez, "Alas! my tender heart must yield, sense you will resist that I be your bride," and so she gin her consent.

"I'm glad to hear that," sez Wick, "I'll cum and see you sum times, but you is quite too fast when you sposes I am for yoking on with you. So good bye to ye;" and he jumped up and sallied off whistling thro the forrest. So when Meg seed he didn't want her arter all the fuss, she went into the high sterricks and the rumytiz, and the fainting fits, and all that sort o'thing, wich she had larnt at the boarding skools.

A Duel---Related by Ben Harding.

Talking of catching whales, Kurnill, puts me in mind of a scrape I wonce seed around on tother side the Horn, so if your gal will jist sit along and give me room I'll tell ye the story. You must no the whalers puts in at a place they call Cokimber, very often. Won day, when I war thar, I war tired of cruising about town, and stepped into a shantee and sot down. Thar war two Nantucket Cappens there, and their ships laid off in the harbor. They war drinking auguadenty, and felt pretty lively. So when they seed me cum in, they jist tipt me the wink, and won of 'em, sez he, "you look dry, Jack; walk up and squeeze brown Betty." "Thank ye, kindly," sez I, and I went up to the little table whar they sot, and poured out a horn—you no, Kurnill, that I aint in the habit of stunting myself; and jist as I war swallering it down, who shood heave in site but two officers from a British sloop of war off in the harbor, with a lobster back between 'em. The lobster lookt at me with all his eyes, and sez he to the other officers, "here is imsponsible cumpany, I think, let us go whar we can find gentlemen to eat and drink with." With that, won of the Nantucket Cappens grinned and sot his teeth as if he war biting a copper spike in 2, and sez he, "thar war none but gentlemen here be 4 you cum in. But if you ar in sarch of sogers like yourself, you'll find graybacks enuff up in the kalibuse." With that the lobster war roaring mad, and he clapped his paw upon his cheese-knife that he wore in his belt, and sez he, "if you war a gentleman I woodn't stand this no how, but as you ar a blubber-hunter, I look on ye with contempt." Then he turned around and war going to hoist sail for another port; but the sailer officers who war in his cumpany wood not stur a step, and won of 'em whispured in his eer, and arter they had torked awhile, the lobster walked up to the table, and sez he, "My ship-mates here, say, that bekase you ar a Cappen, I ort to giv you the satisfaktion of a gentleman. I can't stop long to tork to won of your calling, but you'll heer from me shortly,"—so he put his fingers on his nose as if he smelt whale ile, and hauled his wind. I set as still as the stump of a mast, but arter red fish had showed his tale, the Cappens told me to help myself to bisket and jerked beef, and so I renced it down as I ett it, with the juse of the bottle. We hadn't sot long be 4 one of the sailer officers what war with the lobster, cum in, and maid a low bow like a mainsail be 4 the wind, and handed the Nantucket Cappen a billyduce. So he opened it and redd it, and then the English officer axed him for an ansur. So sez he, "five o'clock to-morro morning, and my weppons will be only a harpoon." The Englishman held up his hands and sez he, "who ever heered of such a unsarcumsized weppon as that to fite a gentleman with. You no, sir, that my principles isn't fish!"

"What's a lobster but a fish?" sez the Cappen, and I hope I may be blown into ribbins, if the Englishman didn't laff rite out, for you must no, Kurnill, that thar never war a blu-jacket who war not fond of heering the marines quizzed. So he went off, and shortly arterward the Cappens hauled their wind and went aboard their crafts.

Arely nixt morning I hauled my corpse out of my hammock, and went ashore to see the fite. The two sea-officers war thar, and the lobster too. The Nantucketman had his coat off and his sleeves rolled up, and he stood leaning on a devilish grate harpoon that war scoured up like silver, so you mite hav seed your face in it. Pritty soon the peeple begun to bundle out and drop down to the battle ground, for the news on it had got wind all over the town. The Nantucketman soon spied me, and sez he, "Jack, do you cum here, and hold on upon this line." So I took the kile in my hand; and pretty soon the ground war marked out. The lobster held up his head, and looked as grum as a shark with his teeth pulled out. He cocked his shooting iron and snapped it. The ball whizzed by my ear, between me and the Nantucketman.

Then the Nantucketer, sez he, "now it's my turn," and then he jist lifted his harpoon, and put one hand over the but eend of it, and steadied the shank with the other. Then he stretched himself out witth a wide spread, like a man that war used to the trade. He took a good aim, right between the two eyes of the red-coat, and the feller looked astonished a minnit—then his lips begun to quiver like a ship's fore-top-mast-stay-sail when she's going in stays. He begun to perseve the Nantucketer war in downright airnest, and he expected that before night his fat wood be peeled off his bones and biled out into ile. He looked as white about the gills as a biled skip-jack, and he dropped his weppon and run as if the devil sent him on eend. Away he went over the hills, and you coodn't see his backside for dust. Then his second blushed like a rooster's comb, and lookt as mad as a red-hot cannon shot. The two officers swore he had disgraced the whole ship's cumpany, and they run arter the lobster and ketched him and brought him back. So when he war brought back, he walked rite up to the Nantucketer, and sez he,—"My shipmates tells me I ort to pologize, and I spose it wont be nothin agin my honor, seein that what I sed to you yesterday was only a *lap-seus-linger*. I own you to be a gentleman and a clever feller."

The Nantucketer didn't like that at all, for sez he, "You've had one good shot at me, and you must let me have one dart at you, be 4 I can be apolligized."

Then the lobster was reddy to bust, he war so mad and so fritened, and he sez, "I'll see you in tofit befour I'll ever stand up to be speered like a whale, by a d——d scrapisland blubber hunter," and he turned about and run like a pirate off Castle Moro, and he war never heern on arterwards, from that day to this.

1841

1841. **JULY.** **31 Days.**

These calculations are on a new plan, whereby much space is saved, and all their usefulness retained. They will serve for all the United States, the Canadas, &c.

D. M.	D. W.	Sun rises. H. M.	Sun Sets. H. M.	Sun's Dec. D. M.	Sun Slow. M. S.	Moon South. H. M.	High Water. Boston.	High Water. New York.	Moon Rises and Sets. Maine.	Massachusetts.	New York.	Washington.	Charleston.	New Orleans.	Aspects, &c.
1	T	4 34	7 26	23 8	3 26	10 42	10 32	8 2	2 3	2 10	2 17	2 24	2 47	3 0	Ⓨ Apogee.
2	F	4 34	7 26	23 3	3 37	11 33	11 10	8 40	2 52	2 59	3 6	3 13	3 36	3 48	*Great alteration in the*
3	S	4 34	7 25	22 59	3 48	m	11 46	9 16	rises	rises	rises	rises	rises	rises	*weather in the space of*
4	**S**	4 35	7 25	22 54	3 59	0 22	a 23	9 53	8 32	8 27	8 22	8 17	8 2	7 52	4th S. Aft. Tr. ☽ Ap.
5	M	4 35	7 25	22 48	4 9	1 10	0 56	10 26	8 58	8 54	8 50	8 46	8 33	8 26	Rather High Tides.
6	T	4 36	7 24	22 42	4 19	1 55	1 29	10 59	9 21	9 18	9 15	9 12	9 2	8 57	*the last three months.*
7	W	4 36	7 24	22 36	4 29	2 37	1 59	11 29	9 42	9 40	9 38	9 36	9 29	9 26	*Many soldiers in the*
8	T	4 37	7 23	22 30	4 39	3 18	2 32	a 2	10 0	9 59	9 58	9 57	9 54	9 52	*streets.*
9	F	4 37	7 23	22 23	4 48	3 58	3 13	0 43	10 18	10 19	10 20	10 21	10 24	10 24	*Dogs plenty.*
10	S	4 38	7 22	22 15	4 57	4 39	3 54	1 24	10 38	10 40	10 42	10 44	10 51	10 54	*Apples rot fast.*
11	**S**	4 38	7 22	22 7	5 5	5 22	4 43	2 13	11 1	11 4	11 7	11 10	11 20	11 21	5th Sun. aft. Trinity.
12	M	4 39	7 21	21 59	5 13	6 7	5 51	3 21	11 26	11 31	11 36	11 41	11 58	m	Low Tides.
13	T	4 39	7 21	21 51	5 20	6 57	7 21	4 51	m	m	m	m	m	0 4	*Fat folks quite uncom-*
14	W	4 40	7 20	21 42	5 27	7 53	8 47	6 17	0 0	0 6	0 12	0 18	0 38	0 48	*fortable. Hard times.*
15	T	4 41	7 19	21 33	5 34	8 51	9 50	7 20	0 43	0 50	0 57	1 4	1 27	1 40	*Several dandies obliged*
16	F	4 41	7 19	21 23	5 40	9 59	10 47	8 17	1 40	1 47	1 54	2 1	2 24	2 37	*to go to work.*
17	S	4 42	7 18	21 13	5 45	11 6	11 37	9 7	2 52	2 59	3 6	3 13	3 36	3 48	*Talk of finishing B. H.*
18	**S**	4 43	7 17	21 2	5 50	a 9	m	9 48	sets.	sets.	sets.	sets.	sets.	sets.	☽ Per. ⊙ Ecl. invis.
19	M	4 43	7 17	20 52	5 55	1 8	0 13	10 27	8 24	8 21	8 18	8 15	8 5	8 0	Very High Tides.
20	T	4 44	7 16	20 41	5 59	2 3	0 57	11 4	8 51	8 49	8 47	8 45	8 38	8 35	*monument.*
21	W	4 45	7 15	20 29	6 2	2 54	1 34	11 42	9 13	9 13	9 13	9 13	9 11	9 10	*Horses complain of*
22	T	4 46	7 14	20 17	6 5	3 41	2 12	m	9 34	9 35	9 36	9 37	9 40	9 42	*flies. Long tails in*
23	F	4 47	7 13	20 5	6 7	4 29	2 57	0 27	9 57	10 0	10 3	10 6	10 16	10 21	*demand.*
24	S	4 48	7 12	19 53	6 9	5 16	3 45	1 15	10 21	10 25	10 29	10 33	10 46	10 53	*A great deal of sweat-*
25	**S**	4 48	7 12	19 40	6 10	6 4	4 40	2 10	10 48	10 53	10 58	11 3	11 20	11 23	7th Sun. aft. Trinity.
26	M	4 49	7 11	19 27	6 10	6 53	5 49	3 9	11 20	11 26	11 32	11 38	11 53	m	Low Tides. *ing.*
27	T	4 50	7 10	19 13	6 10	7 43	7 8	4 33	11 59	m	m	m	m	0 8	*Bathing recommended*
28	W	4 51	7 9	19 0	6 9	8 35	8 24	5 54	m	0 6	0 13	0 20	0 43	0 56	*by the papers.*
29	T	4 52	7 8	18 46	6 8	9 27	9 24	6 51	0 46	0 53	1 0	1 7	1 30	1 43	*Look out for rain be-*
30	F	4 53	7 7	18 31	6 6	10 17	10 18	7 48	1 39	1 46	1 53	2 0	2 23	2 36	*tween now and the end*
31	S	4 54	7 6	18 17	6 3	11 5	11 50	8 20	2 40	2 46	2 52	2 58	3 14	3 26	*of next month.*

PHASES OF THE MOON.

- ○ Full 3d, 1 28 E.
- ☾ L. Q. 11th, 3 29 E.
- ● New 18th, 9 11 M.
- ☽ F. Q. 25th, 3 18 M.

The following are the titles of sundry sacred books which came from the press shortly after the Protestant Reformation:—"A Rusty Saw for the Throat of the Pope and his Cardinals." "The only true Interpretation of Holy Scripture, according to the gift of John Bragg, now put forth for the first time, for the Life of the World, by the Author—price three shillings." "A Slice of Bread and Piece of Meat, spiritually administered, for the Nourishment of Hungry Souls, By Greely Bostruff." "A Sharp Knife for Ripping Open the Pillows which have been put under the Armholes of Sinners, by the Damnable Blasphemies of Papistical Absolution—for the first time whetted and ground on the Grindstone of the Holy Evangelists, by Peter Bulfinch." "A New Wheelbarrow for wheeling away the burden of Corruption from the Church, by Ezekiel Gwynn." "A Rushlight to assist the True Believer in understanding the Fifth Verse of the Ninth Chapter, of the Gospel of Saint Luke, by Benjamin Carver & William Godwin." "A handful of Moss gathered from the Stone which the Builders Rejected, by Obed Sweeting." "A Telescope by looking through which the Humble Christian may peer over the Battlements of Heaven, by Abel Buzzard, one of the humblest of the Lord's Servants."

1841.	AUGUST.	31 Days.

These calculations are on a new plan, whereby much space is saved and all their usefulness retained. They will serve for all the United States, the Canadas, &c.

PHASES OF THE MOON.

- ○ Full 2d, 5 0 M.
- ☾ L. Q. 10th, 1 17 M.
- ● New 16th, 4 33 E.
- ☽ F. Q. 23d, 4 12 E.
- ○ Full 31st, 8 38 E.

D. M.	D. W.	Sun rises. H. M	Sun Sets. H. M	Sun's Dec. D. M.	Sun Slow. M. S.	Moon South H. M.	High Water. Boston.	High Water. New York.	Moon Rises and Sets. Maine.	Massachusetts.	New York.	Washington.	Charleston.	New Orleans.	ASPECTS, &c.
1	S	4 55	7 5	18 2	6 0	11 51	11 23	8 53	3 44	3 49	3 54	3 59	4 16	4 24	8th S. aft. Tr. ☽ Ap.
2	M	4 56	7 4	17 46	5 56	m	11 56	9 26	rises	rises	ises	rises	rises	rises	☽ Ecl. total, part. vis.
3	T	4 57	7 3	17 31	5 52	0 34	a 27	9 57	7 46	7 44	7 42	7 40	7 33	7 30	High Tides.
4	W	4 58	7 2	17 15	5 46	1 16	0 57	10 27	8 6	8 5	8 4	8 3	8 0	7 58	*Grasshoppers dance*
5	T	4 59	7 1	16 59	5 41	1 57	1 28	10 58	8 25	8 25	8 25	8 26	8 27	8 27	*briskly.*
6	F	5 0	7 0	16 42	5 34	2 38	2 1	11 31	8 45	8 46	8 47	8 48	8 51	8 58	*Girls cross.*
7	S	5 1	6 59	16 26	5 28	3 20	2 38	a 8	9 4	9 7	9 10	9 13	9 23	9 27	*Warm weather.*
8	S	5 2	6 58	16 9	5 20	4 4	3 20	0 50	9 29	9 33	9 37	9 41	9 54	10 1	9th Sun. aft. Trinity.
9	M	5 3	6 57	15 52	5 12	4 52	4 16	1 46	10 0	10 5	10 10	10 15	10 32	10 40	*Thunder, at this time,*
10	T	5 5	6 55	15 34	5 4	5 44	5 27	2 57	10 37	10 43	10 49	10 55	11 15	11 25	*will be accompanied by*
11	W	5 6	6 54	15 16	4 55	6 40	7 4	4 34	11 26	11 33	11 40	11 47	m	m	Low Tides. *lightning.*
12	T	5 7	6 53	14 59	4 45	7 42	8 36	6 6	m	m	m	m	0 10	0 22	*Several horses sold very*
13	F	5 8	6 52	14 40	4 35	8 46	9 42	7 12	0 28	0 35	0 42	0 49	1 12	1 24	*cheap.*
14	S	5 9	6 51	14 22	4 24	9 51	10 36	8 6	1 44	1 50	1 56	2 2	2 22	2 32	*Striped Pig* **in** *demand.*
15	S	5 10	6 50	14 3	4 13	10 52	11 18	8 48	3 6	3 11	3 16	3 21	3 33	3 46	☽ Perigee.
16	M	5 12	6 48	13 44	4 1	11 48	11 59	9 29	sets.	sets.	sets.	sets.	sets.	sets.	☉ Eclipsed invisible.
17	T	5 13	6 47	13 25	3 49	a 41	m	10 6	7 15	7 14	7 13	7 12	7 9	7 7	*Great talk of finishing*
18	W	5 14	6 46	13 6	3 36	1 32	0 36	10 42	7 39	7 39	7 39	7 39	7 41	7 42	High Tides. *Bunker*
19	T	5 15	6 45	12 46	3 23	2 22	1 12	11 18	8 1	8 3	8 5	8 7	8 14	8 17	*Hill Monument.*
20	F	5 16	6 44	12 27	3 9	3 10	1 48	m	8 25	8 28	8 31	8 34	8 44	8 49	*Pig run over in Water*
21	S	5 18	6 42	12 7	2 55	3 59	2 29	0 0	8 52	8 56	9 0	9 4	9 17	9 24	*street.*
22	S	5 19	6 41	11 47	2 40	4 49	3 17	0 47	9 24	9 29	9 34	9 39	9 56	10 4	11th S. after Trinity.
23	M	5 20	6 40	11 26	2 25	5 41	4 15	1 45	10 0	10 6	10 12	10 18	10 38	10 48	*A gentleman flogged by*
24	T	5 21	6 39	11 6	2 9	6 33	5 22	2 52	10 44	10 51	10 58	11 5	11 28	11 41	*his wife.*
25	W	5 23	6 37	10 45	1 53	7 25	6 38	4 8	11 36	11 43	11 50	11 57	m	m	Low Tides.
26	T	5 24	6 36	10 24	1 37	8 16	7 57	5 27	m	m	m	m	0 20	0 34	*Old maids very talka-*
27	F	5 25	6 35	10 3	1 20	9 6	9 2	6 32	0 36	0 42	0 48	0 54	1 14	1 23	*tive. Musquitoes*
28	S	5 26	6 34	9 42	1 3	9 54	9 52	7 22	1 40	1 45	1 50	1 55	2 12	2 20	☽ Apo. *bite sharp,*
29	S	5 28	6 32	9 21	0 45	10 38	10 29	7 59	2 51	2 50	2 54	2 58	3 11	3 18	12th S. af. T. *and very*
30	M	5 29	6 31	8 59	0 27	11 21	11 2	8 32	3 49	3 52	3 55	3 58	4 8	4 13	*noisy with their wings.*
31	T	5 30	6 30	8 38	0 9	m	11 32	9 2	rises	rises	rises	rises	rises	rises	

Paying in kind.—A young fellow, numbered among his acquaintances one youth by no means famous for his generosity This youth thought proper to cut the acquaintance of our hero on the plea of a thread-bare coat which the latter found himself obliged to wear. Very soon, however, the death of a relation placed him in opulent circumstances, and then the gentleman who had entertained so much dread of the thread-bare coat, sent him a letter filled with exalted esteem, and reminding him of the friendship which had so long subsisted between them. Our hero answered his letter, and sent at the same time a large square box. He opened the letter in which the former acknowledged his obligations for so much good will, and such warmth of friendship, and stated that he thought some return was justly due. The gentleman then turned to the box, with glistening eyes, and doubting whether it contained Spanish dollars or costly apparel. What was his astonishment to find, upon taking off the top, that it was filled with a quantity of *soft soap*, together with the remnants of the identical thread-bare coat which had occasioned the breach between them.

A Scienterifical Courtship---See page 23.

1841. **SEPTEMBER.** **30 Days.**

These calculations are on a new plan, whereby much space is saved, and all their usefulness retained. They will serve for all the United States, the Canadas, &c.

PHASES OF THE MOON.

☾ L. Q. 8th, 9 19 M.
● New 15th, 1 11 M.
☽ F. Q. 22d, 8 43 M.
○ Full 30th, 11 32 M.

D. M.	D. W.	Sun rises H. M	Sun Sets. H. M	Sun's Dec. D. M.	Sun Fast. M. S.	Moon south. H. M.	High Water. Boston.	High Water. New York.	Moon Rises and Sets. Maine.	Massachusetts.	New York.	Washington.	Charleston.	New Orleans.	ASPECTS, &c.
1	W	5 32	6 28	8 16	0 10	0 2	a 2	9 32	6 36	6 36	6 36	6 36	6 36	6 36	*Several gallons of rum*
2	T	5 33	6 27	7 54	0 29	0 43	0 32	10 2	6 54	6 55	6 56	6 57	7 0	7 2	High Tides.
3	F	5 35	6 25	7 32	0 48	1 23	1 6	10 36	7 15	7 18	7 21	7 24	7 34	7 39	*purchased and sent*
4	S	5 36	6 24	7 10	1 8	2 9	1 41	11 11	7 40	7 44	7 48	7 52	8 5	8 12	*home in oil jugs.*
5	**S**	5 37	6 23	6 48	1 27	2 56	2 20	11 50	8 7	8 12	8 17	8 22	8 39	8 47	13th Sun. aft. Trinity.
6	M	5 38	6 22	6 26	1 47	3 46	3 13	a 43	8 42	8 48	8 54	9 0	9 20	9 30	*Days grow shorter.*
7	T	5 39	6 21	6 3	2 7	4 40	4 9	1 39	9 27	9 34	9 51	9 48	10 11	10 24	*Ladies put on their In-*
8	W	5 41	6 19	5 41	2 28	5 39	5 28	2 58	10 24	10 31	10 38	10 45	11 8	11 21	*dia-Rubbers.*
9	T	5 42	6 18	5 18	2 48	6 41	7 5	4 35	11 32	11 38	11 54	11 50	m	m	Low Tides. *Pigeon*
10	F	5 43	6 17	4 55	3 9	7 43	8 33	6 3	m	m	m	m	0 10	0 20	*pies very wholesome at*
11	S	5 44	6 16	4 32	3 29	8 44	9 33	7 3	0 50	0 55	1 0	1 5	1 22	1 29	*this season of the year.*
12	**S**	5 46	6 14	4 9	3 50	9 41	10 24	7 54	2 10	2 14	2 18	2 22	2 35	2 42	14th S. aft. Trinity.
13	M	5 47	6 13	3 46	4 11	10 36	11 4	8 34	3 32	3 35	3 38	3 41	3 51	3 56	☽ Perigee. *Horse*
14	T	5 48	6 12	3 23	4 32	11 27	11 42	9 12	4 51	4 53	4 55	4 57	5 4	5 7	*shoes found very ser-*
15	W	5 50	6 10	3 0	4 53	a 17	m	9 48	sets.	sets.	sets.	sets.	sets.	sets.	*viceable in keeping off*
16	T	5 51	6 9	2 37	5 14	1 6	0 18	10 25	6 34	6 36	6 38	6 40	6 45	6 50	High Tides. *witches*
17	F	5 52	6 8	2 14	5 35	1 57	0 55	11 2	7 0	7 4	7 8	7 12	7 25	7 32	*Much talk of finishing*
18	S	5 54	6 6	1 51	5 56	2 47	1 32	11 44	7 30	7 35	7 40	7 45	8 2	8 10	*B. H. Monument.*
19	**S**	5 55	6 5	1 27	6 17	3 39	2 14	m	8 3	8 9	8 15	8 21	8 41	8 51	15th S. aft. Trinity.
20	M	5 56	6 4	1 4	6 38	4 33	3 6	0 36	8 48	8 55	9 2	9 9	9 32	9 45	*Much sneezing in*
21	T	5 57	6 3	0 41	6 59	5 27	4 2	1 32	9 38	9 45	9 52	9 59	10 22	10 35	*State Street.*
22	W	5 59	6 1	N 17	7 20	6 19	5 4	2 34	10 35	20 42	10 49	10 56	11 19	11 32	*Cabbage plenty.*
23	T	6 0	6 0	S. 6	7 41	7 10	6 16	3 46	11 38	11 44	11 50	11 56	m	m	Very L. Tid. Aut. Eq.
24	F	6 1	5 59	0 30	8 1	7 58	7 32	5 2	m	m	m	m	0 16	0 27	☽ Apogee.
25	S	6 2	5 58	0 53	8 22	8 44	8 37	6 7	0 42	0 47	0 52	0 57	1 14	1 22	*Evenings grow cooler.*
26	**S**	6 4	5 56	1 17	8 42	9 26	9 23	6 53	1 47	1 51	1 55	1 59	2 12	2 19	16th Sun. aft. Trinity.
27	M	6 5	5 55	1 40	9 2	10 8	10 4	7 34	2 50	2 53	2 56	2 59	3 9	3 14	*Change in the fashion*
28	T	6 7	5 53	2 3	9 22	10 50	10 33	8 8	3 53	3 55	3 57	3 59	4 6	4 9	*of Ladies bonnets.*
29	W	6 8	5 52	2 27	9 42	11 32	11 9	8 39	4 59	4 59	4 59	4 53	4 59	5 2	St. Mich.; Mich. Day.
30	T	6 10	5 50	2 50	10 2	m	11 41	9 11	rises	rises	rises	rises	rises	rises	*Pedlars walk briskly.*

A couple of young gentlemen having resolved to blow each other's brains out, according to the rules of etiquette in such cases provided, took care to have word conveyed to an officer of the peace on the preceding evening in order to prevent any disastrous consequences. It so happened that the officer was taken ill during the night, and neglected to depute some person in his place. The seconds and others in attendance were, therefore, much mystified when upon arriving on the ground the heroes kept constantly looking about them, as if expecting some other person to be present. As the fatal moment drew near, the anxieties of the principals increased to that degree that one of the seconds asked his gentleman whether anything was wanting before they fell foul. At mention of the approaching crisis, and already bursting with disappointment, the hero broke forth in a rage with "Devil take that infernal justice, I'll have him broke!" The seconds blushed and left the field to the combatants, who slunk off very lovingly together, swearing that there ought to be a reformation in the judicial department of the country.

An old bachelor having died of an *affection of the heart*, a young lady declared she did not wonder that he died when such a circumstance took place with *his* heart.

A Duel---Related by Ben Harding. See page 24.

1841. OCTOBER. 31 Days.

These calculations are on a new plan, whereby much space is saved and all their usefulness retained. They will serve for all the United States, the Canadas, &c.

PHASES OF THE MOON.

- ☾ L. Q. 7th, 4 27 E.
- ● New 14th, 11 44 M.
- ☽ F. Q. 22d, 4 20 M.
- ○ Full 30th, 1 17 M.

D. M.	D. W.	Sun rises. H. M	Sun Sets H. M	Sun's Dec. D. M.	Sun Fast. M. S.	Moon South H. M.	High Water. Boston.	New York.	Moon Rises and Sets. Maine.	Massachusetts.	New York.	Washington.	Charleston.	New Orleans.	ASPECTS, &c.
1	F	6 11	5 49	3 13	10 21	0 15	a 17	9 47	5 55	5 58	6 1	6 4	6 14	6 19	High Tides.
2	S	6 13	5 47	3 37	10 40	1 2	0 52	10 22	6 23	6 27	6 31	6 35	6 48	6 55	*Frogs complain of the*
3	**S**	6 14	5 46	4 0	10 59	1 52	1 31	11 1	6 55	7 0	7 5	7 10	7 27	7 35	17th Sun. aft. Trin.
4	M	6 15	5 45	4 23	11 17	2 45	2 16	11 46	7 38	7 44	7 50	7 56	8 16	8 26	*cold. Lodgers on*
5	T	6 17	5 43	4 46	11 35	3 44	3 8	a 38	8 29	8 36	8 43	8 50	9 13	9 26	*Boston Common talk*
6	W	6 18	5 42	5 10	11 52	4 44	4 15	1 45	9 33	9 40	9 47	9 54	10 17	10 30	*strongly of withdraw-*
7	T	6 19	5 41	5 33	12 9	5 45	5 35	3 5	10 44	10 50	10 56	11 2	11 22	11 32	*ing their patronage.*
8	F	6 21	5 39	5 56	12 26	6 45	7 4	4 34	m	m	m	m	m	m	Low Tides. *Look*
9	S	6 22	5 38	6 18	12 42	7 42	8 20	5 50	0 2	0 7	0 12	0 17	0 32	0 40	*for rain in all this*
10	**S**	6 23	5 37	6 41	12 58	8 34	9 16	6 46	1 21	1 24	1 27	1 30	1 41	1 45	18th S. af. Tr. ☽ Per.
11	M	6 25	5 35	7 4	13 14	9 24	10 6	7 36	2 57	2 39	2 41	2 43	2 50	2 53	*month. Strong talk*
12	T	6 26	5 34	7 27	13 28	10 14	10 47	8 17	3 56	3 56	3 56	3 56	3 58	3 59	*about finishing Bun-*
13	W	6 27	5 33	7 49	13 43	11 4	11 23	8 53	5 12	5 11	5 10	5 9	5 5	5 4	*ker Hill Monument.*
14	T	6 29	5 31	8 12	13 56	11 51	m	9 32	sets.	sets.	sets.	sets.	sets.	sets.	*Lobsters plenty.*
15	F	6 30	5 30	8 34	14 10	a 44	0 2	10 10	5 36	5 41	5 46	5 51	6 8	6 16	High Tides.
16	S	6 31	5 29	8 57	14 22	1 36	0 40	10 52	6 8	6 14	6 20	6 26	6 46	6 56	*Complaint of hard*
17	**S**	6 33	5 27	9 18	14 34	2 30	1 22	11 34	6 51	6 57	7 3	7 9	7 29	7 41	19th S. aft. Trinity.
18	M	6 34	5 26	9 40	14 46	3 24	2 4	m	7 40	7 47	7 54	8 1	8 24	8 37	*times, and scarcity of*
19	T	6 35	5 25	10 2	14 57	4 18	2 53	0 23	8 33	8 40	8 47	8 54	9 17	9 30	*money.*
20	W	6 36	5 24	10 23	15 7	5 9	3 42	1 12	9 33	9 39	9 45	9 51	10 11	10 21	*Rats very shy.*
21	T	6 38	5 22	10 45	15 17	5 58	4 39	2 9	10 37	10 42	10 47	10 52	11 8	11 17	*Several poets starve*
22	F	6 39	5 21	11 6	15 26	6 44	5 38	3 8	11 41	11 45	11 49	11 53	m	m	☽ Apogee. *to death.*
23	S	6 40	5 20	11 27	15 34	7 29	6 46	4 16	m	m	m	m	0 6	0 13	Very Low Tides.
24	**S**	6 42	5 18	11 48	15 42	8 11	7 50	5 20	0 45	0 48	0 51	0 54	1 4	1 9	20th S. aft. Trinity.
25	M	6 43	5 17	12 9	15 48	8 51	8 43	6 13	1 49	1 51	1 53	1 55	2 2	2 5	*Boots with tassels, and*
26	T	6 44	5 16	12 30	15 55	9 33	9 29	6 59	2 52	2 53	2 54	2 55	2 58	3 0	*hoop petticoats seldom*
27	W	6 45	5 15	12 50	16 0	10 15	10 11	7 41	3 56	3 55	3 54	3 53	3 50	3 48	*seen in the shops—go-*
28	T	6 47	5 13	13 10	16 5	11 1	10 47	8 17	5 2	5 0	4 58	4 56	4 50	4 46	*ing out of fashion.*
29	F	6 48	5 12	13 30	16 9	11 49	11 21	8 51	6 12	6 9	6 6	6 3	5 53	5 48	*Much doggrel poetry*
30	S	6 49	5 11	13 50	16 12	m	a 1	9 31	rises	rises	rises	rises	rises	rises	*appears in the papers.*
31	**S**	6 50	5 10	14 10	16 15	0 42	0 42	10 12	5 33	5 44	5 50	5 56	6 16	6 26	High Tides.

An old lady said her husband was very fond of peaches, and that was his only fault.

"Fault, madam!" said one, "how can you call that a fault?"

"Why, because there are different ways of eating them, sir. My husband takes them in his brandy"—meaning that he was in the habit of swigging peach brandy.

Those who drink spirits for sickness have this advantage, that they never will be well, and can, therefore, always have a sufficient excuse for taking a swig at the black bottle.

The times are so bad that honest men can't live—as the fellow said when he stole a Beef's Liver.

I love cleanliness—as the fellow said when he washed his shirt entirely away, and went to bed naked.

Never fear me, I'll keep your secret—as the felon promised Jack Ketch, when on the point of being turned off.

A Rail Herowine.

Speeking of human natur, thar's more of it to be seen aboard of a broad horn than enny whar else except in Kongress; tho I think thar's much resemblance between 'em, only the won that steers the broad horn is called a skipper, and him as steers the Kongress is called a speeker. Ruel Gwynn took a broad horn for won seezon, and I used to like to go down the Mississippi with him, tho I didn't let the peeple aboard noe that I war Kurnell Crockett, or I should a had no piece nor elbow room, as thar is alwise a squirminiverous jam to get site of me when I'm vissuble.

I war standing on the shore won day, and I seed Ruel's broad horn poking down the river, and I hollered out for him to stop. So he laid as stil as he could while I swum off to him. As soon as I got in the bote, thar war a passle of fellers cum round me; for they had heered how my name was Crockett, and they stared at me as if I war a mammouth from forty leag beyond the head of Salt River. Won feller cum up rite be 4 me, and leened on his rifle, and gaped at me with his mouth wide open, as if he war going to swaller me up like an arthquake taking down a meetin house. "Mister," sez I, "I take it people are scarse in your diggins."

"How so?" sez he, and then he shuved his nose up to me as sassy as a hungry wolf.

"Why," sez I, "you is so free with your squintifications that I ar thankful your eyes aint a gimblet, or I should ha' been bored threw be 4 long."

"I take it you ar a public man," sez he; "and the peeple has a rite to xamine thar representatives."

Howsever I telled him he needn't xamine me as a Yankee jokky xamines a hoss, for thar war won way to inspeck hosses and niggers.

and another way to inspeck white humans. That war like putting a butt behind his ear, and he lookt as mad as a cat up to her neck in a snow-bank. Fust he turned red, then he turned white, and then he looked blue, and arter that he pushed his hand into his hare. I lookt rite at him, and felt hungry. Thar war a nawing at my stumark like when I feel sharkish arter a day's hunt.

"Stranger," sez I, "do ye meen enny insinnivations?"

Sez he, "I'll see you agin at the 'lection whar I can hav fare play, and I'll chaw you—I'll dubble you down, and screw you into the shape of a cork screw—I'll persuade you I'm pluck and grit united in won individdle."

"Don't tantavrillize me," sez I. "If you arn't reddy to fite now, jest obsquatulate—stand cleer, I tell ye, for I'm rising inwardly. Thar's a hot place in my gizzard, and my gall is reddy to bust, and besides all this my feelins is hurt."

He nodded his head, and stepped back, and sed, "I tell you Kernill Crockett, I'll see you agin about this." So he strutted off like a tree standing perperendicular with the branches lopped off. I sorter kynder got an idee that the feller warnt true grit, but I never judges a stranger, only I ment to give him a chance to meet me agin, for I took it that it war a fare challenge. They called his name Willikins and I got Ruel to rite it down on the seat of my trowsers with a peace of chork so that I needn't forgit it.

The bote had gone on a smart distance further when we turned Great Puddle Point, and thar won of the fellers seed a painter squeezing in among the bushes. So we stopt the bote and a passle of us what had rifles went ashore. This Willikins went ashore with the rest of us, bekase he had a rifle. We went up a smart peace but didn't see nothin of the painter, and wile we war going back to the bote that pesky Willikins thort he seed a white burd jest over the bushes, and he drew a lead upon it; but it war an old woman's cap that he fired at, and if he had fired strait, he would hav put haff an ownse of lead under her hare, but he misst her hed, and hit a bran new shift that she had on the line. She riz rite up, for she had been leaning down over her close basket, and when she seed the feller cuming to look for his burd, she picked up a club, and went at him. Now it's no lye that I'm tellin on, deer reeder, but it's a sartin truth, that he showed this old woman the tale of his cote, and run as if a hole tribe of wild injuns war on his trale, and he bawled for help, but our fellers stood and laft at him; and as for me, I war so mad to think I had been challenged by sich a funk that I grit my teeth till they struck fire.

Mrs. Cuttle and the Catamount.

One day I fell in with Jo Cuttle. Jo war an honest ruff-and tumble sort of a chap, and arter we had jogged on a little way, sez he "Kurnel, thar war a pesky queer scrape onct happened to me in these diggins. It war arter this sort: It war late one arternoon when my wife war cuming home from a tea-squall. She war passing rite thro' the forrest, and had forgot to bring her rifle with her. But she never war afeard of any thing less than a bull mammoth, and so she jogged along as merry and contented as a she bear. She cum to a deep hollow whar war a large pond of water, and she saw a big log lying near, and she rolled it in. As soon as the log war afloat, she got on one eend of it with her face towards the opposite shore, and begun to paddle across. When she got about haff way over, she happened to hear a low growl, and when she looked behind she saw that a great catamount sot on the other eend of the log. He had took passage with her when she fust started, but she did not see him then. As my wife war sitting straddle, it took sum time for her to turn round, and face the catamount. He showed his teeth and grouled because she had left off paddling; so she concluded that he meant to behave civil, if she wood only carry him safe across; but she had an idee that arter they war fairly landed, he would try to make a breakfast of her. So she would not paddle another stroke. He kept growling, as much as to say, "Row away you infarnal jade!" That made her mad, for she cood understand his language jist as well as if she had been born to it; so she dashed water on him with her paddle. This made him wink a little, and he showed his teeth. When she seed he war going to spring rite at her, she jist canted the log and he tumbled into the drink, but he put his paws up to get hold of the log agin, and kept trying to gain a foothold on it, which kept it turning round and round like a grindstone, till my wife's legs war chafed most ridiculous. At last she found she must get upon her feet, and then she war forced to keep hopping up and down all the time—she danced while the catamount fiddled upon the log.—She then stomped on his paws, but he minded no more about that than a flea bite. So she watched a chance and gave a jump rite on the feller's back, and caught hold of both of his ears. When ever he tried to bite her, she wood bowse his head under and haff drown him. Then he set out to swim for the shore, and she kept upon his back, and guided him by pulling his right or left ear, jist as she wanted he shood go. Well, he got safe ashore with her, and she didn't dare let go of his ears, or to get off, for fear he wood be into her like a buck-shot.

Now I happened to be out hunting, with one Kit Weatherblow, at this time, and Kit cum running to me, and told me he saw the strangest cretur going through the woods that he ever seed in his life before. He said it war a wild varmint in petticoats. I told Kit to go with me to hunt it up, for I had seen every cretur in the forrest, and this must be a stranger. We soon cum in sight of it, but I new my wife's petticoat as soon as I got a glimpse at it, and then I seed her head a little while arterward. So sez I to Kit, sing dumb, and let me get a blizzard at the obstropolous varmint, for he's runing off with my wife. I lifted my rifle and put a hole rite through his gizzard: but I shot away one of my wife's cap-strings at the same time, which war made of buffalo sinew. The varmint tumbled amongst the leaves pretty quick, and my wife picked herself off the ground in less than no time. When I seed she want hurt, I felt a little mad, and telled her never agin to clasp around the neck of any living thing but her own lawful husband.

Mrs. Cuttle and the Catamount---See opposite page.

1841. NOVEMBER. 30 Days.

These calculations are on a new plan, whereby much space is saved, and all their usefulness retained. They will serve for all the United States, the Canadas, &c.

PHASES OF THE MOON.

☾ L. Q. 5th, 11 34 E.
● New 13th, 0 49 M.
☽ F. Q. 21st, 1 28 M.
○ Full 28th, 1 54 E.

D. M.	D. W.	Sun rises. H. M	Sun Sets. H. M	Sun's Dec. D. M.	Sun Fast. M. S	Moon South. H. M.	High Water. Boston.		Moon Rises and Sets. Maine.	Massachusetts.	New York.	Washington.	Charleston.	New Orleans.	ASPECTS, &c.
							Boston.	New York.	Maine.	Massachusetts.	New York.	Washington.	Charleston.	New Orleans.	
1	M	6 52	5 8	14 29	16 17	1 40	1 28	10 58	6 28	6 35	6 42	6 49	7 12	7 25	*Parsnips plenty.*
2	T	6 53	5 7	14 48	16 18	2 42	2 13	11 43	7 29	7 36	7 43	7 50	8 13	8 26	*Much talk of finishing*
3	W	6 54	5 6	15 7	16 18	3 43	3 8	a 38	8 41	8 47	8 53	8 59	9 19	9 30	*Bunker Hill Monument.*
4	T	6 55	5 5	15 26	16 17	4 44	4 8	1 38	9 56	10 1	10 6	10 11	10 28	10 36	☽ Perigee.
5	F	6 56	5 4	15 44	16 15	5 40	5 12	2 42	11 16	11 20	11 24	11 28	11 41	11 48	*Much visiting during*
6	S	6 57	5 3	16 2	16 13	6 33	6 32	4 2	m	m	m	m	m	m	*the evening.*
7	**S**	6 59	5 1	16 20	16 10	7 23	7 49	5 19	0 30	0 33	0 36	0 39	0 49	0 53	22d Sun. aft. Trinity.
8	M	7 0	5 0	16 38	16 5	8 12	8 52	6 22	1 45	1 46	1 47	1 48	1 52	1 54	*Cool weather.*
9	T	7 1	4 59	16 55	16 0	8 59	9 41	7 11	2 59	2 58	2 57	2 56	2 54	2 52	*Turtle soup at Tom*
10	W	7 2	4 53	17 12	15 54	9 47	10 25	7 55	4 12	4 10	4 8	4 6	4 0	3 55	*Barr's Pantaloon*
11	T	7 3	4 57	17 29	15 48	10 36	11 4	8 34	5 25	5 22	5 19	5 16	5 6	5 0	*straps in great demand.*
12	F	7 4	4 56	17 45	15 40	11 26	11 43	9 13	6 38	6 33	6 28	6 23	6 6	6 0	*Drizzly rain——Scotch*
13	S	7 5	4 55	18 1	15 32	a 19	m	9 54	sets.	sets.	sets.	sets.	sets.	sets.	*mist with wind at S. W.*
14	**S**	7 6	4 54	18 17	15 22	1 13	0 24	10 40	5 29	5 36	5 43	5 50	6 13	6 26	23d Sun. aft. Trinity.
15	M	7 7	4 53	18 32	15 12	2 7	1 10	11 16	6 21	6 28	6 35	6 42	7 5	7 18	High Tides. *Very*
16	T	7 8	4 52	18 48	15 1	3 0	1 46	m	7 22	7 28	7 34	7 40	8 0	8 10	*wet under foot and mud-*
17	W	7 9	4 51	19 2	14 49	3 50	2 28	0 0	8 24	8 29	8 34	8 39	8 56	9 4	*dy over head.*
18	T	7 10	4 50	19 17	14 37	4 37	3 12	0 42	9 29	9 33	9 37	9 41	9 54	10 1	*A pig with five legs*
19	F	7 11	4 49	19 31	14 23	5 21	3 57	1 27	10 31	10 34	10 37	10 40	10 50	10 55	☽ Apogee. *born in*
20	S	7 12	4 48	19 45	14 9	6 3	4 44	2 14	11 33	11 35	11 39	11 39	11 46	11 48	*the Empire state.*
21	**S**	7 13	4 47	19 58	13 54	6 43	5 36	3 6	m	m	m	m	m	m	24th Sun. aft. Trinity.
22	M	7 14	4 46	20 11	13 38	7 24	6 38	4 8	0 34	0 35	0 36	0 38	0 42	0 42	Low Tides.
23	T	7 15	4 45	20 24	13 21	8 6	7 42	5 12	1 37	1 37	1 37	1 37	1 37	1 35	*A toad with two tails*
24	W	7 16	4 44	20 36	13 4	8 48	8 40	6 10	2 41	2 42	2 40	2 38	2 32	2 28	*will be exhibited in*
25	T	7 16	4 44	20 48	12 46	9 34	9 28	6 58	3 50	3 47	3 44	3 41	3 31	3 26	*Queen's county in Mas-*
26	F	7 17	4 43	20 59	12 27	10 25	10 16	7 46	4 59	4 55	4 51	4 47	4 34	4 27	*sachusetts.*
27	S	7 18	4 42	21 11	12 7	11 21	11 0	8 30	6 12	6 7	6 2	5 57	5 40	5 32	*Asses freeze the tips of*
28	**S**	7 19	4 41	21 21	11 47	m	11 46	9 16	rises	rises	rises	rises	rises	rises	Advent Sunday.
29	M	7 19	4 41	21 32	11 26	0 22	a 31	10 1	5 10	5 17	5 24	5 31	5 54	6 6	*their ears.*
30	T	7 20	4 40	21 41	11 4	1 25	1 15	10 45	6 18	6 25	6 31	6 37	6 57	7 8	Very High Tides.

"Reasoning from analogy, you must be a great dunce,"—said a man to his neighbor.
"How do you make that out?" returned the other.
"Because you keep an *ass* in your barn, which disturbs my family o' nights by his braying."
"Then, reasoning from analogy," said the other, "I should say you were born to be hung."
"How do you make that out?" was the question.
"Because there is a pine tree growing on your land as high as Haman's Gallows."

"I hear Jim has reformed," said one loafer to another.

"Indeed, you may well say that," was the reply—"for he used to get his liquor at the dram shop, where they sell the real slop stuff, and now he buys none but the pure spirit."

"Ah! well," returned the other, "it's an easy thing for a man to lead a *virtuous* life when he can afford it. I had an uncle that was rich, and he never got drunk till after dark when he could tumble upon his bed like a gentleman and get up a sober man in the morning."

Cure for Love.—Visit the damsel to whom you are attached, on washing day.

1841.	DECEMBER.	31 Days.

These calculations are on a new plan, whereby much space is saved and all their usefulness retained. They will serve for all the United States, the Canadas, &c.

D. M.	D. W.	Sun rises. H. M	Sun Sets H. M	Sun's Dec. D. M.	Sun Fast. M. S.	Moon South H. M	High Water. Boston.	High Water. New York.	Moon Rises and Sets. Maine.	Massachusetts.	New York.	Washington.	Charleston.	New Orleans.	Aspects, &c.
1	W	7 21	4 39	21 51	10 42	2 28	1 58	11 23	7 38	7 43	7 48	7 53	8 10	8 18	☽ Perigee. *Weather*
2	T	7 22	4 38	22 0	10 19	3 29	2 48	a 18	8 58	9 2	9 6	9 10	9 23	9 30	*feels like winter.*
3	F	7 22	4 38	22 9	9 55	4 24	3 38	1 8	10 15	10 18	10 21	10 24	10 34	10 39	*Appearances of snow*
4	S	7 23	4 37	22 17	9 31	5 15	4 35	2 5	11 29	11 30	11 31	11 32	11 37	11 40	*in this month.*
5	S	7 23	4 37	22 25	9 6	6 3	5 43	3 13	m	m	m	m	m	m	2d Sund. in Advent.
6	M	7 24	4 36	22 32	8 41	6 50	6 55	4 25	0 42	0 42	0 42	0 41	0 41	0 40	Low Tides. *Consid-*
7	T	7 24	4 36	22 39	8 15	7 36	8 7	5 37	1 54	1 52	1 50	1 49	1 41	1 40	*erable talk about finish-*
8	W	7 25	4 35	22 45	7 49	8 24	9 6	6 36	3 6	3 3	3 0	2 57	2 47	2 42	*ing B. H. Monument.*
9	T	7 25	4 35	22 51	7 22	9 12	9 59	7 29	4 16	4 12	4 8	4 4	3 51	3 44	*Boys break through*
10	F	7 26	4 34	22 57	6 54	10 3	10 42	8 12	5 27	5 22	5 17	5 12	4 55	4 47	*the ice in several places*
11	S	7 26	4 34	23 2	6 27	10 55	11 22	8 52	6 34	6 28	6 22	6 15	5 56	5 46	*Bed bugs freeze up.*
12		7 26	4 34	23 7	5 58	11 49	m	9 30	sets.	sets.	sets.	sets.	sets.	sets.	3d Sund. in Advent.
13	M	7 27	4 33	23 11	5 30	a 41	0 0	10 9	4 58	5 5	5 12	5 19	5 42	5 40	*Ice freezes two feet*
14	T	7 27	4 33	23 15	5 1	1 32	0 39	11 45	6 0	6 6	6 12	6 18	6 38	6 48	High Tides. *thick,*
15	W	7 27	4 33	23 18	4 32	2 20	1 15	11 21	7 3	7 8	7 13	7 18	7 35	7 44	*accompanied by cold*
16	T	7 27	4 33	23 21	4 3	3 5	1 51	m	8 6	8 10	8 14	8 18	8 31	8 38	*weather. Pigs squeel*
17	F	7 27	4 33	23 23	3 33	3 47	2 27	0 0	9 8	9 11	9 14	9 17	9 27	9 32	☽ Apogee.. *much in*
18	S	7 28	4 32	23 25	3 3	4 28	3 5	0 35	10 11	10 13	10 15	10 17	10 24	10 27	*the night. Change*
19	S	7 28	4 32	23 26	2 33	5 7	3 42	1 12	11 12	11 12	11 13	11 13	11 15	11 16	4th Sund. in advent.
20	M	7 28	4 32	23 27	2 3	5 47	4 24	1 54	m	m	m	m	m	m	*in the fashion of ladies'*
21	T	7 28	4 32	23 28	1 33	6 29	5 17	2 47	0 14	0 13	0 12	0 12	0 7	0 6	Winter Solstice.
22	W	7 28	4 32	23 28	1 3	7 13	6 19	3 49	1 20	1 18	1 16	1 15	1 7	1 4	Low Tides. *bonnets.*
23	T	7 28	4 32	23 27	0 33	8 1	7 33	5 3	2 28	2 25	2 22	2 19	2 9	2 4	*Sausages begin to*
24	F	7 28	4 32	23 26	F. 3	8 53	8 45	6 15	3 40	3 35	3 30	3 25	3 11	3 2	*grow ripe. Cold water*
25	S	7 28	4 32	23 25	S. 26	9 51	9 44	7 14	4 53	4 47	4 51	4 35	4 15	4 4	Christmas. *discovered*
26		7 27	4 33	23 23	0 56	10 53	10 38	8 8	6 5	5 58	5 51	5 44	5 21	5 8	*to be a valuable ant-*
27	M	7 27	4 33	23 20	1 26	11 57	11 27	8 57	7 8	7 1	6 54	6 47	6 24	6 11	*dote to thirst.*
28	T	7 27	4 33	23 18	1 55	m	a 12	9 42	rises	rises	rises	rises	rises	rises	*Several gigantic fleas*
29	W	7 27	4 33	23 14	2 25	1 0	0 54	10 24	6 21	6 26	6 31	6 36	6 53	7 2	☽ Perigee. *captured*
30	T	7 27	4 33	23 10	2 54	1 59	1 34	11 4	7 41	7 45	7 49	7 53	8 6	8 12	Very H. Tides ☉ Per.
31	F	7 26	4 34	23 6	3 22	2 54	2 14	11 44	9 2	9 4	9 6	9 8	9 17	9 20	*and put to death.*

PHASES OF THE MOON.
☾ L. Q. 5th, 7 29 M.
● New 12th, 4 46 E.
☽ F. Q. 20th, 9 54 E.
○ Full 28th, 1 37 M.

One poet, not remarkable for his originality, having stolen the idea of another, and made the most of it in a poem of three cantos, claimed the right to consider it his own, to which the other replied, "would you claim my son as your own, because you had dressed him up in a new coat?"

To lie with address and propriety, to adhere consistently to a lie once told, and to act, on every point, as if the said lie was neither more nor less than the truth, is an accomplishment which few people can boast of. A bungling, awkward lie is worse than none; and a person who contradicts himself, falters, and retracts, when he tells a lie, had better always stick to the truth than thus to disgrace himself. All respectable liars are careful to avoid suspicion.

An itinerant schoolmaster in search of a situation, being examined before the school committee of a town in the interior, called Squagville, exhibited his budget of learned lore in vain until he enumerated Squagville among the principal cities of the East, when he was taken into employment immediately.

Colonel Crockett and the Honey Bees---See page 22.

1841

INDEX

This edition of *The Tall Tales of Davy Crockett* was designed by Dariel Mayer, composed by Graphic Composition, Inc., printed by Thomson-Shore, Inc., and bound by John H. Dekker & Sons. The facsimile pages for the 1839 and 1840 almanacs were reproduced by Photographic Services of the State of Tennessee, Nashville. The 1841 almanac was photographed by Ron Dorsey, Austin, Texas.

5/13